W9-BRH-453

# Break the Ceiling, Touch the Sky

Success secrets of the world's most inspirational women

# Break the Ceiling, Touch the Sky

Success secrets of the world's most inspirational women

## Anthony A. Rose

House of Rose

Singapore

***Break the Ceiling, Touch the Sky***
Success secrets of the world's most inspirational women

10 9 8 7 6 5 4 3 2 1
PCPL
20 16 15 14

When ordering this title please use **ISBN 978-981-09-1061-7**

*Why I wrote "Break the Ceiling, Touch the Sky."*

Let me state at the very outset that I am not an expert on diversity. I am simply an ordinary man who respects and supports the advancement of women, because it is needed in a current and future world. It makes business and social sense. It is the right thing to do.

The primary reason for me writing **Break the Ceiling, Touch the Sky.** is my mother Leonie Rose. I learned so much from her and my Dad, Charles Rose. It was not easy for them to bring us three boys up given their financial circumstances. Yet they did that with gusto, gave us great educations and ensured that we had the basics to go on to be contributing members of society. My mother was an amazing woman. She was the constant factor in my life till Dec 30, 2012 when Alzheimer's finally stole her away and she passed peacefully surrounded by all of us. She taught me grit. She taught me patience. She taught me how to give back to society. Never expecting anything back. She taught me tough love. And my father attempted to teach me to be a gentleman. His respect for my mother and the manner in which he treated her taught me more about diversity and respect for women than anything else.

All my life women have played a huge role in my development.

I have been influenced by extraordinary women – Unnita D'Souza, my very first female Manager; my professor and mentor Jane Swamy, India's number one communication guru in her time; Joanne Crewes, one of my earliest bosses at P&G Asia; Deb Henretta, also from P&G now ranked as one of the most powerful women executives in the world. My female bosses always stood out. They were more versatile. More relentless. More focused. Masters of multi tasking. I learned much from watching these exceptional women rise to the top of their respective fields over the years.

Women have always inspired me. Just like my mother did.

In mid 2012, I had a life changing moment when I published my first book *Daddy's Logic* (McGraw Hill, CITIC) in English and Chinese and donated all of my royalties from the book to Habitat for Humanity. A tribute to my father, it opened my eyes to the possibility of making a small individual difference to society. It spurred me on to think about the possibility of writing another book, this time as a tribute to my Mum, and to contribute all my royalties to charity yet again.

As a corporate executive now for over two decades, I also see how brittle female careers are. For a variety of reasons. Lack of genuine support from their employers, social stereo types, pregnancy, playing a supporting role to successful husbands or partners, lack of role models and mentors to guide them on their journeys, or sometimes simply being promoted to the wrong roles to fill a diversity quota. I have watched women with the highest qualifications, degrees and skill sets often fail.

Around the time, I was also somewhat influenced by the huge focus that several leading organizations across the world were putting on diversity. I was touched by the efforts that many of these companies are making to change the gender imbalance in the world and to do more to enable contribution of women to their full potential in the workplace.

My interest was also piqued by a unique article in Psychology Today magazine that highlighted how gender influenced many areas of cognition and behavior, including memory, emotion, vision, hearing and the brain's response to stress hormones.

And so I started to talk to women all over the world about the challenges they faced and the opportunities they needed. It slowly dawned on me how much of a need there was for today's female professional to get the right kind of advice from women who had already succeeded on the world stage.

I began to think ahead that if I wrote a book that highlighted the experiences and success principles of some of the most successful and inspirational women from around the world, across cultures, and across both the Corporate and social sectors, it would be a huge enabler for women everywhere to succeed. Equally important, it would give male professionals everywhere deep insights into how women thought, worked and succeeded.

And so in July 2012, at the launch of Daddy's Logic, I announced that I would be doing another book in honor of my Mum and the book cover would be PINK!

On the 2nd of Jan 2013, exactly three days after my Mum passed away, I got down to serious work on *Break the Ceiling, Touch the Sky.*

100% of my royalties from *Break the Ceiling Touch the Sky,* will go to *Save the Children.* This esteemed NGO will utilize my royalties from this book to prevent maternal anemia across 150 villages in India, touching 20,000 women. I thought that it is fitting that the book benefits women in multiple ways. For professional women reading the book, they get access to the best advice to fast track their success from some of the most inspirational women in the world. And women also benefit as beneficiaries of the royalties from this very same book. To me that's women supporting women at it's very best.

For my male friends and readers, I believe if you read this book, it will forever change the way you look at and support the aspirations of your sisters, daughters, wives, partners and every woman in your life. It will help you be more successful in your professional relationships with women. It will help you understand better the women you work for, who work for you or whom you work alongside.

Read it and you will be changed. Just as *Break the Ceiling, Touch the Sky* changed me.

### How I wrote Break the Ceiling, Touch the Sky.

My journey on *Break the Ceiling, Touch the Sky* started by talking to my personal and professional female contacts from all over the world. I wanted to understand first hand what women were facing all over the world. I have looked at different studies and much data, but what I wanted was to find out for myself through women whose point of view I trusted and could use as a baseline.

I took every single opportunity to connect with successful women and simply listen to what they were saying and feeling. What surprised me was the similarity in challenges and themes that were emerging. The need for work family balance, aspiration to make a difference, the sense of loneliness and hopelessness sometimes without the right mentors, the frustration of career slowdown after having the first child, the hesitation to say "yes" to promotions and more challenging roles, the hesitation to promote self, the aversion to networking, the inability to break into the "boys club", the sadness of being labelled harshly; whether I spoke to someone in Hong Kong, in the USA or in India, the themes were starkly similar.

I finally landed on around 20 common themes. And then I moved to stage two. I started identifying some of the most inspirational women around the world to see if they were experiencing the same issues and what their success secrets were to deal with these challenges.

And over the next few weeks I reached out to close to 150 "targets" to secure additional support.

Responses slowly came in. By March 2013 I had locked on 14 chapter titles and started interviewing each of the inspirational women on my list. After writing up a draft interview I would then place a particular woman leader under a specific chapter head/ principle for success based on the leaders top couple of stated success principles. Some frustration and teeth gnashing occurred as several of my target heroines appeared to be best examples of the same chapters. Further filtering followed. By round two of the drafts I was broadly able to ascertain the heroines that would appear in each of the 14 chapters.

And then the real writing began. From hundreds of pages of notes taken over weary interviews at late evening or night via Skype, telecon and email responses (I do not mix work on my book with the timings of my day job) I was able to construct 43 simple overviews of these great leaders' sharings. The complexity they manage on a day-to-day basis blew me away. I then returned the drafts to them and asked for inputs. Back and forth we went till we got resolution on the messaging and anecdotes that would inspire our readers . By then I was writing 3 hours x 4 nights a week with a few more hours every weekend. I had become a hermit.

Every author wants to publish with a good publisher. My first book Daddy's Logic had a great publisher – McGraw Hill. Unfortunately no publisher wanted to publish a book on women and for women written by a man. That set me thinking. I also realized that as an author who publishes through traditional publishing I would only get 10 % royalties from book sales to donate to charity. I realized that if I wanted to give more back to the charity the book would support, I would have to take on more work in the value chain myself. Result – I opened my own publishing imprint **House of Rose** to maximize my royalties and hence maximize my donation to charity. By doing this I would at the very least double my charitable donations.

In April 2014 I finally got formal approvals from most of the women leaders in the book. Some last minute surprises ensued with me having to replace a couple of leaders who were unable to stick to the deadlines with more willing and equally inspirational women. Apology letters had to be written. In May we went into print production.

By the time you read this, **Break the Ceiling, Touch the Sky** would have launched in Singapore/India/Hong Kong as a first wave. From there on it will go on to touch millions of lives across the world.

It has taken every evening, weekend and vacation day of 2013 and likely 2014. I use no researchers or ghost writers. I am passionate about giving my readers an authentic product of value for their own careers.

I hope my little effort to be the change will make a difference. If we do nothing but cry about the inequalities in the world, nothing would change.

"Intent changes nothing, but action does," my parents would say.

We must act. And act now.


*Anthony A. Rose*

When I wrote my last book *DADDY'S LOGIC* as a tribute to my father and donated the royalties to HABITAT FOR HUMANITY, I never realized it would change my life. In the acknowledgements for *DADDY'S LOGIC* there were several dozen people I thanked for their love and support. For those of you who are curious about having so many people to thank… go get a copy of *DADDY'S LOGIC*.

For *Break the Ceiling, Touch the Sky*, I have been equally fortunate to have many more people rally around to support me as my mission to make a difference became clearer. I have to state upfront – writing and publishing *Break the Ceiling, Touch the Sky* has been far more difficult than writing Daddy's Logic. I've written *Break the Ceiling, Touch the Sky* in half the time I took for Daddy's Logic but by putting in several more hours at night, on weekends and vacation days for the last 18 months.

One hundred percent of my royalties as author of *Break the Ceiling, Touch the Sky* will go to *Save the Children.*

I would like to start with my mother, Leonie Rose, to whom this book is dedicated. My mother was a "working Mum" – she, along with my Dad raised me and my two brothers through sheer grit and determination. She is the bravest woman I have ever known. The most generous woman I have ever known. And the most determined. Very tough, very gentle. When we lost her to Alzheimers in 2012, it was at the end of a beautiful life that had brought so much joy to all around her. I travelled often to India over the last several years. Sometimes the journey was long, but it was all worth it when I finally would reach my parents' home in India and see her beaming face waiting at the door.

I want to thank my family for their support, starting with my two brothers Joseph (Joe) and Dominic (Domy). Dominic's wife, Monica and their daughter Sacha. Joseph's son (and my god son) Keegan. Mum's sisters, Celine D'Sa and Tessie Boyle and Mum's brother Joe Dias. Uncle Joe D'Sa. My cousins Priscilla (Dinky), Gerald (Rabby), Martin, Tiernan, Alethea, Kevin (Puttu) and Lew.

I would like to thank in a very special way Tim Love, a dear friend, who helped me connect with several of the women leaders in *Break the Ceiling, Touch the Sky.* A truly generous individual. Thank you Tim.

Thanks to a few other very special people who helped me through the year just by simply being there for me in some way or other. To encourage me when my energy flagged, challenge me into completing this commitment or simply serve as a sounding board for my incessant questions.

Smita, my friend, philosopher and guide. At the time of going to press with Break the Ceiling, Touch the Sky, I continue to benefit from her sage advice.

Hiten, my dearest friend. I wish I could see more of him nowadays.

Chester, my dearest friend and his family (wife Harpreet, daughter Maxine and son Mathew – who is also my god son) They are like family to me.

My dear friend Shankar and his wife Uma, who have been so generous towards me in their support on Daddy's Logic and on *Break the Ceiling, Touch the Sky.*

My oldest friend Jamshed Bamji, like a brother to me.

Belita Vaz, who passed many years ago, my dear friend who I remember often.

Tulip Abraham, my childhood friend.

Samina Kapasi, my old friend and writing buddy.

Roopina Coutinho, my beloved childhood friend.

Jennifer Tang, my dear friend who has always been supportive.

Jessica Lam, my dear friend and sounding board, soon to be Hong Kong's leading counsellor.

Deepak Acharya my life long friend. Wish I could see him sometime soon.

Donny Rumsby, my dear friend who is always so supportive of my writing. Thanks Baba.

Tee Lee Lian, my dear friend who looks after many of the legal matters of my small charitable effort.

Elvie Lins my dear photographer friend for all her great support.

Dr. Robert Da Costa and Dr. Celine Rodrigues for the medical care and affection they each showered on my Mum.

Dilip Thakore, the man who taught me how to write.

Veena Gidwani, my dear friend. Sharjil Sajid, Preyash Thakrar as well.

Angela Chan, my dear friend from McGraw Hill. Angela, thank you so much for always patiently responding to my (many) questions.

Kash, my friend and former colleague. Now CEO of his own Company called *#besomebody*. My little brother.

Colin Dilaire, my dear friend, who has been out of touch for a while. I hope he is safe and well.

Jamie Ang, my Daddy's Logic ambassador, my dear friend. Jamie, I miss you. Please get back in touch with all of your friends.

Estee Teo, unofficial chairperson of my "fan club." My very dear friend. I can depend on her to ask about my book in every conversation we have.

Susanna Liu, my protégé who connected me to the designer of the front cover and who is always so helpful. I am proud of her.

Banny Choi, the Hong Kong based designer who did this eye popping cover design.

Edwin Lam, my friend who always has a point of view on most everything.

V. Bharat, who is always giving me perspective on the financials.

Mary Carmen Gasco-Buisson and Sonali Sharma for both helping me with their suggestions.

Sam Balsara, Hasan Basar, Muhammad Fadhil Choong, Jimmy Tay, Sunil Gautam for helping me with publicizing *Daddy's Logic* and again offering support. Also, Glenn Osaki and his team for connecting me to a couple of unique women leaders.

My very dear friend Mahesh Parkar, CEO of Parkar Communications Pvt Ltd and his team led by Raj Dusane and Shridhar Chitnis for working on the print production of the book. Mahesh, Raj, Shridhar, thanks so much for helping me on this journey. Raj, a very, very special thank you to you for all your long hours of work!

Chris "Jumpin" Samuel, another of my proteges.

Desiree Hwang, my dear friend.

Each of the heroes in this book, for giving of their time and energy and agreeing to be interviewed. *Judith McKenna, Dr. Lois Lee, Anne Kershaw, Angie Halamandaris, Phyllis Marwah, Joanne Soo, Maria Fernanda Mejia, Umran Beba, Carolyn Miles, Cathy Smith, Deb Henretta, Barbara McFarland, Banali Malhotra, Kiran Mazumdar-Shaw, Eriko Sakurai,*

*Yue-Sai Kan, Anna Whitlam, Pat Martin, Leanne Cutts, Jue Yao, Gail Klintworth, Kristen English, Dominique Reiniche, Valerie Khan, Ella Stewart, Miki Tsusaka, Chanda Kochhar, Dina Howell, Lynne Anne Davis, Cilla Snowball, Louise Beehag, Francoise Hostalier, Yifei Li, Ninie Wang, Kristin Engvig, Su-Mei Thompson, Christine Tan, Clarisse Reille, Micho F. Spring, Emily Sperling, Laura Desmond, Marina Maher and Hiroko Wada.*

My business leaders who have been so generous to me.

First of all, the one and only Bob McDonald. The leader I have always admired and trusted the most. For his ongoing support and mentorship. The most honorable man I know.

Bharat Patel, Sumit Bhattacharya, Helmut Meixner, Gary Cofer, Ashok Chhabra, Jim Stengel.

Scott Price, Tom Waldron, Sharon Orlopp, for their support and encouragement within Walmart.

Harish Manwani  and Irene Rosenfeld for their generous testimonials for **Break the Ceiling, Touch the Sky.**

All of my female bosses throughout my career. Jane Swamy, Unnita D Souza, Joanne Crewes, Charlotte Otto and Deb Henretta. My dear colleague Linda Ulrey, for teaching me so much about PR in the years gone by.

I'm grateful to all my colleagues at my  past employers - The Datamatics Group, Glaxo (now GSK), Clea PR, P&G and to my current employer - Walmart.

I'm thankful for all the support I received from my professors and faculty of the Xavier Institute of Communications (XIC).

At the time of going to press with **Break the Ceiling, Touch the Sky,** there are many changes going on in my life. I'm excited about the future and what it could hold.

One thing I do know. If each of us did just a little something to make this a better world, it would *be* a better world. It doesn't take anything or anyone extraordinary to do that. It just takes commitment.

Thank you for buying this copy of **Break the Ceiling, Touch the Sky.** I hope you enjoy it as much as I have enjoyed writing and producing it. Have a great life. Go **Break the Ceiling, Touch the Sky!**

This book is dedicated to my mother, the late *Leonie Rose.*

Ma, I want you to know that we will never forget all that you sacrificed for us boys. I hope you're rocking heaven with Dad.

# Chapter 1

# AIM TO MAKE
# A DIFFERENCE

Of all the 14 power principles that feature in this book, this one was the most universal amongst women. It seems like every single woman professional I spoke to for **Break the Ceiling, Touch the Sky** had this fundamental aspiration to matter. To *want* to make a difference. Neurological research dubs it as a basic human need of 'contribution.'

In Maslow's hierarchy of needs self esteem and mattering are linked. Research shows that when human beings belong and matter, they perform better, feel more engaged and innovate better.

I spoke to four of the greatest women leaders who are truly making a difference. **Judith McKenna,** *Chief Development Officer, Walmart US;* **Lois Lee,** *President and CEO, Children of the Night;* **Angie Halamandaris,** *Co-Founder and President, The Heart of America Foundation;* and **Anne Kershaw,** *CEO, 2041.*

**J**udith McKenna was named Chief Development Officer, Walmart US just a few days prior going to print with **Break the Ceiling, Touch the Sky.** Till june 2014, Judith was the executive vice president of strategy and international development for Walmart International, a fast-growing segment of Walmart's overall operations with more than 6,100 stores and over 823,000 associates in 26 countries outside the United States. In that role she lead several areas including international strategy, real estate, mergers and acquisitions, integration, global format development and purchase leverage.

Her life's philosophy has always been to do a great job and through that make a difference!

"I was born in the town of Middlesbrough in England. Both my parents were teachers and my overwhelming desire growing up, was always to make my parents proud, especially my Dad", shared Judith.

Judith always wanted to achieve in whatever she participated. At the age of 10, Judith joined in the Girl Guides and just kept collecting badges until there was no room on her arm for them. She eventually became a Queen's Guide, the highest attainable award for members of Girl guiding. It typified her approach to everything she did.

> *"I do not believe my gender has ever stopped me from being successful. Diversity in business of thought and approach, of gender and of culture is the key to balanced decision making, innovation and success. Most importantly, you must want to make a difference in whatever role you are in."*
>
> **Judith McKenna,**
> *Chief Development Officer,*
> *Walmart US.*

"All my life I have tried to do what I am most interested in versus doing something that may be the most direct route to advancement. I have tried to make a unique contribution in every single role I have taken on".

It was this attitude that encouraged Judith to pursue a law degree at the University of Hull. After which, she quickly moved on to gaining her ICAEW accounting qualification at KPMG – one of the U.K.'s leading accounting firms.

Choosing to join KPMG in London was a momentous decision.

"I still to this day don't know why I decided that I wanted to work in London having lived all my life in the North of England and knowing no one there - I think I had only ever visited the City three times in my entire life but I had set my heart on it. I just had to work out a way of doing it and that's where accountancy came in. Accountancy was a means to an end and it paid relatively better than other jobs. I decided I would do it for a couple of years and then move onto something else," she shared.

As it turned out Judith really enjoyed the work despite claiming to not be very good at maths.

"It was about relationships and people and getting to understand businesses as much as it was about doing the maths and that's where I found I could make a difference.

I believe that if you set yourself the goal of doing your very best in the job or task at hand, leveraging what it is that makes you different, you are able to make a bigger, more long lasting impact. I've always loved working with people and developing teams," she added.

In 1992 Judith moved on from KPMG to work in the brewing industry for the Leeds-based Tetley Pub Company - a brewing and pub retailing company which was one of her audit clients she had got to know well.

Judith shared, "The brewing industry was a very tough business for a woman back then. I was the youngest person on the team by at least 15 years. There were some unique challenges as a female leader and in my first job outside of the accountancy profession. I still remember walking into a working men's club in Liverpool and the Steward (the landlord) refusing to speak to me as a 'young lass' like me couldn't know what I was talking about! I had to work out ways to get people to give me a chance and show I not only knew what I was talking about, but I was good at it too."

Judith took it all in her stride. She picked up important tips on how to manage and lead in this male dominated industry and earned the respect of her colleagues. Her focus was on three things - doing the basics of the job she had to the very best of her ability and standing out from others who had gone before by tackling head on problems such as unreconciled accounts that hadn't been tackled for years; by using the knowledge of her team and making sure they got credit for the work that they did (instilling real pride and a will to win attitude) and finally by not doing the job from behind a desk.

By getting out into pubs and talking to the landlords her understanding of the broader business increased and that made a difference to the credibility with which she could talk about business challenges. She turned her perceived weakness of being a 'young lass' into an advantage by getting people to open up more and talk more to her.

Then in 1993, Carlsberg merged with Tetley and moved its accounting team to Birmingham. Judith was challenged with seeing all of her team made redundant. She did her best to place most of them in new roles, including some at one of the biggest companies in town – ASDA. At the time her daughter was just seven months old and she was hesitant to move to Birmingham despite being offered the opportunity. Then suddenly she got a call from ASDA saying that they were very impressed with the people she had sent over and wanted her to come in for a chat. Initially hesitant, Judith took the plunge, went over and had a conversation. In 1996, Judith joined ASDA.

At ASDA, Judith truly found a place where her aspiration to make a difference could blossom.

"I loved the people, loved the values of service to the customer and striving for excellence. Most of all I loved the fact that as I progressed I was also able to manage large teams and increasingly complex projects."

Judith worked her way through the Finance organisation starting with a small accounting team.

Over the years the most valuable lesson Judith learned was it wasn't all plain sailing and sometimes setbacks in careers can be the very things which make you better and more effective if you persist.

In 2000 she was devastated when after being told she was on track in her career, she was passed over for promotion to deputy Chief Financial Officer and a male colleague got the job.

"The feeling of failure was huge and I was concerned about how people would see me and how I would be able to carry on at the Company. But my husband sat me down and gave me a simple piece of advice."

"The only person who will lose your credibility is you," he said.

"He was actually quoting Eleanor Roosevelt but didn't know it at the time! Eleanor Roosevelt is now one of my role models," commented Judith.

Judith decided to focus on making a difference in the areas she could control and lead. Throwing her energy into her team and in communicating what they were doing both in terms of work and personal development, Judith swiftly earned the reputation of being a "people person" - which at the time was unusual for an accountant. She focused on not just being great at what she did, but she also gathered supporters from around the business – sponsors who over time would 'stand in her corner and support her.'

"It also made me realise that sometimes you can focus too much on promotion and when you stop worrying about that and actually relax into what you are doing, your confidence grows and people see a different side of you- it wasn't an easy lesson to learn, but probably one of the most valuable of my career."

In 2001, whilst eight months pregnant with her second child, Judith was appointed directly as Chief Financial Officer, catapulting past the deputy CFO role.

"That only increased my loyalty to the organization even more. I was proud that the organization I worked for would take that leap of faith in me and had recognized the contributions I was making," she shared.

Another milestone came in 2011 when Judith led the transaction to buy a chain of 190 Netto supermarkets to begin ASDA's small supermarkets division. Having done the deal she had the opportunity to lead the integration into the ASDA business and then to run the division seeing the whole deal through from end to end.

She added, "I had never done anything like it and a really stretched me and gave me a few sleepless nights but again with a great team and a logical approach we just worked through it - failure was never an option and we knew success was critical for the company."

During this time she also began to expand her influence through a unique initiative which helped her make a difference not just in the workplace but in the community – *Tickled Pink* – the breast cancer campaign that ASDA supports in aid of Breast Cancer Care and Breast Cancer Campaign.

"Cancer negatively impacts so many people. *Tickled Pink* gave me a real opportunity to contribute something back. If you find something you are truly passionate about that creates a unifying force way beyond your company and amongst people in your community itself, what a great thing that is," said Judith.

"For me this was indeed a great opportunity. Although *Tickled Pink* had been running successfully for years, it wasn't getting the attention it deserved. We had a CEO at the time who was very passionate about cycling and directed the company's efforts into supporting a charity to provide bikes for kids around the company as he cycled the length of Britain. Although I knew it was a worthy cause, it just didn't touch our customers and colleagues in the same way as *Ticked Pink* did so I made it my mission to get it back front and centre. We even persuaded the CEO to make it his charity of choice the following year when he did the bike ride all over again," she shared.

It was an easy task to get people enthusiastic, especially in our stores and the action was to talk about it more and start to share some of the ways our funding was helping the two charities we supported under the *Tickled Pink* banner to combat cancer and support those going through it. I'm pleased to say the baton is still being carried and *Ticked Pink* has gone from strength to strength," added Judith.

In 2011 Judith was appointed as COO of ASDA, the largest subsidiary in Walmart International, with over 560 stores and an annual turnover of $34bn. As COO, Judith had direct responsibility for more than 180,000 associates and her role included leadership of retail, logistics, ecommerce and financial services.

"In the retail business, the thinking can be linear and quite traditional. We introduced into ASDA operations the concept of sparkle," shared Judith.

"Sparkle is about personality and having colleagues who enjoy their work and have an opportunity to make a difference. That involved a number of different ideas from stopping Checkout operators from using prescribed scripts to greet customers and instead encouraging a natural conversation to dressing the stores for events such as Halloween or Christmas and encouraging our colleagues to decorate their departments and even to wear costumes. We even issued every store with a "Sparkle box" of props to use! But Sparkle wasn't just about fun - simply put we wanted to sell more and that was at the heart of it - better customer engagement and experience and showcasing product all helped drive sales," she added.

Judith was the first female COO at ASDA and she knew that diversity was one of the areas that she needed to focus on. Interestingly the sparkle concept helped as it appealed to women as much as to men.

"I was determined to make a difference by being myself, and if that was different from the traditional stereotype that was okay. I knew that I could only get a focus on diversity if I was myself. If I was not sincere I knew my store and distribution colleagues would see right through me. I knew I had a team that was very well equipped to manage the day-to-day operations and I trusted them to deliver. I focused my efforts on people. I did little things that sent a message to the organization, from walking the stores with my kids along with the store manager, to making sure I always viewed the store through a customer's eyes - to having pink sofa's in the meeting room behind my desk or wearing sparkly boots on stage as a presenter at the annual business meeting! We also created more development programmes for women. Sometimes, I had my moments of self-doubt and temptation to revert to being more traditional but I knew it wouldn't have worked so I stuck to my path of "making a difference by being myself."

Judith was also the driving force behind ASDA's multichannel business and in making technology-enabled retail a key part of ASDA's growth strategy.

Being different from a traditional retailer allowed Judith to see the evolving opportunity in eCommerce and include it as part of the operations agenda and move the ASDA business towards a truly multi-channel approach. She understood how the customer shopped with ASDA and saw synergies between the bricks and mortar (physical) stores and the eCommerce business, that the two could work together and be more effective than the sum of the parts. She enabled this change by engaging the stores and providing store managers with tools such as iPads which they were encouraged to use on the shop floor to help drive home the message that the world had changed for ever and ensure that employees were best equipped to embrace the change.

One of the other key innovations that Judith was involved with was the ASDA MUMDEX report. This is a panel of over 5000 ASDA mums of varying ages and backgrounds that provides deep insights into the challenges households are facing in the UK as seen through the eyes of the Mums. This helped the business to understand what innovative solutions were needed to make life easier for the customer.

'The MUMDEX gave us so many valuable insights into the minds of our primary target audience – Mums across the UK. It pointed us in the direction of how mums wanted easy meal solutions for dinner for the kids but they also wanted them to be healthy, that in turn led to the development of the *"Chosen by Kids"* range of foods in ASDA's private brand range. In another issue it showed us what Mums really worried about for the future of their children including them finding employment which helped us refocus our efforts on programmes to create opportunities and the chain to gain qualifications whilst at work," Judith added.

In September 2012, the winners of the prestigious *'Specsavers Everywoman in Retail Awards'* were revealed. The awards recognize the achievements of charting change and leading the way in the retail industry whether as business owners, entrepreneurs, or executives within large organizations. Judith was *awarded the prestigious 'Retail Woman of the Year'* award in recognition of her 'vision, innovative approach and success, making her an outstanding role model that will inspire more women to choose a career in retail.'

"I do not believe my gender has ever stopped me from being successful. Diversity in business of thought and approach, of gender and of culture is the key to balanced decision making, innovation and success. Most importantly, you must want to make a difference in whatever role you are. Good businesses understand that and those that embrace it are more successful in today's competitive business world. That's why I love working in retail and at Walmart."

Judith is a passionate ambassador for diversity and has been a respected judge for a number of equality and diversity awards in the U.K. including the 'Women Of Achievement awards' who recognise women under the age of 35 who are making a difference and being successful in whichever field they operate ... from racing car drivers, through medics and politicians to business women and entrepreneurs.

"I never cease to be amazed by the extraordinary talent that is out there and what women can do and it's humbling to meet some of the nominees. The job of the awards is to shout loudly about their success and celebrate their achievements as role models to others," she shared.

She continues to be the proud ambassador for ASDA's *Tickled Pink* campaign which has raised 45 million USD for breast cancer charities over the last 16 years.

In 2013 she was awarded an honorary doctorate in law from Hull University that was bestowed in Jan 2014. Judith was asked to make the commencement address at the University's graduation ceremony.

In her speech she shared, "I stood out and got on because I loved working with and leading people and I worked hard. I found ways to communicate at all levels in organizations and because, most of the time, I retained a sense of humor ... I could do all of that because I truly enjoyed what I did. I learned that being myself was the path to the next adventure.

Of course I have had amazing sponsors and mentors along the way too who let me stand on their shoulders and be more than I was – something incidentally that has left me with a lifelong passion for mentoring and developing others."

"My other passion that I have to mention is leading ASDA's "Tickled Pink" breast cancer charity. I get my greatest buzz from this work and it's not all about what you put in the workplace but it's about finding ways to pay it forwards as well. That is part of enjoying what you do," she added.

"I know getting a foot on the career ladder is much harder today than it was when I graduated but I do believe that if you start out with the mindset of making a big difference in whatever role you are doing, it will help you make the best of that assignment." She left the new graduates with 4 simple messages spelling out the name of the University "HULL."

- **H. Have courage:**
  Courage to take risks and to take chances in life. Don't be afraid of failing – it only makes you stronger. Not everything will be a success. But pick yourself up and just go again!

- **U. Understand yourself:**
  What makes you tick, what's important to you and what do you believe in. Be true to yourself! Dare to be authentic and different.

- **L. Learn, learn, learn:**
  Graduating is the start of a life of learning not the end. The world is a very small and interconnected place. The more you learn about the world we live in, its history, its culture and its future the more enriched your lives will be and the more you will stand out for your knowledge and understanding in whatever path you choose

- **L. Love your life:**
  Do what makes you happy and fulfilled … make sure you can look in the mirror in 30 years time and say I think life was worth it. Do things because you want to do them… dream big and work hard.

One of my rules of business is never to reinvent the wheel if there is a perfectly good one out there so I leave you with a quote from an American called Harvey MacKay that I have on my office wall.

"Life is too short to wake up with regrets. So love the people who treat you right, forget about the ones who don't, and believe that everything happens for a reason. If you get a chance, take it. If it changes your life, let it. Nobody said life would be easy, they just promised it would most likely be worth it."

Judith concluded, "I am so proud to be here today – many congratulations on your graduation. I wish you all things good as you start your life's adventure. I hope you make every moment worth it. I hope you make a difference."

Judith McKenna is loving every minute of her life. She is exploring life in America with her husband and two children. Outside of work she loves to cook, spend time with her kids and keeps planning to get back to running but never seems to get around to it!

She has truly made her parents proud. She is making a difference. **Dr. Lois Lee** is a pioneer in saving the helpless children who are victims of human sex trafficking, blazing the trail for academics, researchers, law enforcement, social service providers and legislators.

She is the **founder and president of Children of the Night**, the first-established and only comprehensive sex trafficking program in North America. Since 1979, she has rescued over 10,000 American children from prostitution in the United States—that is more children than all of the other sex trafficking programs combined.

Dr. Lee's mission to make a difference began in 1975 as a young PhD student at UCLA.

A previous professor and mentor, Dr. Jeanne Curran, hosted Lois at the American Sociological Association Conference in San Francisco in 1976.

> *"I believe my life is about making a difference. My goal has always been to take social services to the people who need it the most – the people on the street."*
>
> **Dr. Lois Lee,**
> Founder and President,
> Children of the Night.

One morning Dr. Curran learned from the local newspaper that the Glide Memorial Church was hosting The First National Hooker's Convention – for Coyote, founded by the notorious civil rights activist Margo St. James.

At the conference, Lois met two American Civil Liberties Union (ACLU) lawyers who had initiated a lawsuit against the Oakland police for not enforcing prostitution laws equally and only arresting the prostitute. They suggested to Lois that she replicate their work and sue the Los Angeles Police Department for the same activity.

"So we started with one prostitute who was willing to challenge the law. Soon many lawyers joined our constitutional challenge when defending other prostitutes. Private lawyers, the Public Defender's office and even the ACLU joined our court challenge. It created a huge stir and at one point the presiding judge removed the Commissioner who granted the motion for discovery to allow me to research the case. When he took over the case, he demanded my presence in the courtroom and it was rumored that if I stepped in the courtroom he would have put me in jail. The criminal justice system and old boy network were furious with me," shared Lois.

She added, "During that case one of the prostitutes I had met was strangled and tortured and dumped in a cemetery. I was told the community and later the Los Angeles Police Department (LAPD) had gone to UCLA and complained about UCLA giving me credibility to sue the Los Angeles Police Department – both government entities."

Lois was subsequently informed by UCLA that they would not accept any research she had done on prostitution.

That however did not stop Lois.

She shared, "I have always enjoyed being in the thick of the action and tend to get bored very easily. Fortunately I was admitted at USIU, an experimental graduate school who hosted famous lecturers, intellectuals and academics around the world. My work was accepted and supported by the esteemed Dr. Herbert Blumer, a former President of the American Sociological Association."

One fateful evening in December 1977, Lois received a call from a young woman she met in the courtroom. The young woman told Lois about a girl sent to meet a man for the purposes of prostitution; the man was not answering his telephone and his address did not exist on a map. Concerned for the girl's safety, Lois proceeded to call the police and went to the police department to insist they send out a car to check on the young woman. At the police department she was told they had no interest in information about a missing "whore". The next morning the police identified the body of that girl nude, strangled, and dumped on a hillside- she was only 17 years old and was the 11th Hillside Strangler victim - a serial murderer that terrorized women in Los Angeles so much that the police announced women would no longer have to stop for police cars if being pursued.

Lois was so furious with the lack of attention by the police that she went on KNBC news and announced, "If you are in the prostitution business and you think you know who the Hillside Strangler is and don't want to call the police, call me" and put her home telephone number on national news. Thousands of telephone tips flooded her phone line, and she worked tirelessly to answer each call and distribute the tips on possible murders – giving the pimp tips to Warren Wilson at KNBC, bad cop leads to Wayne Satz at KABC and Outcall/Escort Operators to Jim Mitchel at KFWB. They were a team as they hit the streets to research the leads that came from Lois' home telephone. Lois worked most closely with Warren Wilson and visited all of the nightclubs where pimps frequented and worked with all of the young women who were prostituting on the street.

In response to the Hillside Strangler incident, Lois established the first sex trafficking hotline and street outreach program for victims of sex trafficking.

These tips and meetings with young women who worked as prostitutes on Sunset Boulevard led to the arrest and prosecution of Angelo Buono – one of the murderers.

At 27 years of age, Lois Lee was a legend on the street, in the courts and among social services and the police.

But even after the search for the serial killers concluded, those in the prostitution business continued to call Lee's home telephone for help. Some of the people calling for help were children, and because they had nowhere else to go Lee offered to let them stay with her.

From 1979 to 1981 over 250 children passed through her apartment – marking the humble beginnings of Children of the Night.

By 1981, she was profiled in television news magazines and caught the attention of two philanthropists who were conservative republicans. They offered Lois grants to move the program from her home to the heart of Hollywood where she opened America's first drop-in center for sex trafficking victims.

It took almost 10 more years to raise the necessary private funds to open the Children of the Night Shelter Home. Children of the Night has operated a licensed shelter home for America's child prostitutes ages 11-17 since 1992. The Children of the Night home receives America's child prostitutes from all over the United States and accommodates up to 24 residents at a time, providing an on-site school, individual case management, wholesome recreational outings, and a chance to experience a childhood free from sexual exploitation. The Children of the Night onsite school places five children a year in college and to date has placed over 100 children in colleges and universities throughout America.

In the last three decades, Lee has raised over $40 million to provide these crucial services. Children of the Night graduates have gone on to become lawyers, executives and educators, among other professions.

Lois shared, "Diplomats and social service providers come from all over the world to observe the work we are doing at the Children of the Night home — which is a model for similar programs in the U.S. and abroad. We have been sponsored by other countries — Japan, Romania, Mexico, Canada — to assist in developing such programs and to teach law enforcement organizations how to respond and intervene in the lives of sex trafficking victims while they pursue their efforts to prosecute the vile criminals who prey on these victims."

Recently, she has established a presence in Rome to teach others all over the world how to create life-changing programs for victims of sex trafficking and she is currently working on developing financial, law enforcement and political resources for those already working to help sex trafficking victims.

I asked Dr. Lois how she went from struggling under-grad student to Founder and President of one of the most unique organizations in the world.

She responded, "How did I get to where I am at Children of the Night? Many people think it is luck, looks and contacts but it was hard work. What many people do not recognize is that I am an accomplished academic so when I work with politicians, police, social systems I'm armed and dangerous. I am always armed with facts, research and well thought out programs and I am a doer. I'm committed to make a difference."

"Many times I was challenged by the police or prosecutors to prove that I could change the world for young women victimized by prostitution. My compassion and expertise allowed me to immediately connect with victims of prostitution – I was able to obtain the critical information needed to investigate, arrest and prosecute pimps. I could produce a witness in court - dressed, stable and confident which is the key to a successful prosecution of a pimp. I gave the police a resource for their work that they never thought possible – I was revered for this. The police who I worked with learned firsthand how much work was involved in the process of turning the life around for a victim of prostitution – those in the know became my cheerleaders and advocates – they gave me the respect I earned. Chief Daryl Gates of the LAPD was an early advocate," added Lois.

As a result of her efforts police departments now treat America's child prostitutes as victims instead of criminals and juvenile courts divert these children to shelters, foster homes and treatment programs rather than detention. The U.S. Department of Justice and other government agencies have developed tough laws against pimping and pandering and have developed sex trafficking task forces across the country. Several states have developed specific laws and sentencing practices to punish people that pay children for sex and law enforcement operates special investigations to arrest the customers of prostitutes.

The government has also created multiple organizations to end human sex trafficking in America.

Since 1988, Lois has served as an expert witness for federal and state prosecutors enforcing laws against dangerous pimps. Chapter Five of her PhD dissertation, "The Pimp and His Game", continues to be relied upon by vice officers, district attorneys, FBI and U.S. attorneys as a guide for the treatment of child prostitutes.

"While the police taught me a lot, I too taught them a lot about investigations, arrests and prosecutions of pimps. Many were in awe of me. As my popularity grew and higher-ranking law enforcement and politicians tried to befriend me I stood up for the "street cops" (the experts in prostitution) who had no status within law enforcement and that loyalty and reputation spread like wildfire. When street cops called me sometimes at the wee hours of the morning I answered my phone, I was ready to work – I was the real deal not some fast talking academic," shared Lois."

Lois has been profiled on national television including appearing on CBS' *60 Minutes,* and her life was portrayed in a 1985 CBS Movie of the Week entitled "Children of the Night". She was lauded by rock musician/songwriter Richard Marx in his song "Children of the Night," which appeared on his 1989 Repeat Offender album.

Lois has received countless awards for her humanitarian work, most notably the prestigious *President's Volunteer Action Award*, presented to her by President Ronald Reagan at the White House in 1984. She also received the *1994 National Caring Award*, and her permanent memorial portrait hangs in the Frederick Douglass Museum and Hall of Fame for Caring Americans in Washington, D.C.

Lois continues to lead the field in the treatment of child prostitutes. In 2012, Lee forged a relationship with backpage.com in an effort to rescue even more children from prostitution by advertising Children of the Night's Nationwide Hotline among escort advertisers. In response, traffic on the Children of the Night website went from 7,000 to 30,000 hits a month and the hotline continues to provide lifesaving work to both adults and children who want to escape prostitution.

"I'm not afraid of anyone whether it be a street pimp or a politician who tries to intimidate me. I am who I am and I have integrity and a high moral value for the victims of prostitution who I have helped. I don't mince words and I don't waver no matter whom I'm talking to. I focus on the facts. I am consistent," shared Lois.

Looking back over the years, Lois recalls that her biggest challenge was 'to be seen as an intelligent activist rather than a cute blonde who probably had some sexual adversity in her life that created an interest in prostitution.'

"I know little of the challenges women face today in corporate careers because I have never had a 'corporate career'. But I knew when I was 19, I was going to be different. This is the key challenge that women all over the world face – being recognized by men in social gatherings as professionals rather than as women. The interesting thing is that I recall participating in a study regarding successful women. The common thread amongst all of us is that we don't see barriers or discrimination – we don't recognize it," she shared.

Lois shrugged off the obvious dangers of her area of work. "If I were to let that affect me, there is no way I would be effective," she said nonchalantly.

Lois believes she had many outstanding role models growing up that helped her shape her love for the facts and making a difference.

"I looked up to so many uniquely successful people. And have tried to learn from them and their stories. My teacher Dr. Jeanne Curran in undergraduate school - she mothered me through graduate school and later law school. Helen Keller – her journey and commitment to achieve skills unthinkable in her time. Theodore Roosevelt – for doing what he wanted to do without fear and being smart enough to pull it off. Malcolm X – his journey and overcoming adversity to being a great leader – against all odds," she added.

Dr. Lee believes that for women across the world there are no limits to what they can achieve and had some simple tips for women intent on making a difference in the corporate or social sector.

- *Know your area of expertise better than everyone else. Get as much education as possible:*
  Know your material before you open your mouth.

- *Always focus on the facts and tell the truth:*
  No matter how unpopular. Be real and do not let political opinion or social pressure sway you from your commitment to your work. Stand up for what you believe in.

- *Never accept no for an answer:*
  There is always a way – you may have to rethink your strategy – but if you know your material the answer will appear to you after a good rest and some additional thought.

- *Learn from your failures:*
  Know in your heart that when you feel you have been beaten there is something good in it and only time will reveal what it is…time reveals everything.

Lois today lives in Los Angeles and has a son who is 27 who works in advertising and marketing.

I shared with Dr. Lee the huge admiration I have for the work she does day in and day out to help these women whose lives she has touched through Children of the Night.

She responded, "I believe my life is about making a difference. My goal has always been to take social services to the people who need it the most – the people on the street. And nothing will demonstrate that commitment more than the recent expansion of my work which has been named Children of the Night WOW – Children of the Night With Out Walls."

In a world full of boundaries, Dr. Lois Lee knows none.

Making a difference has taken on a unique form for **Anne Kershaw.** Anne is **CEO of 2041**, an organization working to save the Antarctic from mining and drilling in the future if the need for oil and gas continues to grow and we deplete other areas and must then look to Antarctica for a solution.

Anne was born in Glasgow and shared that she started her first job at the age of 12.

"I grew up in a working class environment so we all 'worked'…it taught us responsibility, respect and accountability which I think is lacking in much of society today. My perception of growing up was what we could do for others rather than 'what's in it for me.' My parents worked hard, were generous and kind but also wonderful teachers. Always reminding us that we must be tolerant and that listening would help us though many of our struggles. Tolerance is something I feel strongly about and teach to my children," shared Anne.

"For better or worse work has been a constant in my life. From the age of 12, I delivered milk before school with my brothers and after school we delivered newspapers. On reflection, I think it was also a good bonding time for us. We always worked and we enjoyed it," shared Anne.

"At 13 years old I wanted to be an aeronautical engineer but in Glasgow at that time there were no such classes for women. I studied civil engineering instead and had to take an evening class for technical drawing, as there wasn't a class available for girls at school during the day. Without it being a negative I have always felt that women have to put in more effort than men at most things to get the same results," she added.

Anne's adventure started in 1983 when she met Giles who was then a Cathay Pacific pilot. They married shortly thereafter. Anne first visited Antarctica in

1985 with Giles, one of the early adventurers to the South Pole, to which he operated flights through a small company that he founded with three others called Adventure Network International. In March 1990, tragedy struck when Giles died in a gyrocopter accident in the Antarctic. He since has a mountain range named after him called the Kershaw Range.

With an enormous void and change to her life, Anne took over Giles' airline and resolved to make it safer and better.

"It was not without its challenges," shared Anne. "I parallel the Antarctic and aviation world as similar to my College days. No one wanted to listen to a woman about aircraft, landing on ice runways or making logistical and business decisions about the Antarctic. But I had a great mentor and a good sense of self," she added.

"I wanted to provide people that "safety blanket" that had not been there for Giles. I wanted other families to know that their loved ones would return home safely. They included many personalities such as Michael Palin, Sir Ranulph Fiennes, Ted Turner, Richard Gere to name a few. Then in 2000, a larger organization offered to buy the Company. It was a difficult decision but I knew it was time. Time to start a life again for me and this time to give back," said Anne.

> "Making a difference by helping save the Antarctica has been the most rewarding work of my life. I do believe I personally have been much more successful and satisfied after I truly set my sights on making this bigger difference."
>
> Anne Kershaw, CEO, 2041.

To date, Anne is the only person in history to be awarded an MBE for services to Antarctic Aviation.

The difference she wanted to make presented itself in the form of 2041 – named for the date (2041) when the ban on mining in the Antarctica is due to be reviewed. Anne was persuaded by old friend, renowned explorer and eco-campaigner Rob Swan to take up the role of CEO of 2041. As CEO of 2041, Anne partnered with Robert to make a unique difference – to encourage young people to take action to change how we impact the Earth before the 2041 deadline!

"The Antarctica is so precious to me. Giles is buried there. It's the last untouched and pure place on Earth. It is truly the last wilderness and is such an important factor to the entire planet," added Anne. "I had supported rich and famous people to make their dreams a reality with Adventure Network and now it was my time to engage and inspire with Robert Swan all those who had a bigger dream...to make the Earth sustainable for all future generations.

In order to fulfill my goals I had learned over the years that sometimes to get the job done you have to be a chameleon. To be adaptive, to be a leader, or the manager, to roll up my sleeves to get the job done. An incredible skill I believe mostly women are blessed with and use as the situation requires. Women have this special ability to adapt quickly to changing environments and must leverage this special skill," said Anne.

Over the years Anne has made significant progress through 2041 in saving the Antarctica.

"Robert learned quickly that saving Antarctica is not relevant in places where food is not available, where a government is not for the people and where AIDS and other diseases are of so much concern. So always stop, think and check if you are relevant," shared Anne.

"The work with 2041 has allowed us to connect people and organizations that perhaps would not have come together. Linking young leaders with those already established. Connecting many different countries and cultures. Last year we had 28 different countries represented on Robert's annual Leadership on the Edge Antarctic Expedition.

One of the great achievements is the creation of EBase (educational bases) all over the world that allows students, teachers and educators to see the world from their classrooms. We are working to put one on each of the 7 continents. To date we have one in Antarctica, Asia, USA and working on Europe, Africa, Australia and South America," shared Anne.

Women face many challenges today – "Balancing family and work, finding "me" time, keeping updated on current news about our professions, working harder than other men in your field to show we are competent and dedicated and reminding ourselves that we are doing a good job," shared Anne.

She added, "In order for us to make a difference people have to believe in what we are saying and doing. I have found over the years that I truly connect when someone believes firstly in himself or herself. It is not always easy to find strength and belief in who you are and what you do, but this is fundamental to making a bigger difference. Passion and honesty will take you far. Belief in yourself will take you all the way to your goals."

"Making a difference by helping save the Antarctica has been the most rewarding work of my life. I do believe I personally have been much more successful and satisfied after I truly set my sights on making this bigger difference," added Anne.

Anne believes that "making a difference in society" is critical not just to professional success but also in having a fulfilled life.

"I've been very fortunate to travel and as I've travelled I've come to realize how fortunate many of us in the developed world are compared to less developed parts of the planet, Africa for example. In the less developed parts, people still dream, but it's so much more difficult to achieve those dreams. I realized over the years that people with better circumstances just have an obligation to do so much more for society.

If you live in Africa for examples (the Sudan) you can dream but it's so difficult to change your life. In the western World I realized we had more, and hence had an obligation to do more. I realized working with Robert that we could create a healthier world. Working with Robert gave me that opportunity," she shared.

Little wonder that Anne's "making a difference" transcends her work with 2041. She is today a single mother of four boys. One biological, one adopted from Thailand and twin boys adopted from Ethiopia.

"They were my dream and now they are my reality. How blessed am I?" she shared.

And in an interesting way she is shaping the next generation of young people wanting to make a difference in the World – starting with her little boy from Thailand.

Anne's little boy from Thailand is following in her footsteps. He often says jokingly to friends; "I am not adopted, I am recycled."

Today, 2041 is working with Robert on his upcoming expedition back to the Antarctic where he will complete a crossing he started in 1985 with Giles in support at that time. The crossing of Antarctica will be on solely renewable energy.

"If this can be done in Antarctica, the highest, driest, coldest and windiest continent.... then surely we can use more renewable energy at home," shared Anne.

Anne shared her top tips on making a difference:
- *Start with yourself:*
  It's the simple things – like re cycling things at home, then soon it's the neighbors, and very soon you have a whole community involved.
- *Start small:*
  Do what you can and don't beat yourself up because you are not in the front lines. Very soon, before you know it, you move beyond yourself and are influencing things on a much larger stage, hopefully global one day.
- *Name three things you are grateful for today:*
  That's another great way to train yourself to be positive and to make a difference.
- *Take a little time everyday to day-dream:*
  Its good to day-dream, just as long as you are willing to work towards making those dreams come true.
- *Be yourself and believe in yourself :*
  It takes too much energy to be someone else.

Making a difference was something **Angie Halamandaris, Co-Founder** and **President, the Heart of America Foundation** discovered and nurtured early.

Angie grew up in Rocky Mount, North Carolina and was 22 when she finished College at the University of Florida in 1986.

That very next year her mother developed a cerebral aneurysm (similar to a stroke), and Angie became her primary care giver. Angie's dedication to her mother ensured that she kept going back and forth with her mother from home to the rehabilitation center. In one such instance a new rehabilitation center had to "interview" her Mum for admission to the rehab center program. They also had to "interview" Angie.

"I was surprised when the rehab center called me the next day not just to tell me they were very happy to receive my Mum into their program but also to offer me a job! I was soon working for Learning Services Corporation, a national post-acute rehabilitation company," shared Angie.

In time Angie moved her Mum to Florida to enjoy sunnier climes where she found work with an organization called Give Kids The World Village. *Give Kids the World* was created to to fulfill the wishes of terminally ill children wanting to visit Orlando, Florida.

"The move to Give Kids the World came with a 50% drop in salary but increasingly I felt I was making a difference in the world." As Director for Development for Give Kids the World, Angie helped the charity's inspirational founder, Henri Landwirth, create a 75-acre resort for terminally-ill children in Orlando and raise more than $10 million through corporate partnerships to support that effort.

"I learned a lot of things from Henri but maybe the most important is that why you do what you do is often more important than what you do. Henri helped me see every decision through the eyes of the children we served," shared Angie.

> "Making a difference has always been my key leadership principle. It is infectious and impactful. People can see it when a person is intent on making a difference."
>
> **Angie Halamandaris,** Co-Founder and President, The Heart of America Foundation.

One of the many gifts Henri gave her was an introduction to the man she would marry – Bill Halamandaris. Bill had spent his life in public service, first at the U.S. Senate and then as a founder of several charities. Looking for something to do together that combined their interests, the couple founded the Heart of America Foundation in 1997. The organization was so named because Bill and Angie believe it represents the "heart of America" – people who represent the best instincts of man and the best in society.

"Few things surpass the satisfaction of knowing you have made a difference in the life of a child. We wanted to do whatever we could to make sure every child has a chance – a chance to learn to read, succeed, and make a difference in the world," shared Angie.

Angie leads the organization, which focuses on inspiring acts of service and a love of reading. The charity builds community by asking those who have to help those who have not. Key programs are committed to education and volunteer service. The Heart of America Foundation engages volunteers by putting books into the hands of children who need them the most. Through the Books From The Heart® and READesign® programs, the organization revitalizes school libraries and reading spaces in under-resourced communities into vital and vibrant centers of learning that become the heart of a school.

Since 1997, through Angie's leadership on a national scale, The Heart of America Foundation has provided over one million children living in poverty with over 3.5 million library and take-home books (a value in excess of $22.3 million) and has replenished, redecorated and revitalized more than 260 school libraries and education spaces in high-need areas through its library makeover program across the USA. In addition, Angie has engaged community and corporate volunteers in giving back more than one million hours of service in their communities. Further, Heart of America has helped to introduce more than 500,000 students to community service.

"Making a difference has always been my key leadership principle. It is infectious and impactful. People can see it when a person is intent on making a difference," shared Angie.

As an example, Angie recalled what happened when Hurricane Katrina hit New Orleans.

"I will never forget how my son reacted," she said. "He was just in first grade then but when he saw the hurricane's impact, he wanted to donate all of the money from his piggy bank. İt showed me just how fundamental the desire to make a difference actually is. İ was so moved by my son's act we designed a program to help children like him respond. From that humble effort grew Operation BuddyPack which grew to involve over 16,000 children. We were able to deliver 40 tons of backpacks filled with essential supplies in six weeks to the children in the Gulf Coast region who had nothing!

After losing everything, now at least they had something they could call their own," shared Angie.

Angie shared that her desire to make a difference has helped her personally manage so many challenges she has faced as a woman – both professional and personal.

"First, there are so many expectations from me as a leader, mother, wife and care giver to my mum. Second, I believe women are often under estimated and have to work harder to prove themselves. So doing what you love and knowing that you are making a difference can mean the difference between a good job and spectacular success," said Angie.

Making a difference has truly sparked spectacular success for Angie and has enabled her to touch countless lives. From establishing the national "Heroes of the Heart®" recognition program to highlighting heroes of all ages throughout the US for their community building efforts; to reaching out to students to provide a 'Day of Hope' a year after the Columbine High School massacre in Denver, Colorado; to responding to needs and creating a national awareness campaign to aid families after the September 11 attack on the World Trade Center in New York in 2001; to engaging 250,000 students in restoring Gulf coast school libraries, classrooms and home libraries destroyed by the storms by providing books for children in need.

Angie now leads her staff and volunteers to focus their efforts on the needs of children living in areas of poverty through the Books From The Heart® and READesign® Library Makeover programs; not just in disaster plagued cities, but around the country in other areas experiencing hardship. These projects engage corporate volunteers, youth volunteers and other members of the community in service and community involvement through library beautification and improvement activities, book distributions and one-on-

one reading activities with children. These programs are supported with lasting relationships with premier organizations such as Target Corporation, Capital One, Federal Express, NFL Players Association, and many others.

"In our business, we have to lead by example. You have to walk the talk," she explained. "This is to me the only way to live. Traveling around the country, visiting schools. Every single person has to stay true to the mission. You can never lose when you are being authentic. I speak in front of thousands of people every year, so it is important for them to feel that they are part of something that is real and is making a difference," she shared.

You get what you give. Angie is often reminded of the rich rewards of making a career out of helping people.

Angie commented, "During President Obama's first inauguration it was a big week in DC," she recalls. "We were participating in a very large Project with many other non profit organizations. There were a lot of celebrities such as Oprah, Usher, and Tobey Maguire, involved. Often times when events become highly visible, people can lose their focus on what is truly important. I started sharing that I felt that at an event like this we should be involving the children themselves more. Immediately following the discussion a little boy walked across the foyer of the event school hugged me and walked away without saying a word. I felt like he spoke for all the children whose names we would never know. I was so touched."

As another example, she spoke of the aftermath of 911. "We went up to the District Attorneys Office in New York to ask how we could help. They told us that many of the victims' families would have no health insurance and asked if we could arrange insurance for as many of the families as possible. We were able to raise funds for the health insurance of 30 families. One woman I will never forget had two small children and was pregnant when it happened. She was devastated by the loss of her husband. When I called to check on her I found this loss was compounded by the loss of the baby at birth. Her mother said she didn't know what she would have done without our support," added Angie.

Angie believes that her passion for making a difference has been influenced by several people including her mentor, holocaust survivor Henri Landwirth, famed environmentalist Dr. Jane Goodall, and Leila Macauley, co-founder of AmeriCares. "I am in awe of Henri's ability to forgive and answer hate with love," Angie said. "Jane's unyielding commitment to the environment is an inspiration not only to me but to all who know her and Leila Macauley has taught me it is possible to address the problems of the world one child at a time."

Angie has demonstrated her commitment to improving the lives of children in need through volunteer service to organizations such as the National Capital Area Foundation of the March of Dimes, WETA-TV, The Caring Institute, The Frederick Douglass Museum and Hall of Fame for Caring Americans and other foundations and committees. She has been recognized by the Junior League of Northern Virginia as the 2007 "Woman of Vision Award" recipient. She is also a graduate of the 2009 class of the Leadership Greater Washington program.

Under her leadership, The Heart of America Foundation has been honored with the 2008 Target 'Best of the Bullseye Award for Innovation,' the 2009 Morris and Gwendolyn Cafritz Foundation *Youth Partnership Award* Finalist designation and was named 'One of the Best' by the 2009-10 Catalogue for Philanthropy, Greater Washington.

Angie shared with me her top five tips for how young women professionals could cultivate the habit of 'making a difference':

- *Be Positive*:
  Know that anything is possible with great love and determination. Winston Churchill once said, "A pessimist sees the difficulty in every opportunity; an optimist sees the opportunity in every difficulty." I believe attitude is a choice. Choosing to live a positive life predicts and ensures success.

- *Listen:*
  Make a conscious effort to truly hear and understand what people are saying. Becoming a more active listener will not only help you create deeper relationships but will help you to better understand your world and have a greater impact in the lives of others.

- *Forget Yourself:*

  An amazing and humble woman by the name of Rachel Rossow once shared with us the basic lesson that she taught her 22 children of all ages and disabilities. She taught them, that first you need to learn to know yourself, to love yourself, and then forget yourself in service to others. This is a powerful lesson and one that I have continued to remind myself of over the years.

- *Think Small* :

  Some people think that to make a difference in the world you have to make some grandiose gesture or give away millions of dollars. Sometimes it is the small things that can make the biggest difference. People that try to do too much at once often do nothing at all. Do what you can, when you can.

- *Don't Forget to Take Your Heart to Work:*

  Make sure to filter every decision through the head and heart. Whenever we are hiring new team members at The Heart of America Foundation, we always look for those that possess both head and heart. This combination has proven to be very successful in helping our organization to grow and make a difference.

Angie clarified that being a woman professional definitely held challenges over her career but her guiding principle of 'making a difference' had helped her through every challenge she faced.

"Early in my career, I found that being a woman professional came with several challenges. One such challenge was feeling like I needed to be over-prepared in most every situation. I often found myself having to work much harder than my male counterparts in demonstrating my strengths and abilities.

With this hard work and determination, came a confidence that was both helpful and a hindrance. As I gained confidence and trust with those in my work, I quickly learned the importance of letting go of my ego. Too much ego can inhibit great learning and growth.

When I learned that I could do anything, I learned I could not do everything.

In letting go, I have been able to learn some of the greatest lessons both in work and life. This has also allowed me to truly follow my passion and do what I love.

In the end, the decision I made to take a 50% drop in salary and go do something I was passionate about has defined who I am and helped me touch people's lives in a way I myself never fully imagined," said Angie.

I am sure the millions of people touched by Angie would agree.

# Chapter 2

# HAVE A
# CLEAR GOAL
## PLAN FOR
## SUCCESS

Research shows that simply SETTING a goal raises the chances of achieving that goal significantly. Given the multiple priorities that women face in professional and personal life this becomes increasingly significant.

In a Harvard study, students were surveyed on their goals after graduating. 84% had no specific goals, 13% had goals but they were not written down. 3% had clear written goals.

Fast forward ten years and those grads were interviewed again. The 13% who had goals were earning, on average: twice as much as the 84% without goals. The 3% with written goals were earning, on average ten times as much as the other 97% of graduates.

In exploring this challenge, I spoke to three of the most focused individuals I have ever met – **Phyllis Marwah,** *Chairperson, Mothers Choice;* **Joanne Soo,** *CEO, ACE Adventure;* and **Maria Fernanda Mejia,** *President, Kellogg Latin America* to understand their success via good goal setting.

I first met **Phyllis Marwah** at the American Chambers of Commerce (AMCHAM) Women of Influence Awards 2012, Hong Kong where she was being recognized for her many achievements. In the first few seconds that she spoke, I realized how extraordinarily focused she was. There was no self-congratulation or overt celebration of her achievements. She was a woman there with a goal, a mission. To continue to garner support for the NGO that she and three others set up in 1987 called Mothers Choice.

Setting goals and exceeding them has been a key success factor for Phyllis Marwah. Phyllis is the **Chairwoman** of the NGO **Mothers Choice** that helps single women, their families and boyfriends coping with crisis pregnancy.

Phyllis grew up in Taos, New Mexico. She studied Education at Grace College, the University of Hawaii and the University of Washington.

Phyllis' father was a pastor. She remembers how her mother played the piano at every single service her father gave, and even taught Sunday school. She saw first-hand the power of her parents being focused on their life goal – doing good and helping the poor.

Phyllis comes from a family of six children. An environment where every one of the kids had to pull their own weight.

Her father Sam continued to preach and build strong communities through his missionary work for close to 30 years, often surrounding his family and children with hardship to enable the contributions they had to make in the community.

> *"Being clear about the goal ensures that you give your focus and capacity to the things that are most important."*
>
> **Phyllis Marwah,**
> Chairwoman,
> Mothers Choice.

She started her first job at the age of 14.

As a young Professional, Phyllis found her goal to be loving, kind and patient often challenged.

In 1974, Phyllis moved to Hong Kong to complete her field study for the East-West center of the University of Hawaii. She taught school in Hong Kong and fell in love with the city. She continued to teach and interact with young people for several years.

In 1987 Phyllis was brought face to face with a situation that would change her life and give her a goal, which would last over 30 years.

Phyllis shared, "In 1987 we saw a series of articles in the South China Morning Post which highlighted an alarming and sad situation that no one was addressing. Hundreds of teenage girls every month were experiencing crisis pregnancies. With no one to talk to for good information or advice on their options, many were keeping their situation secret as long as they could, then crossing over from Hong Kong to Shenzhen, China, for abortions that were often in third trimester, and dangerous, even life-threatening."

"During the 1980's, pregnant and unmarried teenagers faced intense stigma and criticism that their actions brought disgrace to their families. There was a wide gap in the Hong Kong community and the schools with regard to sex awareness and education; sexuality and pregnancy were simply not talked about at home or at school. Many of these girls felt that their pregnancy had to be kept secret from their families or they would be kicked out of their homes. They had nowhere to go, no support from the community and knew of no other choice than abortion," she added.

"We found out that all the places that pregnant girls could go to in Hong Kong then were juvenile delinquency centers. They treated them as if they had committed a crime. We wanted to provide a loving home for them until they gave birth, and help them get back into society after their deliveries," shared Phyllis.

"So a small group of us started Mothers Choice to help Hong Kong's single women, their families and boyfriends coping with crisis pregnancy.

Many girls who come to us are so desperate they just want to commit suicide. We have three options for them - terminate the pregnancy, give birth and give up the baby for adoption, or give birth and be a teenage mother. All three options are painful," added Phyllis.

What started as a simple effort to help Hong Kong's single women has today evolved into an inspirational movement. With Pregnant Girls Services Pregnant Girls Hostel, Counseling Services, Referral Services, Adoption Services, a Child care home and emergency foster care.

Mothers Choice has over the last 25 plus years remained focused on its original goal - to provide and promote loving, nurturing care for babies and children needing permanent homes, and for single girls and their families facing crisis pregnancies.

The organization has impacted thousands in Hong Kong and inspired sister organizations in India, China and Cambodia.

Phyllis shared that a Chinese woman living in Hong Kong called Dr. Barbara Chan helped shape her life goal as well.

"Barbara and I went to the same church. She had seen me have all of my children. She once told me that I always need to keep my hand open. She explained that if I always keep my hand open, I would be happy with what I have and never even know if something is taken away. If I kept my hand open, I will always be ready to give to others, but will also receive. She taught me never to count the cost of giving to others!" said Phyllis.

"But generosity must be focused. To do good, one must be deliberate about it. What has been most instrumental in my success is my ability to have and focus relentlessly on a clear goal. From the moment we decided to set up Mothers Choice there have been tremendous ups and downs along the way, but what has sustained us is our clear mission of promoting loving, nurturing care for babies and children needing permanent homes, and for single girls and their families facing crisis pregnancies," commented Phyllis.

Phyllis goal of giving love to the hapless women she has encountered has truly tested her resolve.

"When we started Mothers Choice in 1987, we really didn't know what we had gotten ourselves into. The first building we got on Borrett road was full of rubbish and everyone was a volunteer. Even my six kids at the time (I had one more later) came in every single day after school to help clean and pick up rubbish. The simple goal at that point was to turn the former military barracks which had been unused for over 15 years into livable quarters," shared Phyllis.

"I can remember clearly like yesterday, the first lady we helped," added Phyllis.

"The very day after we opened Mothers Choice, we received a call from

Queen Mary hospital about a girl who was wandering around in a housing estate and was obviously about to deliver a child, and was scared and depressed. The hospital had tried everything but the girl just refused help. In desperation they called us, believing we could help.

We agreed to help and we managed to get to the girl. The next day we left a nurse with her. The girl was lying in the room and the nurse told her that she was going to get her some biscuits and tea. By the time the nurse got back to the girl's space, the girl had given birth," added Phyllis.

"So we called in the ambulance. What was shocking was as the girl was being taken into the ambulance the girl started shouting hysterically that she did not want to see the baby. So within 24 hours of opening Mothers Choice we had our first baby.

Later when we visited the baby we were told the baby would have to go to an orphanage. When we visited the orphanages we realized it wasn't the best place to leave the child. And that lead us to set up our own on-site care and facilities for these children," shared Phyllis.

Phyllis shared that the challenges facing women in todays corporate and social sector are still many and women need to be more focused about what it is they want to achieve.

"Despite the day and age we live in, there are still so many challenges facing women and possibilities for support. My own daughter has even done things like breast feed her baby in the lobby of the building in which she worked even though she was working for a leading Corporate at the time."

"The biggest challenge for a woman in career today is to be taken seriously. And to know what she wants. Distraction is what makes a professional less effective," shared Phyllis.

Over the years Mothers Choice has grown significantly to cover many things but Phyllis has always kept the organization well anchored and focused on the basic mission. To help single young women cope with unwanted pregnancies.

"This central goal has guided most of the important choices we make every year. One such choice was the need for Mothers Choice to have its own social workers. In one instance a while back, our staff noticed an old man consistently walking around our facility. It was odd, so I went out to ask him why he was here," shared Phyllis.

He simply said, "I work at the railway station and I see many girls coming to Shenzhen to abort their babies. İ often have to clear up their blood off the floor. I heard about you and wanted to see what it is you do. Even if I can pass on your information to a few of these who are aborting their children, it may help save the babies lives... that's why I was looking around your facility."

Phyllis commented, "That opened my eyes for us to have our own social workers who would not only be available onsite to help with the kids but also proactively work to identify the girls most at risk.

Being clear about the goal ensures that you give your focus and capacity to the things that are most important. Over the years we have been sorely tempted to move Mothers Choice into different areas but that would only distract us from our core mission. First and foremost we are there for the girls and finding families for their babies. This is our core idea and objective and we have to let go of some of the other things," she added.

Phyllis' relentless pursuit of her goal of establishing Mothers Choice as an extension of her personal goal to be kind, loving and patient has rubbed off on her children.

One daughter was inspired to take up medicine; another works for an NGO; one son aims to work in human rights after his law studies in London; and another, who is a barrister, helps her with work on improving laws to protect children. Alia, her eldest child, showed signs early on that she might devote herself to charity work.

In August 2012, her daughter Eyres (Alia), a lawyer, who also practiced in the United States, joined Mothers Choice as its CEO. This came with a huge drop in salary.

Alia shared at that time: "It's no sacrifice. I am grateful that I got to work for something that I am passionate about. We are continuing a mission that my parents started out decades ago. Now it is my goal. My choice, my mission. In doing this I am carrying on a family legacy."

Today Mothers Choice employs over a hundred people and has helped over 35000 single women, their children and families. The phenomenal success of the organization can best be seen by the fact that there is a four-year waiting list of volunteers waiting to help support Mothers Choice!

"I couldn't be happier with what I am doing in my life. İ have seven kids. I have devoted my life to helping these young girls and children, and the satisfaction and delight I have got in seeing these peoples lives change sustains and inspires me on to greater effort. Yes, there have been sacrifices along the way, financial and other hardships, but it has all been so worth it," smiled Phyllis as we ended our meeting.

Walking around the Mothers Choice facilities I cannot help but admire the hundreds of happy pictures and cards that Phyllis and Mothers Choice receives every week. Some thanking her for their newfound kids, some thanking her for her support, some just thanking her for her love.

In 2012, Phyllis Marwah won the 2012 'Entrepreneur of the Year' at the AMCHAM Women of Influence awards in Hong Kong. There were tears shed in the audience as Phyllis acknowledged that her life's goal of helping these young girls was only made possible by the love and support shown to her by her mother and the many other women who had played a role in shaping her own values.

But the ultimate testimonial came from her daughter Alia. She said: "My mum is the most goal oriented and focused person I know. And also the kindest person I know."

Phyllis is a deeply religious person and shared with me that the five tips that have helped her be very focused on her goal came from the Bible, Proverbs, Chapter 11.

These were:

- *Be Honest in all that you do:*
  The Lord abhors dishonest scales but accurate weights are his delight.
- *Be humble:*
  Pride comes, then comes disgrace, but with humility comes wisdom.
- *Have integrity:*
  The integrity of the upright guides them, but the unfaithful are destroyed

by duplicity.

- *Be kind:*
  A kindhearted woman gains respect, a kind man benefits himself.

- *Be generous:*
  A generous man will prosper; he who refreshes others will himself be refreshed.

Phyllis concluded, "I feel that it is everyone's responsibility to take care of the poor and needy in their own community. There are many ways to give other than money--your time, your talents, and experience. If we all work together, we can make a difference and change our world.

In Singapore in the meantime, **Joanne Soo**, is focused on entirely different goals but as challenging.

At 10, Joanne Soo had already started her first vacation job. By 15, she was completely independent and had saved enough to pay for her own school, books and education.

Joanne is no ordinary person. She is one of Asia's top climbers and a member of the all women team of climbers from Singapore who successfully summited Mt. Everest on May 22, 2009.

Her mission in life is to be the best climber she can be and to teach young Singaporeans life skills through adventure. Little wonder that Joanne is also **CEO** of **ACE Adventure**, a Singapore based Company that she set up in 1999 that organizes mountain climbing trips for students to develop their character and leadership qualities.

"My clarity about my mission and passion in life did not come overnight. I had many dreams such as being a teacher, an architect, and a graphic artist. But when I discovered climbing at the age of 19, I invested all my energies and finances into it. From then on there was literally no turning back," shared Joanne.

Joanne and her sister were both adopted by their parents when the parents were well past 40.

"My parents were born before WWII, and the war deprived them from having a proper education. My dad used to work as an apprentice in a restaurant. He later became a school bus driver after being jobless for a long time trying to be a cook. My mum used to work in the shipyard and worked very long hours. I recall that when my dad was jobless, my mum worked round the clock to provide for the family. She would leave home at 6 am only to return after midnight. Between the ages of 7 and 12, I hardly saw my mum, and my dad stayed home to look after us including cooking good meals for us. The fundamentals of my work ethic started with my parents who have been so good to us," shared Joanne.

Joanne believes it was the challenging circumstances of her growing up that helped her focus on what she wanted to do with her life.

"Life was really simple and tough at times. My older sister and I started to do part time work during school holidays to earn pocket money to celebrate Chinese New Year, to ease my mum's burden," she added.

> "Being the best mountaineer I can be has helped me negotiate between life and death. Having a clear goal has helped me to stay focused despite the most challenging of circumstances."
>
> **Joanne Soo,** CEO, ACE Adventure.

To compound matters, Joanne did not perform well academically.

"I stopped school after my O levels because my results were not impressive. I could have gone on to study commerce in one of the institutions, but that was not what I wanted. I wanted to be an architect, or a graphic designer, but my grades were not good enough for our local polytechs. I had tried attending the foundation course at the Nanyang Fine Arts to prepare for a diploma course in the design field, but the course fee was very difficult for me to pay, so I stopped. I later took up advanced diploma courses in business management after I started working and when I had a stable flow of income," she added.

Then on a fateful day shortly after her 19th birthday Joanne started climbing.

"I went on my first climb without much physical preparation yet I did extremely well. Not only did I enjoy the climb, I was able to support my climbing mates. I helped to carry extra loads for friends who were too weak to press on. That raised my self-esteem. I finally felt that I was actually good at something. I wanted to return to the mountains because I was more confident when climbing."

That set Joanne thinking. Climbing was an expensive affair and she was enjoying it as a "weekend warrior". Yet she acknowledged that climbing was becoming important to her.

"I wanted to move away from what others deem 'that's the way to go'. I just wanted to live a life that I would have no regrets in my later years. I also knew that I was not good at academics but great at sports. I was also on the basket ball team in school so I knew I had some aptitude for this," she added.

But pursuing her goal did not come easy. Joanne had to fund creative ways to supplement her income.

"The first step was making sure I earned enough to meet the expenses of this very expensive sport. So I worked part-time with McDonald's while holding a full-time job. My weekends, and some weekdays evening, were spent working at the fast food restaurant. When I was in my mid twenties, adventure camps for schools became popular; I worked as a part-time camp instructor. Once I had enough savings, I would plan for a mountain trip. But these mountain trips were restricted to Malaysia and Indonesia as the costs were relatively lower. The climbing duration span from three days to a week," she shared.

Joanne continued to climb, and made her first major trip when she was 25 - a three-week trek in Nepal, and another one in 1998, also to Nepal.

Then at 29, she realized that if she wanted to truly pursue her goal she would have to be responsible for her goal and in control of her time.

"I realized that if I continued to work as a salaried worker and additional part time worker I would just not have the time to do more. I would continue to be trapped in a vicious cycle – of working for the money, versus working towards my dream. So I decided to go full time into outdoor adventure. That was the first big piece," commented Joanne.

The idea of setting up an adventure company came in 1999, after some planning, Joanne left my salaried job in 2000 to open ACE Adventure.

"My motivation to start on my own was that I wanted to create a climbing culture among Singaporeans. Climbing allows me to appreciate the little things in life; it has humbled me, and gives a broader perspective about many iffy issues in our fast moving society. I want more people to have that same opportunity. To do so, I have to engage myself fully," she shared.

But gaining support for her mission was no easy task.

"I had to share my mission with my parents. We had to travel to Malaysia to climb, and I wouldn't dare let my parents know that I travelled overseas, because both of them didn't even have a passport to travel at that time," she added.

While Joanne's parents did not fully approve of her climbing, they did not try to stop her either. Joanne slowly won them over by getting them involved.

"I made an effort to show them the photos I took of the places I visited. I would especially focus on the culture of the country and avoid showing them any images that looked overly dangerous. More importantly, as I returned home safely after each climb, that gave them the confidence that I knew what I was doing," shared Joanne.

And then there were the risks.

Joanne commented, "I had a couple of near fatal encounters in my early days of climbing. The first when I was just about to turn 21. I still had no formal training for climbing back then. I had zero knowledge of rock climbing specifically which is different from mountain climbing. I made an attempt on a route without much knowledge about the risk involved and I fell, and all of my protection points didn't hold me except for one, I was hanging less than a feet from the ground. I could have been injured badly or even died, and my belayer could have been injured too. I was stunned, but ignorance kept me going."

"Not until I acquired formal training and eventually became an Instructor that I realized how lucky I had been," she added.

A second incident after scaling Mount Kinabalu wherein she immediately went white water rafting, was thrown out of the raft after it capsized, and almost died, left Joanne with a healthy respect for the outdoors.

"By then I was clear that I wanted to make climbing my life. I realized that I had been so fortunate to escape both those near death experiences and resolved never to take my life or the lives of those with me lightly again. I learned to assess the risk involved in climbing," shared Joanne.

Joanne took up a basic rock-climbing course and started regular climbing practice. From there, she met many rock climbers who shared their experiences. She also went to Batu Caves, a popular rock climbing site near Kuala Lampur in Malaysia, to rock climb to gain exposure on various natural rock formation. She took up an instructor course and became a climbing instructor in 2000. In the midst of learning climbing, she also took up abseiling.

"As the saying goes, what goes up must come down. I picked up the skills and successfully became an abseil instructor," she added.

Amazingly, Joanne has not attended any formal training in mountaineering.

"I did not manage to plan for one mainly because the more reputable courses were only available overseas like in New Zealand or the USA. And closer to home was the course in India, but it requires 28 days to complete the course. As a twenty - something young adult, I could not afford the time (long leave from work), and it was too expensive for me to travel to New Zealand or the USA," she added.

Joanne compensated for her lack of formal mountaineering education by reading umpteen books on mountaineering.

"I borrowed books on mountaineering literature from the library, and I also bought mountaineering books. "Freedom of the Hills" by the Mountaineers is a book that I always referred to, even till today. I am also inspired by the stories of Sir Chris Bonington, Doug Scott, Reinhold Messner, and Alison Hargreaves. Alison Hargreaves had summited Mt Everest without bottled oxygen and without a Sherpa support in 1995. The same year, she went on to summit K2, the 2nd highest in the world, but perished with her team when they made their descent. The infamous Mt Everest tragedy in 1996 killed 11 climbers. These two tragic mountaineering histories served as a learning for me," added Joanne.

In 2003 Joanne set her sights on the most prestigious and ambitious challenge of all – an assault on the highest peak in the world – Mount Everest. Joanne teamed up with five of her fellow climbers to form the first ever all women team representing Singapore to make the attempt on Mt. Everest.

For Joanne, it was also a moment of introspection and coming face to face with her own fears.

"All of my team mates were in their early 20s and super fit. I felt age and experience were against me," she shared.

Yet, she steeled her resolve and told herself to focus on her mission.

"I recommitted to both the physical and mental training required, and pushed myself to the limit," added Joanne.

"I also had to balance out the needs of my business ACE Adventure and the time needed to climb. It was a five-year commitment. By then my business ACE adventure was picking up. I did have doubts about my ability to maintain my four old business. Unlike the others who would have a steady income as long as they reported to work diligently, finished work at 6 pm then headed for training, I had to balance out looking after my business and stepping up my training as well. My challenge was to ensure I would not lose income no matter how tired I would be after each training session. Spending time on expeditions would mean a loss of income for me as an entrepreneur," she shared.

What followed were five years years of arduous training to prepare them for the 8850-meter climb up Mt. Everest. The preparation was as physical as it was mental. To physically deal with the stresses and stamina needed for the climb Joanne and the team put in brutal four hour workouts every day including stair climbing at their apartment blocks sometimes as late as midnight.

"10 km runs, weekly circuit training up hills, with 25 kg weight packs and ankle weights all became part of the daily routine," shared Joanne.

Joanne also dealt with the mental challenge of whether an all women team from Singapore could make it up Everest.

"Finally it all came down to how badly we wanted to achieve our goal, our mission. The mountain of course did not care whether we are male or female," added Joanne.

Between 2004, the women team scaled the peaks across New Zealand, Tibet, Nepal, and China. Day in and day out Joanne and the team stuck to their mission. Joanne says she spent about 30,000 dollars of her hard earned savings on these expeditions.

On 22 May 2009 Joanne and one of the team made it to the top of Mt. Everest. Two days earlier three of the other climbers had made it.

Joanne and her team returned home to Singapore to a heroines welcome from Prime Minister Lee Hsien Loong and then President S.R.Nathan.

I asked Joanne why she was so passionate about climbing and why she had made it her life's mission.

She responded:

"To me, climbing is a very personal affair. We may climb together in a group, but it is the individual experience that is attractive. There are so many external factors to consider - relationship with our climbing teammates, respecting the culture and the people we meet in a country, dealing with the environment, dealing with fear and the unknown- all these external factors will contribute to our individual experience, and each of our experiences is unique."

She continued: "This is exactly what I like about climbing. Some people call it self-discovery, or self-actualization. When I climb, I can see myself very clearly because when in the mountains the environment is so harsh that none of us can disguise our true selves. Or our behaviors. We become who we actually are! It is this experience that will guide me to be a better person that attracts me to climbing. The breathtaking scenery is motivating, the summit is a bonus," she added.

As a woman, Joanne has faced several unique challenges in her chosen field.

She commented, "Especially in the field I have chosen, it can be challenging being a woman. Mountaineering is a male dominated sport. Less than 2% of the climbers who reached the summit of Mt Everest have been women. And coming from an island with the highest point standing at 164m, it is hard for anyone to imagine how Singaporeans would tackle the harsh environment of a mountain, let alone being a woman climber,"

Today, Joanne continues to pursue her passion for climbing, but is also seeking other avenues to continue her mission of being the best climber she can be, yet at the same time

Joanne shared that having a clear goal has been the most important factor in her success.

"Being the best mountaineer I can be has helped me negotiate between life and death. Having a clear goal has helped me to stay focused despite the most challenging of circumstances," she shared.

Joanne's tips on setting goals and achieving them:

- *Listen carefully to understand your own purpose:*
  Find happiness in what you do. So that when adversity strikes, you know exactly why you need to push through it.

- *Acknowledge that your goal will have consequences:*
  Think through these consequences and ask yourself if you are willing to bear them. Make sure you are willing to deal not just with the returns that may come, but more importantly, the many challenges that will likely come before you taste success.

- *Build a bridge towards your goal:*
  Learn from mistakes. Build a plan that is flexible towards your dream or aspiration. Acknowledge that there may be tweaks along the way, just as long as you are progressing at an acceptable pace.

- *Adapt to change quickly:*
  Circumstances can change quickly. The most successful people are not necessarily the smartest but the ones that adapt fastest.

- *Avoid burn out:*
  Set milestones towards your goals and reward yourself for achieving them. This will re energize you and motivate you on towards the long-term objective.

Joanne has over the years enabled thousands of young people to experience 'leadership on the mountain.' She has also climbed the highest peaks across

India, Nepal, South America, Korea, China and Indonesia.

She maintains that her positive outlook, commitment to fitness, ability to learn constantly and most important, her focus on her goal has helped her live a life without limits.

"I believe that my goal has helped me share my love of climbing with so many students through ACE Adventure. Through my Company, I am not only helping people to climb, or to have an outdoors adventure. We are also helping them to develop life goals, learn to deal with challenge and adversity and finally drive towards the success that they so want," she concluded.

**M**aria Fernanda was just a little girl when she first heard the words her Mum shared that would stay with her all her life.

"Plan big, get big. Be clear about what you want to achieve and stay flexible," said her Mum.

Maria Fernanda has done exactly that in a career that has so far spanned 25 years.

> *"I learned at a very early age that having a clear goal and planning for your own success is key. No one else is going to do it for you."*
>
> *Maria Fernanda Mejia, President, Kellogg Latin America.*

This includes the Colgate-Palmolive Company where she held a variety of roles since 1989 including corporate vice president and general manager, Global Personal Care and Corporate Fragrance Development, corporate vice president of marketing for Europe/South Pacific, and president and CEO of Colgate-Palmolive Spain.

In November 2011 she joined Kellogg as President, Kellogg Latin America. She is a Corporate officer and a member of the Kellogg Global Leadership team.

Born in Cali, Colombia and a US citizen, Maria Fernanda was only four when she moved to the United States with her family.

She saw the power of her Mum's single-minded goal.

"My Mum had a very clear plan – to assimilate into US culture but also help us remember our Colombian roots – she dreamed of us being successful in the United States," shared Maria Fernanda.

She added, "My parents' focus was that we embraced the best of the American culture; learn and thrive in our new environment and become part of the community."

"I learned at a very early age that having a clear goal and planning for your own success is key. No one else is going to do it for you," shared Maria Fernanda.

So she started planning. And set about exploring her life's mission – to be a global business leader.

"I was always proactive and took ownership of my dreams, goals and my responsibility in achieving results with others. I have been blessed to have the support of many leaders that helped turn that proactivity into real leadership. Becoming a leader starts with believing in leadership and understanding its role in delivering exceptional results, building successful relationships and developing ourselves and the people under our responsibility. It has required an enormous amount of time, resources and hard work. It has been worth every minute," she shared.

Maria Fernanda received her engineering degree in 1985, with a concentration in Industrial Distribution from Texas A&M University.

In 1989, she achieved the first phase of her mission of being a global business leader by joining Colgate (now known as Colgate Palmolive).

"I am a highly focused, obsessive strategist and planner and very disciplined and rigorous in the management of all aspects of my life. I have also learned to be flexible. I have achieved more than I ever dreamed, but not always in the manner I and perhaps others had planned. I have been able to balance my role as a wife, mother and business leader by always maximizing the career development tools available in the organizations where I worked and ensuring that I always had an overall life plan that aligned to my career plan. The two must be living, reviewed with certain frequency and aligned for maximum impact," she shared.

She added, "Life is constant and our goals and priorities naturally evolve or change. We must be deliberate in our career and life planning. The most important thing for me in achieving my goals and aspirations was to make my family my inspiration to succeed and to be relentlessly focused, open and flexible and have fun while doing it all."

While being flexible was a journey in itself and did not come easy, openness combined with flexibility to achieve her mission has paid rich dividends for Maria Fernanda.

In 1993 as a young mother with two kids aged one and three, Maria Fernanda went through an amicable divorce.

"It was a challenging time. Clearly divorce was not part of the life plan. But my ex-husband and I talked and planned together how best we would make the divorce least disturbing for us both and still be good parents to our two kids. That commitment helped our family thrive and prosper and our children to grow into exceptional human beings and global citizens. We stayed the dearest of friends right till his passing in 2010," she said.

The divorce however left her with a tough choice. To leave Puerto Rico where she was based at the time and move back to the USA.

"My household shipment was on its way to Houston where I was moving to take on a new role in a new company. Then three weeks before the date I was to physically move to Houston, my General Manager at Colgate called me into his office, looked me in the eye and said to me "Maria Fernanda, we need you here. You must consider staying on in Puerto Rico and then join us as we continue to develop your global career at Colgate," she shared.

She continued, "So I talked to my Mum and my ex-husband and they both said I should stay."

"That moment changed my life. It took courage, flexibility, loyalty and commitment to my company as well as my ability to adapt to the situation impressed my bosses. They invested heavily in me. I experienced an accelerated global career and held a number of positions of increased responsibility in North America, Latin America, Asia and Europe/South Pacific. In just a few years I was promoted multiple times across functions and geographies. Most importantly, my commitment, agility and demonstrated success in delivering results and developing talent created a tremendous trust and respect between my organization and myself. As I stayed on, it became increasingly apparent that I would have a global career, just like I had dreamed when I was a child." shared Maria Fernanda.

After a successful 23 year global career at Colgate, in November 2011 Maria Fernanda took the next step on her life journey with a move to The Kellogg Company as President of Latin America.

"I found a great Company (Kellogg) with whom I shared the same values and beliefs, business and leadership philosophy and where I believed I could contribute by leveraging my global experience," shared Maria Fernanda.

That "journey" is an exciting new growth agenda for Kellogg – a Company that Maria Fernanda says is "taking exciting new steps in not only going to the next level of global growth, but also continuing the journey of social responsibility and giving back to the communities where we live and work through the legacy of our founder W.K. Kellogg and under the helm of our CEO John Bryant."

"I believe that my work today in our great company integrates my love for building global brands, developing people and making money through my passion to live a life of meaning. I hope to play a small part in continuing the great legacy of our founder Mr. W.K. Kellogg," added Maria Fernanda.

At Kellogg Maria Fernanda has been instrumental in helping the global team craft a new Global strategy and growth agenda, drive transformational change, lead a new vision and strategy for the Latin America Region and create an environment for growth where our leaders can develop and thrive. Talent and Leadership development is Maria Fernanda's number one business priority.

Maria Fernanda outlined her top tips for planning of success:

- *Align your professional and personal goals:*
  I realized at a very early stage the power of alignment. Understanding where I was going and how to get it done. As a leader I have realized that the best way of creating opportunity for self and to aid planning is to align with your company values, vision and strategy as well as operating model. Align with your leaders and the organization! You will simply move ahead in career and life much faster and achieve greater individual and collective results if conflict is minimized and you simply share the same values and beliefs.

- *Stay flexible:*

I believe that ambition is a good thing, but it should be based on good intent. I have always made my ambitions known to my bosses but made sure to they also know my good intention in wanting to do certain roles. Then I have trusted my managers to do the right thing for me. I have never been disappointed.

- *Learn from anyone and everyone:*
  I have never missed a single training or development opportunity in my life. I doodle constantly. I keep a meticulous diary in which I put down ideas, inspirational quotes, and observations from others. Interestingly what's in my diary is mostly about the learning that others can give me, less about self. At the end of the day I will often spend a few minutes to reflect on my notes in the diary and define clear action steps to aid my planning. In 1997 when I moved from Puerto Rico to work in our Corporate Global Marketing group in New York I was responsible for developing global Strategy for one of our principle categories and I worked for an exceptional strategist and people developer. On our first day together he talked to me about the three questions you ask when developing strategy "Where are we? Where do we want to be? How do we get there? I wrote then down in my notebook (which I still have in my office) and those words have been critical in helping me develop successful strategies and initiatives and deliver consistent results.

- *Make your family your inspiration to succeed:*
  Planning big also requires a support team to keep me moving and on track. I have been blessed to be supported by amazing personal assistants. I can honestly say that they have been huge enablers in my planning process. So have family. Much of what I am today is because despite all the challenges she faced when moving to the USA, my Mum never let me wake up a single day without telling me that I was the best no matter what anyone believed or said "I was the best". Not one day went by that she did not tell me what a great daughter, student, and professional I was. Till this day she still does that. I have counted on the unconditional support of my children and husband and today I can say that all that I have achieved is not my success, but my family's success. You cannot succeed without them!

- *Commit and put in the hard work:*
  Be courageous Finally no amount of planning will get you to where you

want to go, unless you are willing to put in the hard work and learn from others and every situation. I have been relentlessly resilient in my career and life. I have made mistakes, had failures and dealt with several painful moments. In every instance, I have assessed, analyzed, self- reflected, course corrected and forged on always with the help of my family, my peers and my leaders.

Maria Fernanda concluded our discussion with a simple quote:

"I can still hear my Mum's words ringing in my ears. Whatever you do, do with a positive attitude and fiercely committed. Believe that you can do anything you set your heart and mind to. Make a success of it. If you plan big, you get big."

# Chapter 3

# DEFINE YOUR
# LEADERSHIP COMPASS
## What are the values by which you will lead?

The power of a 'leadership compass' – or consistent principles or philosophy by which a leader can lead is well established. A leadership compass lets people know what to expect of a leader, what the leader values, how the leader values performance and contributions and how the leader navigates challenges and opportunities. In sum total it makes the workplace a consistent, more productive environment in which employees can give of their best. **Umran Beba,** *Senior Vice President and Chief HR Officer, PepsiCo AMEA (Asia Middle East Africa);* **Carolyn Miles,** *President and CEO, Save the Children; and* **Cathy Smith,** *former Chief Financial Officer, Walmart International* are living proof of how women leaders are far more effective when they operate with a personal leadership compass.

**U**mran Beba is **Senior Vice President** and **Chief Human Resources Officer, PepsiCo AMEA** (Asia Middle East Africa) and one of the most unique women leaders I have met in recent years. Her enthusiasm and passion to enable women leadership around the world is infectious.

"When we are true to ourselves and our values, we can lead with conviction. These values form our own unique leadership compass. They guide us in the most challenging times. Because the most powerful leadership principle there is, is to be yourself, authentic and guided by what most matters to you." shared Umran.

> *"My success is largely due to the values I live by and the support of my husband and broader family. I try to bring 100% of me to the workplace and to life every day."*
>
> **Umran Beba,** *Senior Vice President and Chief HR Officer, PepsiCo AMEA (Asia Middle East Africa).*

Umran is driven; driven to succeed as a professional and driven to make a difference in the community.

Umran's span of influence covers 90 markets with approximately 30,000 direct employees of more than 50 nationalities and 250,000 indirect employees.

Umran also has a lead role in PepsiCo's famed diversity and inclusion program and its many community initiatives.

Umran has held a wide range of roles since joining the company in 1994. Before assuming her current position, she was President of the Asia Pacific region of PepsiCo responsible for 25 markets, with approximately 4,400 direct employees of 27 nationalities, 70,000 indirect employees. Prior to that she served as President of PepsiCo's South East Europe Region, covering 14 markets including Turkey, Greece, Cyprus, Israel and the Balkans. Umran has also served as the Business Unit General Manager for East Mediterranean, comprising Turkey, Lebanon, Jordan, Syria and Iraq and started her PepsiCo career at Frito-Lay in Turkey, where she held positions including Marketing Director, HR Director and ultimately General Manager.

Umran shared that her leadership compass is based on six key values,

Passion; determination for achievement; giving and taking support; listening, understanding and empathy; openness, respect and trust; perseverance and resilience.

"Values are formed whilst one is still very young. Family life, school life, marriage life, becoming a parent, social activities and the obstacles and accomplishments experienced in one's lifetime constitute a person's values. These become a part of our business life and gradually form our leadership compass. This compass affects the way we work, how we get results at work and our style of building and developing teams as well as our role in the team. I believe a person's effectiveness, sincerity and happiness as a leader depends on how much one knows about herself/himself and one's 'set of values and strengths and weaknesses demonstrate how well we know our leadership compass,' shared Umran.

Umran shared that she has been heavily influenced by the book "True North" and that the concept of personal values and personal compass is very much reiterated in that book.

Umran grew up in Turkey; having been born in Aydin she then moved to Ankara and finally to Istanbul. Her values were influenced early on by her parents and her early mentors.

"My parents were my earliest influences," she says.

"Growing up in Turkey I was also influenced very heavily later in my life by Prof.Turkan Saylan as a role model who had dedicated her entire life to leading an NGO for young girls' education in Turkey," she added.

Passion for Umran surfaced in her school days when she was involved in folk dancing as a dancer, team leader, mentor/coach but always primarily as a team member.

"In order to succeed in folk dancing you have to practice every week. You practice as a team. It is not an individual hobby, but rather a team activity and you learn a lot. You prepare for a performance by organising costumes, music, musicians and all the key performance elements," shared Umran.

"It was not easy continuing to be involved in dance. I sometimes had to sacrifice my weekends and evenings and invest at least 10-15 hours a week which meant I often missed out on enjoying life with family and friends. Of course you make a lot of friends at the folk dancing club but still it is a choice. However it fuelled me with a passion like no other! Combining music and rhythm and turning this into dance has always excited me. If I had another chance, I would like to be a ballerina," shared Umran excitedly.

She continued, "I wanted to feel this passion for all the work I have done, and if I didn't feel it, then I knew it was time for a change. This doesn't necessarily mean changing a job. It may mean changing a system, developing a new project, making the work more rewarding. If there is still no passion, then it's likely that the job is unsuitable."

Umran was involved in folk dancing for twelve years and during this time, she performed on stage many times, entered competitions representing her school and visited different cities in Turkey and also Baghdad in Iraq during the war with Iran. At the graduation ceremony at her University she received the Rector-President's award for combining academic and social activities in the best fashion.

"My determination for achievement actually came from my Mum, who was a housewife but also a part time teacher to add to our family's income. She was always asking for more and wondering how I could do better with my studies, 'B' is good but you could aim for an 'A'?"

Armed with an Industrial Engineering degree from Bogazici University (and later an MBA from the same university) Umran took her first job as a research executive with a market research company. This was part-time whilst she was studying for her MBA.

"I come from a family of moderate income and was always determined to work and earn my own money. At an early age, during summer vacations I had various jobs at a pharmacy, fashion store, the reception of my school social club and as a hostess at business conferences. When I was pursuing my MBA, I wanted to continue working alongside my studies, hence my part time research executive job. This became full time after my first year in MBA school and I was working on my thesis at the same time, so it was truly a busy time but so worth it," added Umran.

Another value in Umran's leadership compass is giving and taking support.

"My first boss, who was the owner of the research company that I worked at in my first professional job was a Professor of Statistics. She was a woman and also a great role model. She had children but also led a successful, large business. She started her own business which still operates today," said Umran.

Umran learned from this first boss the power of giving and taking support.

In 1994, Umran joined PepsiCo.

Umran believes that giving and taking support" includes "how can I support others?" and being able to express that "I need support" and experiencing the feeling of accomplishment while working together as a team.

"In 1999 during the earthquake in Turkey I was the Sales/Marketing Director. We had a plant on the major earthquake fault line which resulted in serious damage to our factory. The building was still standing but inside it was badly damaged. We were not able to produce anything for three to four months, our employees were affected, their houses were damaged and most of them needed new housing. We worked together as a team and got the business back up to speed in record time but also supported our employees. This happened with the support of the broader PepsiCo family," shared Umran.

She continued, "I was based in Turkey during the economic crisis in 2001, and was the General Manager there. We were hit by the massive financial crisis with 40% devaluation of our currency in a day. I was announced as General Manager and was also pregnant at the time. During this time I definitely needed a lot of support. To successfully deal with the crisis I needed help not just from my manager but also from different levels in the organization. I also needed tremendous support from my husband and my family. By giving and taking support, I was able to transition smoothly into these significant roles as a GM and as a mum, and by 2002 we were back to 'business as usual'. We reset our business strategy and during my tenure as GM we, as a team, doubled our revenue and tripled profits so despite the tough start we managed to do well. The bonding and interaction I experienced with key people during that difficult time has been instrumental to my success during the many years since," shared Umran.

"Listening, understanding and empathy" is another value which Umran believes to be very important in the workplace and specifically in leadership roles. Umran stated that she learned this in good measure when she took the position of Human Resources Director for PepsiCo Turkey's snack business from 1997 to 1999. Umran had a major in industrial engineering, had completed her MBA and worked in marketing for about ten years before being asked to take the Human Resources Director job at Frito Lay.

"I had very little time to think about it and after a night of consideration, I said, "yes" because I believed that I could bring a new perspective to the role. During my three years in this position, I learned a lot and was able to contribute significantly to the company. I have learned the importance of building a rapport with every employee in every department in the company and know the importance of being able to listen well, make fair decisions and knowing that we cannot achieve success without listening to and understanding our employees and being as transparent as possible. This was a crucial and enlightening experience after my marketing role," she shared.

Umran introduced several innovative but simple HR programs during her time in this assignment.

"One of the programs was called Valentines Day where we gathered different functions in a room and they were giving feedback to each other in the format of roses and thorns. This was to make the process more enjoyable as giving feedback can be a difficult process for some. The idea was basically leveraging my marketing background as I wanted to make this program an interesting employee engagement event," commented Umran.

Umran believes that one of her core values is dialogue with employees that is "open, respectful and trustworthy".

She commented, "This value guides us in our jobs and affects communication between our consumers, customers and partners. It frames our position in the company and general standing as a leader whether internal or external. No matter who we are in contact with, the 'openness, respect and trust' triangle is always important. I inherited my approach regarding this subject from my dear father. Unfortunately, we lost him about 20 years ago. He did his job as a government officer in the most proper way, transferring these values to us and making me and my sister always feel a high level of trust. If we can share these values with our employees, I believe we can achieve the best."

Umran shared, " In 1988 when I was a Brand Manager in Colgate Palmolive it was a joint venture with a Turkish family. It was critical to manage the relationship between the global company and the major shareholders especially when managing global brands. I was a junior manager but I tried hard to gain trust, show respect and achieve results whilst aligning those involved. This attitude worked well and overall it was a great experience for me."

"Finally perseverance and resilience have been very critical in my success. To be successful one has to be relentlessly determined and resilient and therefore not be affected by setbacks," shared Umran.

"Our diversity journey at PepsiCo itself is a great example of staying the course. Over the years I was the only woman in the leadership teams and I really wanted to change this. In 2004-2006, I was representing the East Mediterranean region – the markets of Turkey, Jordan, Lebanon, Syria, and Iraq – and we were reporting to the Middle East-Africa region. So I was going from Turkey, where we were best in class on diversity, to Middle East-Africa, a region that was very different with the total female representation of only five percent. After many initiatives, we managed to get up to 20 percent in the region but it took a few years to get this started," added Umran.

Umran described how it was important to get the support of her manager and peers, as well as the HR leads and General Managers. Without the support of her manager this was not possible.

"It is challenging to get everyone aligned. For example some cultures (Pakistan, Egypt, Saudi Arabia) might have difficulty accepting the diversity and inclusion journey. We introduced flexi-time and that became a big success. In Europe however it is a different story. Flexibility exists but childcare can be an issue so we needed long-term solutions such as long-term maternity leave. We kept trying new initiatives, aligning and moving forward," added Umran.

The fact that Umran made the move from living most of her life in Turkey to Hong Kong is further proof of her resilience. "In January 2010 we decided to move to HK for my role and it was a big change for all of us. My husband is a Professor and he had to change his university, our sons had to change location, school, language and make new friends. Whilst it was a big change, we have learnt a lot and perseverance and resilience helped us." She is thankful to her husband and children for their support during this transition and beyond. Umran's husband Prof.Ali Beba has been a great support and counsel for her throughout the years, in good days and tough times.

In 2013 Umran moved yet again to take on her current role based in the United Arab Emirates.

Umran shared that one's leadership compass is even more effective when it is in line with the values of the organization you work for.

"If personal values do not match those of the company, then the person becomes unhappy and unsuccessful. I am fortunate that my values closely match that of PepsiCo. I have also learned a lot from Indra Nooyi, our CEO who is leading a large organization with many opportunities and challenges but at the same time is very close to our people," shared Umran.

Umran believes that it is her leadership compass of passion; determination for achievement; giving and taking support; listening, understanding and empathy; openness, respect and trust; perseverance and resilience that has enabled her success in the Corporate world.

*Umran's top five tips for leading with values:*

- *Understand your own values and personal style:*
  Take time to truly understand what's most important to you.

- *Verbalize these values:*
  Let people know what you stand for and what to expect from you.

- *Learn from leaders with similar and dissimilar values from your own:*
  You will not always work with leaders whose values are the same as yours, so you need to make tough choices where needed.

- *Use your leadership compass as a navigation device:*
  Even through the most challenging of circumstances.

- *Live by the values you preach:*
  If people see consistency, they will trust you. If they see you erratically

change direction, they will not be able to trust or understand you. That will limit a productive work relationship.

"My success is largely due to the values I live by and the support of my husband and broader family" added Umran softly. "I try to bring 100% of me to the workplace and to life every day."

Just like she did when she was a folk dancer at the age of 10.

Working out of Connecticut, USA, **Carolyn Miles** is today **President** and **CEO** of **Save the Children** - one of the world's most reputable NGOs. But it was a moment in the Philippines that surfaced her leadership compass and changed her life.

Save the Children is the leading independent organization inspiring breakthroughs in the way the world treats children, achieving immediate and lasting change in their lives. It serves over 85 million children in the United States and in 120 countries around the world.

> *"Bring your full potential to the workplace. If you work consistently and from your heart and head and people learn to see your key defining values, they respect you so much more."*
>
> **Carolyn Miles, President and CEO, Save the Children.**

"My career and how I have lived my life have always been shaped by three basic values: Integrity, Personal accountability and Compassion and passion.

Growing up with three brothers as the only girl in the family, outside of Pittsburgh, PA, Carolyn believes that her leadership values were shaped most by her parents and family.

"My family shaped me the most. That and the fact that I was a competitive swimmer from the age of 8, were probably the two most important aspects of developing a set of values that have become part of my DNA," shared Carolyn.

"Swimming taught me the value of hard work and the joy of being part of a team. It also taught me accountability. I trained twice a day, five days a week from the age of 11, with swim meets on the weekend and weight training worked in as well. Mornings started early with practice sessions at 6.15 am before school. Swimming was where I learned true accountability as a leader," commented Carolyn. Carolyn swiftly assumed the role of team captain in her high school.

In 1988, Carolyn earned her M.B.A. from the University of Virginia's Darden School of Business.

"Shortly after getting my MBA, I was offered an opportunity to move with American Express to Hong Kong. It was an international exchange program where five people in the headquarters were swapped out with five people in the international markets of the Company. At the time my husband was with Citibank. The amazing part of it was that the Company didn't fully tell you where you were going to be based till very late into the process, you just had to jump in and take a leap of faith," she shared.

A week before she moved, Carolyn and her husband Brendan, received a very pleasant surprise.

"I discovered I was pregnant. It was tough to leave the security of home in the USA, and move to Hong Kong in this circumstance, but we made the decision to move. I felt personally accountable to AMEX for giving me the opportunity. So we moved and it was a full 4 months later before I shared the news with them that we were expecting our first baby. I was nervous to tell the Company the news when they had made such a big investment," added Carolyn.

"The challenge I faced at the time was one of the common challenges women all over the world face," she shared. "How to balance professional life, family life and responsibility to self."

"That initial accountability towards AMEX shaped so much of my professional life. If I had not made that move, I would never have been able to see Asia and would never seen all of the hardship but also beauty of that amazing continent," added Carolyn.

Carolyn threw herself into her work, and created a reputation for integrity quickly in Hong Kong.

"My earliest project was re-launching a loyalty card in Asia for AMEX in collaboration with several leading airlines and hotels. We had tried to do this in the past and had a poor track record. This time I went into the details and identified very solid areas of collaboration and benefit – for both AMEX and for the partner airlines and hotels. It worked!" shared Carolyn.

"From that one launch I had impressed my management with my eye for detail and accountability and finding win-win solutions for the company and our partners," shared Carolyn.

"This gave me a quick start at AMEX in Hong Kong," she shared.

By 1995 Carolyn was a Senior Director for AMEX.

"We had our second child in 1995. My regional job had me travelling way too much and I finally made the decision to leave AMEX after seven great years and move to something which at the time seemed like an option that would give me more time to be with my young kids,"

That opportunity was partnering with a friend from business school to join the start up of a successful chain of Pacific Coffee shops in Hong Kong.

During the time in Hong Kong as our children grew up, we travelled a lot off the beaten path. Thailand, Philippines, South Korea, all over Asia. We met hundreds of families with poor kids. The issue of the lack of opportunity for kids slowly began to register more and more with me," shared Carolyn.

Then in the summer of 1995 on a visit to the Philippines, a drive from the airport through the slums on the way to Makati changed Carolyn's life forever.

"The car in which we were travelling stopped at a traffic light. I was holding my six month old in my arms. My three year old was seated besides me. Outside, a young mother, probably my age came to the window and tapped on the glass. She was holding a little infant in her arms. I looked up and our eyes locked for a few seconds. In that moment I knew I had to do something different with my life. It was the huge gap in opportunity that poverty caused which gave me the impetus to want to do something different with my life," shared Carolyn.

Carolyn came back to Hong Kong and started to do regular volunteer work. A year later she made the decision to return to the USA with her family and work in the social sector.

"I interviewed with a number of social organizations including UNICEF and some smaller organizations. One of the organizations I met with was Save The Children. In a stroke of fate, the person who interviewed me was at the time specifically looking to build relationships with large Corporates. Having worked in the corporate sector for so many years, we hit it off and she helped me fit the right position," added Carolyn.

In January 1998, Carolyn joined Save The Children.

In the first month of working for Save The Children, Carolyn's core values or leadership compass were tested.

She learned that a series of very damaging articles were likely to be carried in a leading US publication – the Chicago Tribune, on a lack of accountability of Save The Children and other leading NGOs on the usage of funds collected from the public.

"On internal investigation, I came to realize that there were some pretty tough things going on at the time. While there was no fraud involved, in essence the money generated was not being traced back to specific programs and executions. There was a disconnect between the marketing messaging and the operations. What was being promised, was not 100% being delivered in our village programs with those funds," shared Carolyn.

"I was in the center of this storm as my new job was about bringing in new sponsors who were the entry level donors at Save The Children. So I recommended a clear course of action. First, we would own up to our mistakes. We would be accountable for every single dollar we received from donors. I worked very closely with our donor services colleagues and travelled out to our country offices. We admitted our shortcomings and publicly shared we would correct the errors. We committed that every dollar that came to us, we would be clear about how it was being used," added Carolyn.

The entire employee group at STC rallied around the mission. And the

NGOs targeted in the media article worked together to make sure that was said in communications exactly matched the reality on the ground.

"In an organization like Save The Children people come to work here because they believe in our mission- achieving immediate and lasting change in the lives of children all over the world. Our employees wanted to preserve the work that we do with children because that is so dear and precious to all of us. People stepped up. I found people in the organization that could help fix the problem," shared Carolyn.

As testimonial to that success, the Chicago Tribune finally did a follow up story recognizing the actions that Save The Children took and how they had resolved the issue. Under the banner of Interaction- a membership organization of NGOs also worked closely together.

That initial display of doing the right thing got the attention of Save The Children management. Over the next few years Carolyn's leadership compass of integrity, personal accountability and personal passion and compassion, got the organization more and more interested in her ability.

Carolyn was given increasing responsibility in both the sponsorship area as well as participating in many cross functional teams to learn more about multiple facets of Save the Children's efforts.

"I was fortunate to be given many opportunities to work in the field and visit operations. I had over 15 visits in those years," she added.

As she grew in her role, Carolyn also found her compassion for the not so fortunate continue to grow.

In 2000, she and her husband decided to adopt a child. After a long process of home study and paperwork, she received their referral in August 2001. Then on September 11, the world changed with the terrorist attack on the World Trade Centre in New York.

"My travel date for Vietnam had been fixed for September 17. Brendan and I decided to go ahead. I travelled to Vietnam on a virtually empty plane. After a long and rough process, with many obstacles to close the formal adoption process in Vietnam, we finally brought home our daughter Molly in March 2002," commented Carolyn.

In 2004, Carolyn was appointed COO of Save The Children.

Over the succeeding years she had ample opportunity to draw on her three basic values: Integrity, Personal accountability and Compassion and passion.

In 2008, the recession struck and Carolyn was faced with one of her biggest leadership challenges - the subsequent downturn in resources for Save the Children.

"This meant lay offs in 2009 and in an organization with such mission focused staff, this was very difficult and painful. As COO, I took on personal accountability to do many of the conversations with team members which took great compassion," she added.

During her tenure as COO, Save the Children doubled the number of children it reached with nutrition, health, educational, and other programs, and helped grow the organization's budget — 90 percent of which is spent on programs serving children — from $250 million to more than $550 million.

In 2011, Carolyn became President and CEO of Save the Children.

Since then the organization has grown to annual resources of over $630 million.

Carolyn had a few simple tips to developing and leveraging a leadership compass:

- *Let people see your leadership compass in action:*
  It's very important for women to establish their leadership compass and for people to see this in action.

- *Be consistent in your behaviors:*
  Career is not just one experience but also a series of experiences.

- *Bring your full potential to the workplace:*
  Work consistently and from your heart and head.

- *Be a good role model for balance:*
  The challenge of integrating professional life, family and personal needs is a very real challenge. Your people will look to you and take cues from your behavior.

- *Be confident in who YOU are:*
  Women have a greater lack of confidence compared to men. But if people learn to see your key defining values, they respect you so much more.

"Even today there are so many challenges ahead. The world has changed tremendously in the last 20 years. The previous CEO was 18 years in the role. I have only 15 years overall with the company. Long-term stability and continuity helps in organizations like Save the Children. I know my leadership compass will help me steer the way. Just like it changed my life after the visit a long time ago to the Philippines," she closed with a smile.

She grew up poor. During the summer months, working in the fields on a farm from dawn to dusk to earn money for school clothes. At age 10 she lost her Dad in a plane crash. Yet she is today one of the most powerful women in business. At the time of going to press with Break the ceiling, touch the sky she had just moved from Walmart International to an exciting new assignment. She fulfills her need for adventure by also becoming one of the world's most accomplished sky divers – with over 3500 dives to her credit, including holding world records for the largest free fall formations. Yet she keeps her feet firmly on the ground, anchored by her own unique leadership compass. Meet **Cathy Smith,** one of the most powerful women leaders in the world.

> *"I think every woman should focus on being who she is. Of being authentic and celebrating herself. It will help your colleagues and peers understand you better in the workplace. With more predictable and consistent results!"*
>
> **Cathy Smith,** *former Chief Financial Officer, Walmart International.*

"My leadership compass is simple – be genuine, authentic. Respect, strive and serve! And don't judge anyone." shared Cathy.

"Every individual, no matter what walk of life or background deserves the utmost respect – with no judgment. None of us have walked a day in their shoes so we cannot judge," she added.

"Strive to be the best you can," added Cathy.

"Never ever complete anything and then wish you could do it over and wish you could do it better. This requires hard work, preparation, being self-critical. Be passionate. Demonstrate high energy. And on those days you cannot find the energy, pretend it is there anyways. Your teams are always watching and taking signals from you. Your energy becomes their energy," she added.

"Serve your team and constituents to make them wildly successful – in turn, the company and you are successful. Find the one thing they are good at – everyone is good at something. Help them be better than they knew they could; set high standards," she added.

"The last piece element of my leadership compass is unbending, unimpeachable integrity," she commented.

Cathy sees herself as "a simple country girl enjoying a complex world". Cathy grew up on a farm in southern California. Her family are farmers. They work very long hours daily. She learned the value of striving hard and developing a work ethic on the farm. In the summer, she worked in the fields to earn spending money for school clothes. Cathy was raised by her father predominately with her two brothers. Her dad worked the farm every day, so her brothers and she were shuffled around to aunts and grandparents' homes often. She learned the value of a village and of helping others!

"We were poor – but honestly, I never knew that. We had all we needed – food, love, clothing, shelter. When my father was killed in the plane crash, my younger brother and I went to live with my mother whom I had not really known," added Cathy.

Cathy's grandparents taught her the value of being the best.

"My grandfather grew a terrific business to be the third largest national rose grower in the USA. From him I learned the value of trust and respect. He trusted and respected everyone immediately. It was only through the other person's actions that he would lose that trust and once a person wronged him once/was not worthy of his trust – that was it. Rarely did someone get a second chance. But, it was a great outlook to trust everyone immediately – expect the best of him or her – most of the time he was not disappointed. My grandmother was motherly – she had eight children (my dad was one of them). She spread her kindness and love equally to all. She welcomed everyone into her home, always. She taught me the value of serving others," Cathy commented.

Cathy also learned tremendously from her mother.

"My mother is a very interesting individual – she has a huge capacity for accepting everyone. We raised our own food (livestock and vegetables). We were still poor. I had jobs from the time I was 12 years old– paper route, babysitting, and retail butcher shop. I always felt my little brother was my responsibility –we were incredibly close. In high school, I was a cheerleader. I was valedictorian of my class. I worked more than 20 hours a week. There was little idle time! But, the biggest thing to mention about my mom is that she instilled a wonderful value in me – no judgment. You have no right to judge people – you don't know from where they have come, their situation or circumstance. This has served me so well in my life," added Cathy.

Over her college years at the University of Southern California at Santa Barbara, Cathy further shaped her leadership values and compass of 'no judgments, being authentic, respect, strive and serve.'

"While earning my undergraduate degree I continued to work 20 plus hours a week. Although I had earned academic scholarships, had access to grants and the generosity of my grandparents, I worked to have money for books, incidentals and skydiving! I struggled trying to 'fit in' -- my roommate took me to sororities and frat houses. I tried to pretend and be something that I wasn't. Once I realized that I needed to stay true to who I was, genuine and authentic, school was just a means to a degree and next chapters in life. At one point during my undergraduate career, I briefly contemplated quitting school—not because it was difficult academically but because I wasn't seeing any value. I was unconnected. However, the 'strive for excellence' element inside me came to life -- I am not a quitter. I knew a college degree was essential. I studied for my classes, went to work, skydived, and graduated with very respectable grades," shared Cathy.

Later in her career, Cathy went back to college for a graduate degree and earned a MBA at the University of Southern California, USC and had a much better experience.

"By then (10 years into my professional career), I had a much better understanding of myself," she added.

It was primarily her leadership compass that got her so enthused about skydiving. Determined to not let the tragedy of her father's death affect her, Cathy worked relentlessly to become one of the world's best skydivers and to stare death in the face and come out winning.

"I started skydiving when I was in college and jumped out of airplanes for almost 30 years. I have jumped around the world with wonderful global teams. Skydivers live at a different speed – but, with that, I have seen more death than one should of people I cared about. I also based jumped (jumping with a parachute off objects) for a while. Fun but very dangerous – you don't get a back-up parachute like you do when you jump out of a plane. But when I look back, skydiving truly encapsulates my leadership compass. In this very dangerous sport, you truly have to respect and trust your fellow jumpers, strive to be the very best and be there for the team. Most important it taught me how to appreciate every single day I have," added Cathy.

Cathy continued, "Sky diving requires absolute trust in your instructors for the first jump several jumps, team mates during a skydive, pilots and equipment. You must respect the sport immensely. You can never be complacent. In 1997, I traveled to Russia to skydive with 300 top jumpers from 27 countries to attempt a world record for the largest free fall formation. We didn't all speak the same language. We were reliant on each team member to do their job, be safe and look out for their fellow teammates. We were jumping at an altitude that required we use oxygen in the aircraft to avoid hypoxia. Under the affects of hypoxia, your reflexes are slow, you mind becomes confused. During one of our record attempt jumps, we had been at a high altitude for a longer-than-normal time and I noticed a jumper that looked delirious. I asked if he was ok. He didn't look ok. I feared he had not gotten sufficient oxygen and was suffering from hypoxia. I told the plane captain. We decided that the rest of the team would jump and I rode the plane down with the skydiver. He would not have been safe for himself or the rest of the 300 skydivers if he had jumped. This meant we wasted a precious attempt for the world record -- but well worth it. We would jump again. My leadership compass of service to others rings loudly for me. I am driven to serve the team first and foremost. After almost two weeks of attempts, we fell short of our goal, a 300 way free fall formation -- we only achieved 297!"

But that record did not elude Cathy.

"Many of us were later able to participate in the 300-way free fall formation World Record in December, 2002," shared a beaming Cathy.

Cathy believes that her leadership compass has helped her tremendously in her corporate career as well, albeit with some initial challenges.

"In the past 5 years, I finally came to terms with leveraging my leadership compass in entirety. Much of my career till then, I had struggled with being completely genuine and authentic at work to some degree. I am really a goofy, outgoing, energetic, casual person. At home, I'm ponytails and jeans. But, I have grown up in a very male-dominated, corporate world professionally. I was challenged early in my career to not be a 'cheerleader' – so I learned to mute my enthusiasm. I learned to conform. But, internally, I struggled with that. Over the course of several years, I realized that this was not who I truly was. With a career job change in 2006, I started to consciously become more comfortable in my own skin. I started to reflect the more 'true me' at work. And it has begun to bear rich results. That also gave me the confidence to make another important career move in 2014," she added.

Cathy acknowledged that many people have helped coach her and have contributed to her choice of leadership compass.

"I have been coached by executive coaches throughout my career to be less "intense." When I was with my last employer Walmart for example, I had a great coach who focused on helping me to be more 'warm and engaging.' He saw that in a small audience or one-on-one, I was warm, engaging, at ease. But, presenting to a large audience, like at the annual analyst meeting, I was 'cold' and almost intimidating. He worked with me to 'lighten up' and have fun on stage and in key interactions. Within a short while folks inside and outside Walmart were approaching me more and engaging me and our interactions seemed so much more meaningful.

Cathy added; "I am a much better leader today because my personal and professional life are more aligned. While I still wear suits, I have found it is ok to laugh out loud, to joke, to have fun, to be warm and enthusiastic. I think every woman should focus on being who she is. Of being authentic and celebrating herself. It will help your colleagues and peers understand you better in the workplace. With more predictable and consistent results!"

Cathy's leadership compass has also helped her in more serious challenges.

"Probably one of the periods that contributed most to my growth professionally was during 2008-2010. I was the CFO of a large national homebuilder. And, during this period, the United States experienced it's most severe housing and credit crisis ever recorded.

At our peak, we delivered approximately 39,000 homes in a year. In 2010 when we sold our company, we were delivering 2,500 homes. The entire industry experienced huge reductions in volumes. Consumer and business credit was almost non-existent. Our entire management team and Board of Directors lived in full crisis management mode for almost three years. During that time, we reduced over 11,000 employees, sold multiple businesses and large land assets. We lived with our cash in a survival mode. Our external constituents (shareholders, bankers, development partners) and internal teams needed the leadership of the company to be calm and balanced," she shared.

She added, "We had to make difficult decisions like to stop projects, lay off people... survival. Now, more than ever, I knew I had to lean on my leadership compass. I was genuine and authentic when speaking with all audiences – let them know the situation, as I understood it at all times. Respect for the individual was essential as we laid off folks. We needed to focus immensely on the fewer customers we did have and be certain of exceptional service. In the end, we sold our company to another national homebuilder and with the two businesses combined made a much stronger company to deal with the low market volumes and weather the environment. I am proud to say the follow-on company is doing well today. Many of my old colleagues and team members remain in contact and are thriving. Our shareholders got the best deal they could and the stock price is rebounding. I am a much better leader and executive today because of the very difficult years I experienced during this nation's worst housing and credit crisis."

Cathy's top tips for building a leadership compass are as follows:

- *Truly understand and know yourself:*
  What is important to you above all else?

- *Align energy to what is most important:*
  Adopt a "right here, right now" mindset.

- *Never give up:*
  Commit daily to education, excellence, and persistence.

- *Never say 'can't':*
  "Can't means you have quit. Instead, say, "I'm having trouble," means there is a solution, ask for help, and keep trying.

- *Never forget the special people who have helped you grow:*
  These very people will be by you through the good times, but more importantly through the bad times as well. And they will always offer you candid feedback if you are (or not) living your leadership compass.

Cathy concluded our discussion by sharing with me how important her husband and her two boys have been been to her development and in helping her define her leadership compass.

"He has tirelessly been my biggest supporter and he also challenges me to be better at everything. He appeals to my strong need to strive for excellence. For example, when I'm tired and needing a break, he'll remind me that whatever I was planning to 'blow off', that I can't --people are counting on me and my contribution. He reminds me everyday to be the best I can be," concluded Cathy.

# Chapter 4

# MASTER THE
# ART OF BALANCE

This topped the list of challenges that professional women universally face around the world. More than half of Americans are stressed to their limits. 27% of employees feel emotionally drained from their work and 42% feel used up at the end of the work day according to a five year study of the American work force conducted by the Families and Work Institute. Yet there is strong evidence to show that earnings make a woman more, not less desirable according to *Time Magazine*. I spoke to a former boss **Deb Henretta,** *Group President, P&G Global Beauty;* **Dr. Barbara McFarland,** *Co-Founder and Partner of FlexLife;* *and* **Banali Malhotra,** *Head of Marketing, RAKBANK* to discover their secrets for work, family and life balance.

Listed seven years in a row on Fortune magazine's 50 Most Powerful Women lists, **Deb Henretta** is currently **Group President, Procter & Gamble Global Beauty**, and is one of the busiest women you could hope to meet.

She leads one of P&G's largest and high profile divisions, with annual revenues of 20 Billion USD, and including iconic brands Pantene, Olay, Head & Shoulders, Rejoice, SK-II, Old Spice, COVERGIRL, Gucci, and Wella. Beyond P&G however, Deb is recognized as an influential leader and effective voice in global business. She served on Singapore's Economic Development Board for several years, and in 2011, received a US Presidential appointment to be the first woman Chair of the Business Advisory Council to APEC (Asia Pacific Economic Cooperation). All of this while being a wife, and actively-involved mother to three teenagers – Connor, Caitlin and Shannon.

Deb is the epitome of "well organized" and "balanced". She is both super-mom and corporate athlete rolled into one. I know this to be true first hand, since I was Deb's Executive Communications leader at P&G between 2008 and 2010.

"The world is significantly faster, more complex and more demanding today compared to even a few years ago and women face the daunting challenge of operating at peak performance in a very competitive landscape," said Deb. "Balance in this world is essential and to me, is not just two-pillared but a triangle," said Deb. "It involves balancing work, family and self. Only when one masters the art of balancing between all three can I say I have achieved ideal balance." She added.

> *"Try to find time for life."*
>
> *Deb Henretta, Group President, P&G Global Beauty.*

Working at P&G over the last three decades, Deb has faced many challenges in balancing her corporate role, while raising and now 'letting go' of her three children to their own careers and life challenges - all the while making time for the important 'self'.

"If I look back over my career, the most important step in creating this balance is recognizing the need to clarify priorities in both work and personal life. You must be 100% clear about what you want to achieve in each of these areas. So balance to me starts with being choiceful and then prioritizing, prioritizing, and prioritizing even more. And never forgetting it is a continuous challenge," she added.

Deb grew up in Rochester, New York and joined P&G as a Marketing Assistant on the laundry business in 1985. One of her first challenges on balance came in 1992. Just after learning she was pregnant with her second child, Deb took on a significant career assignment as Marketing Director for Tide, which was in the midst of a business decline.

"I think that was one of the toughest times in my life from a balance point of view. It was mentally tough and physically tough. Feeding the baby every few hours throughout the night. Having a two-year old who also needed time and attention, and then having an important job trying to turn around one of P&G's largest businesses - all at a very young age. That was not easy".

Still, clarity and perseverance can make a difference. "I am a firm believer that you can have all that you desire on the career, family and personal front, but just not all at the exact same time, so that's where prioritization comes in," she added.

"I managed to get through that period by being relentless about what my priorities were at work, and also at home. This enabled me to focus my time and capacity on those things that mattered most. The reward is that once you make that commitment, the balance does gets easier, and you get better organized. Best of all, when those around you see you living your priorities, they very often also begin to help you achieve them," shared Deb.

With this approach, Deb successfully managed to turn the brand around to a path of success and growth that continues today, and all the while managed to find time for her family and a little time for herself.

Deb's success on Tide – and aptitude for balance and prioritization - earned her a series of promotions. By 1999, she was leading the global Fabric Conditioners and Bleach business for P&G. But life needed to be re-balanced again, when she was appointed Vice President of Baby Care, now with a third child, who at the time was still in diapers.

At the time, Procter & Gamble's Pampers was in a serious decade-long business decline with lackluster sales throughout the 1990s.

"In this particular business situation, I found that being a mom enabled my career in an entirely different way. I had changed diapers. I was living a similar experience with the moms of the world. And it helped me see things differently – through a different lens than just being a business leader". This was important as the brand's single focus for years had been on developing superior innovation. "We'd gotten too exclusively focused on the technology," Deb commented.

Deb challenged the brand to be more in touch with moms and babies. Under her leadership, new products were aligned with baby's development in mind – to great success. The brand bounced back stronger than ever, growing by 2 Billion USD over the next four years. Today Pampers remains P&G's largest brand.

"It's an achievement I'm very proud of because I realize I could not have done this without being a mom, nor could I have done it without being a business woman. Those years of balance – allowing me to be both mom and manager - paid off in a way I could have never considered," she added.

Deb continued leading P&G Baby Care through 2005, when she embarked with her family on yet another adventure that would again test her ability to balance: a move to Asia as President for P&G ASEAN, Australia and India (AAI).

Even with extensive experience in managing global teams, this was the first time Deb had lived outside the USA. It was a completely new challenge.

"Overnight, things changed dramatically for my family and self, fortunately to wonderful outcomes. My kids made the transition to a new culture incredibly well, and as I became responsible for my most complex business to date, my husband played an even more supportive role in helping me achieve my triangle of balance", she shared.

"But the added layer of living abroad is that you have to also balance in your cultural engagement. I made efforts to learn as much about Asia as I could. And I immersed myself in the culture of Singapore, where we lived, as well as across Asia when I traveled," shared Deb.

At work, Deb focused on connecting with and enabling her direct reports in the dozen or so countries to be successful in their own businesses. Enhancing the marketing efforts of P&G's Asia-based billion dollar brands was yet another priority. And, she also maintained deep engagement in P&G's much admired talent management system, to help build Asia's leaders of tomorrow.

These efforts again required a rigorous discipline. "There was so much I wanted to do every day, both at work and at home. But I did not want my time in Asia to be spent only in the office!" Deb's priorities during this time included maintaining strict office hours, spending evenings with family and friends, and then, late into the night it was not unusual to receive emails from Deb as she fit in a few final hours of work.

Deb also found capacity to become involved in the planning and development of Singapore through association with the Economic Development Board (EDB) of Singapore. In 2009 she was invited to be part of an Economic Strategies Committee commissioned by Singapore's Prime Minister, Lee Hsien Loong, which worked to develop a 10-year strategic plan for the country.

"This was an entirely new type of contribution I could make to the world, and one that I thoroughly enjoyed and am so proud of. But again, I would never been able to give my time if my existing approaches on balance in priorities were not so well established," Deb commented.

In 2012 Deb moved back to the USA, taking on the role of Group President, Global Beauty Care, which includes skin care, cosmetics and personal care products, and in 2013 she was promoted to Group President, P&G Global Beauty, adding hair care, prestige fragrances and salon products to her line of responsibility.

When Deb reflects on her thirty years of working and balancing, she believes that people are too often far clearer about their work priorities than they are about their personal priorities.

And, women in particular have a much tougher time prioritizing and making choices versus men. "Women bucket many things into a single priority which means we are not making choices at all," she shared. "I believe it is because women find it more difficult to accept the consequences of choices. This is somehow so much harder for women."

"As an example, spending time with my kids when they were babies was really important. So for two of my three pregnancies I took a little extra time off to really focus as much energy and time as possible on them. It was not without its sacrifices of course, but we believe it was worth it," commented Deb.

Deb also notes that an often forgotten path to better balance is to use creative approaches for building support systems.

"First stop is of course family. But if you don't have any family around, there could be help available at a local church, or even youth groups. Then, as your financial means improve, you can afford more professional help. Regardless, what it does require is for you to ask: to reach out for help, and to be open to accept it," she added.

Deb shared that another of her big enablers to balance was staying healthy and fit – this is her time for 'self' that makes up the balance triangle. "I prioritize my health and well-being. I exercise four times a week for at least 30 minutes. In order to effectively take care of business and family you've got to take care of yourself", she commented.

Deb also underlined the power of setting aside just a few minutes everyday to pursue a hobby. "One of the greatest enablers to performing better at home and at work is to take a little time, maybe even just a few minutes to do something you love. When I was younger I loved to garden. However, given all of the other things going on at work and in my personal life, I de-prioritized gardening for a while. Over the years this is one thing that I have tried to bring back into my life, and every time I do, it's a tangible reward," shared Deb.

"I always encourage young women professionals to have a passion or hobby separate from work. In times of stress and challenge, when I am faced with the toughest of choices and situations, I step back and go do something I love for a couple of hours, and then come back to tackling the problems. The solutions seem just so much apparently after that down time," shared Deb.

Across business, continents and challenges large and small, the art of balance is everlasting and essential to Deb. "Net, balance is truly a triangle of being clear about your work, family and self priorities! If you stop for a minute and acknowledge that you can't be all things to all people, at all times, you will find that you will enjoy a much more productive life," shared Deb.

*Deb's tips for achieving balance:*

- *See balance as multi-dimensional:*
  Career, family, and self. You can't always have everything perfect at the same time, but you can still have a lot.

- *Prioritize:*
  Be clear about what you will do and importantly what you won't do.

- *Set aside a few minutes a day just for yourself:*
  This can be tremendously rejuvenating. Just a few minutes to do something that you truly enjoy.

- *Be willing to compromise:*
  You can't be perfect on every single project. But if you can be perfect on the top few - the priorities that really count – it's easier to live with being 'just good' on the others.

- *Leverage your uniquely female traits of passion and commitment:*
  Use your passion to spur you on to success.

**D**r. Barbara McFarland literally wrote the book on balance.
"If anyone had told me I would not only be a psychologist but also a global corporate consultant when I was a younger I would have laughed out loud. When I graduated from high school, I fell in love and married at 18 and had a son, Casey. Two years later I was divorced and was feeling pretty much like a failure. It was a really a difficult time for me," shares Dr. Barbara McFarland.

And yet today, Barbara has authored 7 books, has a clinical practice as a psychologist, is a corporate consultant, author, trainer, media guest, and motivational speaker. She **Co-founded FlexLife, LLC,** an organization that offers behaviorally based life balance solutions and strategies. In addition, she has been invited to present her clinical work at Harvard

University Medical School, Department of Psychiatry. Dr. McFarland has also designed and delivered diversity programs related to life balance and life mentoring across the world with clients that include Procter & Gamble, General Electric, Cinergy, The Health Alliance of Cincinnati, the State of Nebraska Office of Women's Health, Ernst & Young, the Xavier Consulting Group of Cincinnati, Ohio, and The Network of Executive Women.

"If it hadn't been for the support of my parents, I'm really not sure where I would be today," Barbara says. "Those feelings of failure also propelled me to rise above and make something of my life – for both my son as well as myself."

Barbara was born and raised in Chicago, Illinois. Both her maternal and paternal grandparents immigrated to the US from Poland.

> *"Many people wish they had more time – 'If only there were more hours in a day, I could do it all.' Actually, time is not the major problem in being able to balance your life. Surveying 800 graduates from Wharton, research revealed that the psychological conflicts that come from thinking about work when at home and thinking about home when at work are more of an issue than time."*
>
> **Barbara McFarland,**
> *Co-Founder and Partner of FlexLife.*

"My dad was a great influence on me – The positive side was that he had an amazing work ethic. He frequently said to me, 'Make sure you love what you do.' The downside was the long hours he kept as he tried to build his business. Growing up, I had always missed spending time with my dad. What made it worse was the fact that my mom and sister had a very close relationship so I felt quite isolated," shared Barbara.

"I was also deeply influenced by my Mom's two sisters. Both of their husbands passed away when they were quite young and so, despite the fact that they were uneducated, they had to work. One as a seamstress and the other worked for a telephone company," she added. "They were women with a great deal of grit and resolve."

Barbara's dad provided a middle-class lifestyle for the family while her mom assumed the traditional role of housewife.

"My parents, especially my mom, were devout Catholics so all of us, my brother, my sister and myself attended Catholic schools. My parents shared the same dream for their children – they would each have a college education. It was simply assumed that we would go on to higher education," shared Barbara. "My marriage was a disappointment to them but their vision remained strongly entrenched in my mind. So when I divorced I knew there was only one option for me – college. I worked two jobs as a way to support myself and my son once we moved in with my parents."

Barbara's drive and determination took her far beyond a bachelor's degree. She was the only one of her siblings to go beyond a four-year college degree and received her master's degree. In 1979 she attained her doctorate.

"But there was a long road to travel before that happened. I went to school full time and worked about 30 hours a week - first at Marshal Field selling sportswear and after a few years there, I was hired by a large Chicago bridal salon selling wedding gowns! That was a fun job! The remainder of my time was spent studying while my mom took care of my son."

Barbara added, "Then once I completed my bachelor's degree at Mundelein College, I became a junior high school teacher (a career that at that time was one of two -- the other being nursing--that young women were encouraged to go into) and taught school in the inner city of Chicago in the Cabrini Green projects. One of the most challenging and gratifying experiences I had had until that point." Barbara goes on to say that 'diversity' was unheard of at that time -- schools were pretty much segregated so she decided to take a job in an inner city school teaching language arts.

"I wasn't fully conscious of my sensitivity to diverse cultures at that time. But somewhere inside I felt a need to positively influence kids from lower socio-economic backgrounds".

"After a few years teaching, I decided, with the support of a colleague and my parents, to enter graduate school at Xavier University in Cincinnati where I attended sessions during the summer months. I had been encouraged to enter the Counseling Department. I loved being there – the faculty was incredible as were my fellow students. Once I graduated, I was able to get a job at an all boys Catholic High school in Cincinnati. At that point, my son and I were able to afford our own place -- my greatest life balance challenge was being a single parent. Once we settled in Cincinnati, I really knew very few people. I lost the support system of my parents and siblings."

She continued, "My job as a school counselor was another gratifying experience. But, whenever I had to go to work, or even to go out socially, guilt hovered over me. I felt like I was not being a good parent. My son and I had a good relationship – he was very understanding and supportive of me. What a guy!!"

Then, another rung on the ladder was put before Barbara– some of the faculty at Xavier strongly encouraged her to get a doctorate. She had many self-doubts about her ability to succeed in such an endeavor but her faculty friends assured her she could do it.

"I then made the most difficult decision of my life – I knew I could not attend post graduate school, be a graduate teaching assistant, work 30 hours a week and be a mom. So, after much soul searching and many tearful discussions with my parents and my son, we decided it would be best if he returned to Chicago to live with them while I immersed myself in school. Hard as that was, I made a lot of weekend trips to Chicago and I must say, that since my son and I had limited time, when we were together we were together," shared Barbara.

Once Barbara finished school, her son returned to Cincinnati and they resumed their lives.

"Again, at that time, I really didn't have balance in my life – I was just beginning my practice and working with poor and needy, drug dependent women at Eden Treatment Center, which consumed about 50-60 hours a week. Whatever time I had left I spent with my son but I wasn't a whole lot of fun!! I was increasingly stressed," she shared.

"This was the time I was becoming addicted to being constantly busy," concluded Barbara.

"Somewhere deep within me, I had inherited my grandfather and dad's entrepreneurial spirit – a need to be untethered and free to create and develop without interference from anyone or anything. – I wanted to do what I wanted to do without any restraints. I have a strong need for control and very little patience for corporate politics," she added.

Barbara's clinical practice grew and in 1984, she opened the first free-standing outpatient eating disorders clinic in the tri-state area (Ohio, Kentucky, Indiana).

"I had a staff of 10 people including therapists, nutritionists, exercise physiologists and administrative staff. To be clear that this program was the most effective treatment, the clinic underwent a very strict accreditation review by the Joint Commission Accreditation on Healthcare Organizations (JCAHO) for as long as the center was opened," she added.

In the early 90's, managed care began scrutinizing levels of care within the practice of psychotherapy. As a result, Barbara went to the Mental Research Institute at Stanford University, as well as The Solution Focused Family Therapy Center in Milwaukee, for training on solution focused brief therapy. The entire staff at the clinic was re-trained. Recognizing the resistance most practitioners had to brief therapy, she began training clinicians in North America in this model of treatment. She trained over 1000 clinicians in hospital settings, mental health agencies and private practitioners. In 1994, as managed care became more and more restrictive, and she realized she could not provide the level of care that was needed for patients, Barbara decided to close the clinic and see patients privately.

"So in the midst of all of that, guilt clung to me even tighter– I was very fortunate that I had what I call a 'low maintenance' son – he was very independent and learned at an early age to cook and do his own laundry (his wife can't thank me enough now!) But, mothers are supposed to do all that! Well, I decided that since our time was so limited I would much rather spend time with him – face-to-face – then be a mom by doing laundry and/or cooking. I redefined "motherhood" on my terms. So I decided that I had to establish some one-on-one time together that would diminish my guilt and enhance my relationship with my son. He, of course, had input," shared Barbara.

Thus, we took French Lessons from a diminutive, soft spoken native of Paris, tennis lessons, and then played on weekends -- we were fortunate as we had a park directly behind our apartment building with a somewhat battered asphalt tennis court. We started our own dinner club – he would pick the restaurant as long as it wasn't a drive through! What boy doesn't love to eat??. It was during these times that are most dear to me – we had many, many good conversations – face-to-face, eyeball-to-eyeball as I say. It was the time when we shared our lives and whatever else was of utmost importance. And I was fully present during these times…of course, there were no cell phones, texts blipping, or ipads, so it was a bit easier then it might have been today," she added.

"My brain was constantly filled with my to do list -- what I had to do the next day or should have done the day before. But I made a conscious decision to be focused on him. This is really the basis of the FlexLife program – being present and focused," added Barbara.

As Barbara grew in her professional career, she increasingly realized how difficult it was for women.

"Most of the time, if a woman's definition of success is based on achievement and accomplishment then they tend to be perfectionists. Have to do it all and have it all. Women want a successful career and partner, perfect children, and an immaculate house. Women have the added pressure of being able to fit into a size 0 -- being thin enough, pretty enough, and on and on. I began to realize that most women I interacted with had not reflected enough on their own definition of success. Comparison became a trap. Women I knew continued to look at other women and evaluate their own success with these other women," shared Barbara. "And I was no exception!!"

She continued; "As the world grew more complicated and technology began to invade our lives, I noticed that the women I was treating in my clinical practice began talking more about their physical and emotional exhaustion – their self-described periods of depression and anxiety were now more related to their own felt inadequacies in being able to meet all of the demands placed upon them. Their language was laced with a lot of "shoulds" as they compared themselves to the cultural ideals of being a woman both professionally and physically."

It became clear to Barbara that these women were running themselves ragged desperately trying to be what they, most likely their parents and current day culture defined as "successful."

"This of course led to more depression and anxiety - general unhappiness. I saw women become more and more alienated from their inner experiences, their core values, and their own personal truth," she shared.

"Balance began to become more of a reality for me as during this time I remarried. My husband, Hal, was a tremendous support to my son and me. We laugh as I say -- I am a Type A and he is a Type Z! He served to ground me and kept me focused on my relationship with my son. So now, all three of us played tennis! However, the weekly dinners were off limits to Hal – those continued for the two of us and still do to this day – only not weekly as my son now lives in Syracuse, NY, with his wife. He is a partner and Vice-President of a wealth management firm in Rochester, NY.," she added.

"Marrying Hal was likely one of the most important events in my life. In fact there is research from Stamford University, which shows that one of the most powerful enablers for a woman is to have a supportive and available partner. Slowly over time I began to balance out my own family and work life priorities more effectively. I am not saying single moms can't live healthy balanced lives – they certainly can as I did at certain times. It is less challenging with a supportive partner," commented Barbara.

So, life balance for Barbara McFarland was born.

"But I asked myself 'where do I begin? What do I do?????' It's tough stopping that busyness addiction cold turkey but I did and with the help of my family, I put boundaries around my workday and weekends. I began to say "no" more. It took a little while but I began to feel that guilt dissipate – I began to feel a bit more relaxed – I was laughing more at myself and with myself! That was the first step but I knew it wasn't enough.

Barbara did an inordinate amount of reading and research on the topic – she met with people who emulated (to her) a balanced life and learned from them.

And thus, FlexLife was born.

In 2004, Barbara developed a half-day seminar and was hired by Procter & Gamble to deliver it to their women's regional networks throughout the US.

It was so well received and so needed that P&G invited me to present at a women's symposium in Bangkok, in Bogota and then again in Evian, France.

"In 2007, I met Kristen English at the seminar in Bangkok. We met again in the States a few months later and agreed to take the content and maximize its usability by partnering together and co-developing the FlexLife website."

The FlexLife program was a huge success at Procter & Gamble and continues to be available to employees world-wide.

According to Barbara, life balance is not an event – it is fluid and ever changing, particularly as women progress through different life stages – four life stages.

"The single life stage is normally for most women in their 20's. Work becomes the obsession – success, achieving, establishing credibility, discovering our own talents. Trying to find a partner/mate," over rides everything else," shared Barbara.

She continued. "Married Life without children is the stage when career is still demanding. Living with someone is a new challenge. If the partner is someone who actually is a partner, the challenges aren't as great – if however, the partner is uninvolved, the life balance scales tip significantly for the woman and becomes increasingly difficult to manage.

She goes on to say that the third stage is being married with children. According to Barbara, this is the most challenging of stages when it comes to life balance and particularly so for single moms. "Guilt is a key emotion during this stage which is incredibly draining."

"The last stage is what is known in the USA as the "empty nesters" stage. When a couple gets to the age when their kids have moved away for college or for work. This is the least challenging time – for most. Age and wisdom generally prevail – the need to be perfect is no longer a priority – and there is more time," commented Barbara.

Barbara's believes that her concept for FlexLife was simple and practical and helped her personally find the best possible balance between work and life at each of the four stages.

"The starting point for finding work life balance is being focused and in the present," shared Barbara.

"Many people wish they had more time – 'If only there were more hours in a day, I could do it all.' Actually, time is not the major problem in being able to balance your life. Surveying 800 graduates from Wharton, research revealed that the psychological conflicts that come from thinking about work when at home and thinking about home when at work are more of an issue than time," she continued.

"Balance has two dimensions. The Doing Dimension, which consists of our tasks and responsibilities in each of the four quadrants - Work, Family, Support and Personal and the BEING dimension, which is where we create "space," shared Barbara. It is a place of renewal, reenergizing and replenishing.

"People who solely live on the Doing Dimension over book, over schedule, double schedule, fill their time with one activity, one meeting, one conversation after another. They cannot tolerate any space of time or inactivity often dreading such space will stir up feelings of emptiness or discomfort. This is a major obstacle to experiencing balance," shared Barbara.

"We live our lives in a trance moving at warp speed often wondering where our day went and if we keep the pace up, we end up wondering where the years went. In other words, we go through the motions, but we're not really there. We get so caught up in what we have to do, that we lose sight of the here-and-now, of our values and what's important to us," she added.

According to Barbara, the Second Dimension of Balance - BEING - is the only place we can experience balance.

"While on this dimension, we are focused, fully present and there no matter what we're doing. If we let it, the Doing Dimension can become our master and can seductively pull us away from being present. We end up feeling overwhelmed, out of control, exhausted, resentful and depressed. The Doing Dimension is a fact of life - in fact it is life. The more we can integrate the Being Dimension into the Doing Dimension, the more we become masters of our own lives. The art of balance is being fully present while we're doing the juggling.

It sounds easy – to be. But how does one be? We have to create space while on the Doing Dimension. There are two ways: One is to breathe-- to bring yourself into the present moment. By focusing your awareness on your breath you will find yourself being more present. Even though your mental chatter may be going at high speed, pay attention to the spaces of silence within. Be patient and practice every day, every moment you think of it. Notice that when talking to a colleague or a loved one, how present you are - are you paying close attention to this person? Are you really listening with your fullest attention? When you shake hands with someone are you really present? Are you focused on the experience? Are you there?" she shared.

Barbara added; "The second way to being is to spend time alone - meditate, walk, sit quietly in nature, ride your bike. Many people have difficulty being alone, doing nothing. Practice being present within yourself. By creating this space, you'll be able to reflect -- making time to evaluate and assess your choices and decisions and revitalize your energy and ability to focus, all of which increases productivity."

"One of the most powerful examples of FlexLife came in 2007, with a client who had a very high level job with a Fortune 25 company. She found her female boss to be extremely non-supportive and critical of her style of managing people. She was with the company for 20 years and was very committed to the organization. This new role created an inordinate amount of stress and anxiety for her. She was expected to answer emails whenever her boss needed something from her…some of these came at 4 and 5 AM! Her boss would frequently point out to her that she was single and didn't have any family responsibilities like the other team members so she had nothing to complain about," shared Barbara.

"During the course of therapy, after much soul searching, she decided to resign. Over the last few years she has succeeded in much greater measure as a consultant. She is far happier too," added Barbara.

Two of the key issues that most of the women (Barbara has worked with) identify as challenges for them in having a balance life is being able to ask for help and making time to renew their energy levels. In that context Barbara shared with me two testimonials from P&G executives.

Bonnie Curtis, Vice-President, Procter & Gamble, Product Supply shared, "Stress has always been my issue. Not smoking, not weight loss, not diet, and not exercise. I have a stressful job, four kids, a working husband, and I'm responsible for my 88-year old mother. No time for myself, and a propensity to get trapped into the guilt trip. All of these responsibilities drain my energy."

Bonnie participated in a FlexLife workshop and this really made a significant difference in her ability to experience life balance.

"FlexLife gave me tools to help me evaluate my stress and deal with it. During the past year I have started drinking a lot more water, meditating daily, and acknowledging when I can't do any more…and asking for help. As a result, I have not gotten sick at all this year and am performing better at home and work."

Gale Beckett, Vice President, Procter & Gamble Worldwide Quality Assurance, says, " The FlexLife experience helped me in so many, many ways. It increased my awareness about the decisions I was making particularly in my family relationships. I became more intentional in reaching out to my sisters and focusing on the quality of our time together both in person and through emails and phone calls. We all have become more transparent with each other." She goes on to say the support she now receives from them is extremely beneficial as she faces her personal and professional challenges.

"The FlexLife program taught me to be more selfish in a healthy way – to really make time to take care of myself and most of all – to ASK for help when I need it. When my husband, Dave, sees that I am stressed out he will tap me on the shoulder and say, 'You know, you aren't alone. Just tell me what I can do to help you right now.' And then I take a long, slow, deep breath and smile!"

Barbara shared that she wanted to take her FlexLife experience to millions of women who need it.

In this context she was delighted to share with me her most important habits she has used over the years to achieve work family balance.

- *Practice conscious breathing throughout the day:*
  Create space.

- *Know your values/priorities:*
  Do a daily reflection at the end of each day to see how you put these into action.
- *Make time for yourself:*
  Incorporate one self-nurturing activity into your weekly schedule
- *Set boundaries in your relationships:*
  And with yourself both at home and at work
- *Develop a spiritual practice:*
  Consistently invest in developing a support network

Today, Barbara is an empty nester herself. She has come a long way from that single parent of 20.

"I love writing as does my husband, Hal. We have written a few books together which has been great fun and re-energizing. In addition to the joy I find in writing, I am an avid reader of historical fiction. And remember, there is no balance without exercise -- I enjoy kickboxing daily and last but not least – I meditate daily," concluded Barbara.

**B**anali Malhotra is head of the marketing division of RAKBANK, one of the most successful banks in the United Arab Emirates (UAE). Banali is also mother of two young girls, wife of one the Regions top financial services executives and a dutiful daughter and daughter-in-law.

As the head of the Marketing and Communications unit of RAKBANK, Banali leads a senior team of marketing professionals and is one of the handfuls of female banking executives that are part of the top management team in the entire banking industry in the Middle East.

Her multiple roles require her to be proficient in one great skill – the art of balance.

Banali's career started in 1993 when she joined American Express as a Credit/Risk analyst. She progressed quickly from risk and credit analysis to consumer sales, corporate sales and was finally appointed as head of Strategic Partnerships. At AMEX she racked up accolades and achievements including the Top Sales Achiever Award across JAPA (Japan Asia Pacific) and in 2005 won the Chairman's award, which is the pinnacle of awards globally at American Express.

That success did have its challenges as well for the aspiring Banali.

She commented, "My early years in Amex were rather challenging as I kept long hours at work and had a long commute to get to work. I did not have my own transportation at that time and hence was dependent on public transport or getting a ride from other colleagues. Yet, I persevered because I never wanted to give my boss the opportunity to say 'she can't do it because she is a woman.'"

So eager was Banali to prove her ability that she actually hid her first pregnancy for over six months as she was attempting to get a larger role and was afraid the pregnancy would go against her.

"At the time the corporate mindset in the country was that women leave their career or take a break when they start a family. But for me I did not want to compromise on either work or family so I worked that much harder to prove it. And all that did take its toll on me. I had a very difficult last semester and delivered a premature baby after eight months. It was a very stressful time in my life with the new premature baby and new job both needing extra attention," shared Banali.

She continued, "When my baby was a year old and I was juggling work and home constantly, I got diagnosed with severe Rheumatoid Arthritis (I was 29 yrs. old at the time) at one point I had 26 inflamed joints and could not get out of bed for two months. Over the years I have had several episodes and surgeries related to this condition ...the biggest trigger for it is stress."

*"Increasingly I have come to understand that women can have it all, just not all at the same time. For me, some days work is the priority, on others it is the children who need more attention, and some days it is the support role I play to (my husband) Raghu."*

**Banali Malhotra,** *Head of Marketing, RAKBANK.*

"In 2002 I decided I had to balance my life and my work much better to prevent the extreme stress that was destroying my health. I started to organize and plan much better. I maximized my time at the office and at home. I began to organize around the top priorities. I simply started to work smarter," shared Banali.

"Women faced then and even now some unique challenges. First, women are always fighting against double standards at the workplace. Over the past, I have seen that most organizations have this pre-conceived idea that women are good only at certain kinds of jobs. Often, men start thinking you have got a certain job just because you are a woman. So women don't often get credit for their work. Yet when a man achieves success, people perceive it was because he was very well prepared for it," she shared.

"Second, women are somewhat more emotional or should I say passionate about their jobs. We tend to take things far more personally than men do. We find it difficult to move on from failures or setbacks. And finally, the biggest challenge we face is maintaining a balance between work and our commitments at home," she added.

In 2005 that balance between work and home was severely tested.

"At the time I was at the top of my game at AMEX. I had successfully established myself not just at AMEX but also in the banking industry in India. My career was on an uptrend. At that point in time my husband Raghu was offered a move up at MasterCard in a large regional role, which involved moving countries. We had avoided moves in the past to balance our careers as well as our family life but this time around I was faced with the toughest of choices. I had to resign from AMEX to follow my husband and restart my career in a completely new market or suffer the stress of us working in two different countries. This would be tough on our young daughter and our family. It was a tough call," commented Banali.

After discussing the pros and cons at great length with my spouse and knowing that it made long-term sense for her family, Banali made the move to Dubai with Raghu.

"I did it after some apprehension but secure in the knowledge that it was worth it for the long term success and growth of our family. Raghu and I have one great advantage. We have known each other since we were 16. We sat together in class and were best friends. We realized our feelings one evening when as friends we went to see the movie 'When Harry met Sally' and we have never looked back. We are equal partners in every sense of the word and we are committed to supporting each other. So I made the move and haven't regretted it," she shared.

Within a few weeks of moving to Dubai, Banali was offered the role of Marketing head for RAKBANK.

At RAKBANK, Banali was given a brief to develop a comprehensive, integrated marketing and communications strategy for the Bank, which she did with great success. With a clearly defined strategy which is dubbed as the "Four C's" - Crystal clear, confident, cheeky and combative, Banali has over the last few years lead RAKBANK into a strong consumer brand in the UAE. The bank has won many accolades in the region including the best credit Card in the Middle East and North Africa by the Banker Middle East Magazine in 2011. RAKBANK and Banali have also been featured in Oxford University's Marketing textbook as a case study in Relationship Marketing. Banali acknowledges that this success is a result of the very strong management team and also the strong vision of the bank's top executives.

But it is not just the results that Banali has delivered that are significant. It is the balance she has been able to maintain in her work and family balance.

"Increasingly I have come to understand that women can have it all, just not all at the same time. For me, some days work is the priority, on others it is the children who need more attention, and some days it is the support role I play to (my husband) Raghu," she shared.

I asked Banali to describe a typical day.

She responded, "I wake up at 6.30 am. Get my younger daughter Myra aged 6, ready for school. Talk to her, get her breakfast, get her off to school by 7.15 am. My husband travels a lot so this is my job when he's not in town. Then at 7.15 I settle down to read the newspapers, get current on news, have a cup of tea. I leave for work and get there by 9 am. On my way to work I call my mum, mom in law and other family and friends, both in India and overseas. I do all of these calls enroute to work every morning."

"For the first couple of hours at work, I clear up the work related to my advertising agencies. Then at noon check in with my boss. During the lunch time I call my younger daughter who has just got back from school."

"I then take all calls or return all calls from external parties – pass on the relevant ones to my team. I make sure people know whom on my team they can connect with to take a conversation forward."

"After lunch I settle into meetings with my team, and then work through the afternoon with them. This includes brainstorming sessions, meetings with our advertising agencies and talking about our new campaigns," she added.

Banali leaves the office on the dot of 5 pm.

"I don't keep long hours in office currently and I make sure to offer my team the same flexibility. We are a marketing team and as long as the work gets delivered, I am fine. One has to be punctual but one does not have to be at the office-desk to work. My current organization is extremely supportive and flexible and encourages an environment which is conducive to work life balance. My team has several working Mums and Dads and I fully understand their situations," she added.

By 5.05 pm Banali is in her car on the way home.

She said, "This time I am talking to my elder daughter Taanvi who is in grade 10. Check in on how her day has been. She is majorly into sports so often I need to be at a match that she is in. Between 5.30 and 7.30 pm it's a mix of getting homework done and spending time with the girls. I also often take the opportunity to take a short nap if possible during this time. This is important me time for me and helps me rejuvenate. Myra needs more time. Taanvi is far more independent. We are proud to see her display these qualities early in life. These will hopefully lay the foundation for her work ethic later in life. By 7.00 pm the little one is ready for bed."

"My husband tries his best to get home before the little one sleeps. After she goes to bed, we have dinner with Taanvi around 8.30 pm. After dinner we catch up on news and media developments again before winding down for the day," shared Banali.

Banali added that her husband's high profile role needs support and capacity from her end.

"I also need to balance out my role at RAKBANK and my role as a mother with my role as a wife to a high powered corporate executive. Apart from all the ongoing corporate networking which we must do, twice a year we have to host the members of the board and their partners, which is enjoyable but also needs a lot of careful planning and time," she added.

I asked Banali for the secret to how she maintained this balance between her many responsibilities.

- *Set very clear priorities:*
  Be clear about what you will and wont do. Know what are the things that are most important to you at work and at home. Even when I am traveling out of the country, I ensure I Skype with my girls every night and discuss their day, I involve them as much as I can in my work so they feel part of it and are engaged in it.

- *Manage your time and capacity:*
  Manage around these priorities and taking responsibility for your actions. If you let distractions from your plans come in your way, you are making a conscious decision to do that. Focus. Raghu and I get our calendars synched up months in advance to make sure at least one of us is always home for the children. This takes some discipline. I also use BBM and what's app and outlook mail a lot for work rather than meetings and calls. These are faster ways to communicate and less intrusive...and makes me a champ at multitasking.

- *Build a support system:*
  We are fortunate today to have parents that are willing and able to fly to Dubai in an emergency situation and look after the kids if both Raghu and I are both travelling, but its pragmatic for women executives to actively build a support network of friends, trusted neighbors, relatives who are willing to support your ambitions.

- *Have a transparent alignment with your partner:*
  This really helps. I am blessed to have a partner who supports my aspirations and who does not stereotype the traditional male/female roles. He helps at home. I often joke about the fact that Raghu is far better at the grocery shopping than me.

- *Stop feeling guilty about being a busy executive:*
  One of the biggest frustrations I have seen for young women professionals

is trying to compete with non-working mums. Do not "compete" with non-working Mums. They have made a personal choice and they should respect your choice to work too. Your kids will understand if you don't have the time to bake a beautiful cake the way a non-working mum would.

- *Take short breaks and time to recover and rejuvenate:*
Travel if you can afford it. Or just take a little break off to spend time with your favorite friends and family. It is important to spend time with your friends and family.

Banali acknowledges that throughout her career, especially in the early years of struggle, she has received a huge amount of helpful advice from her own Mother, close friends and confidants.

"Some of the common themes that I heard as advice from very many of my successful friends were: Remain objective and don't get emotional at work, be professional in all your dealings and interactions and stay away from office politics."

I asked Banali about the top three mistakes she made as a young woman professional that she wanted other young professionals to learn from.

She replied without hesitation.

"They are: Manage expectations upfront - don't get pressurized and promise what you cant deliver, be happy and enjoy every phase of your career and finally, never compare your situation with anyone else's.

Today, Banali and Raghu are content with the life they have in Dubai with their two daughters Taanvi and Myra. Both of their careers have done well since the move to Dubai. While Banali has clearly made a mark with the unconventional marketing strategy at RAKBANK, Raghu has been elevated to President, Mastercard, Middle East and North Africa. Both publicly acknowledge the role the other has played in their personal and career success.

It is this balance of work and family life that has been critical to not just their individual but their dual success as well.

# Chapter 5

# THINK BIG

**Brian Reich,** author of 'Shift and Reset: Strategies for addressing serious issues in a connected society' argues that in the current day reality of endless to do lists, the best way to beat overload and achieve success is by learning to think big. I spoke to **Kiran Mazumdar-Shaw,** *Chairman and Managing Director, Biocon Limited;* **Eriko Sakurai,** *President, Japan/Korea region, Dow Corning;* and **Yue-Sai Kan,** *Emmy award-winning TV host and producer, entrepreneur, style icon and humanitarian.* All powerful leaders with that unique entrepreneurial ability. Here are their learnings.

**K**iran Mazumdar-Shaw, Chairman and Managing Director of Biocon Limited, has featured on Forbes World's Most Powerful Women list, Financial Times Top 50 Women in Business and TIME Magazine's 100 Most Influential People in the World.

Kiran's inspirational story of a first generation woman entrepreneur began in the garden city of India – Bangalore. As a child she was fascinated by science and was a frequent visitor to the science museum in Bangalore, a city which is also home to the famed Indian Institute of Sciences.

'Science is about curiosity driven learning' was etched deep on Kiran's mind since school days, which led her to pursue a path of innovation.

"Innovation for me is not just doing different things but also doing things differently", mentioned Kiran. Ever since Kiran began her journey of entrepreneurship, differentiation and creating her own opportunities was her guiding principle, which is the core essence of her leadership style even today. At Biocon every employee takes pride in saying, " The difference lies in our DNA."

> *"There are incredible opportunities out there today. Anybody can become an entrepreneur if they are willing to commit to it. I think glass ceilings are in people's minds. The glass ceiling is a transparent ceiling, so it's up to you to either hallucinate that it is there or to think that it is not there. Break it."*
>
> **Kiran Mazumdar-Shaw, Chairman and Managing Director of Biocon Limited.**

Kiran's father was the Managing Director and Master Brewer for India's largest brewery- United Breweries - and Kiran remembers growing up in the fascinating surroundings of the brewery and its unique processes and odors, in Bangalore. Her father and her mentor also inculcated in her a sense of gender equality – by showing no difference in the way he brought up Kiran and her brothers.

"He was a man ahead of his time in that sense. He expected from society in general that there would be equal treatment of men and women. I grew up believing that there was nothing my brothers could do that I could not," said Kiran.

Kiran studied at The Bishop Cotton Girls' School in Bangalore. After finishing school she wanted to become a doctor but unfortunately did not have the grades to make it to a medical college. Like many of her friends she expected her father to secure a seat for her by paying a capitation fee. However, her father refused to do so which taught her an important lesson in meritocracy and about not having a sense of entitlement.

Narrating the incident Kiran said, "My father told me, 'I have provided you with the best of school education and if your efforts have not helped you to gain admission into Medical College, it means you haven't worked as hard as someone else who has made the grade. Money is not the currency with which you buy favours but a currency with which you make a difference to society.'"

"Since then his words of integrity have inspired me to strive for excellence and be second to none," shared Kiran.

Taking forward her love for science, Kiran pursued a degree in Zoology Hons. from Bangalore University and graduated with a top rank.

Kiran shared how in those times, women in India were stereotyped into being able to do or not to do some roles. Kiran felt this was wrong and that women were capable and intelligent enough to succeed in any field.

Commented Kiran, "From the very beginning I wanted to be a change agent in society and wanted to change the way society perceived and treated women."

Kiran believed that with the inspiration of her father and supportive attitude of her family, coupled with her strong educational background, she was well equipped to do something different in her career.

"I wanted to challenge this concept that women couldn't do some roles that men could," she said.

It was then that her father drew her attention towards brewing which was the oldest form of biotechnology practiced by humans. He suggested to her that she should probably look at brewing as a prospective career.

"Encouraged by my father, I decided to pursue a career path that was unique for women in India, and set out for my Masters degree in Brewing," she added.

The experience at Ballarat College, Melbourne University in Australia was life-changing for Kiran. In India she had lived a somewhat sheltered life, living with the family. In Australia, however she was on her own, living in a land completely new to her, and to make matters worse she was the only woman in a male-dominated career programme. However far from initimidating her, these hardships strengthened her resolve to be successful.

"I blossomed there and developed a lot of self-esteem, which was lacking when I was in India. I learned to fend for myself in an industry that was all male. This boosted my confidence significantly. It set the base for me being able to work with the best in the industry and compete," commented Kiran.

Kiran outperformed all her male colleagues at the programme and two years later she was back in India armed with her Master Brewer certification.

Kiran was all set to take up the exciting job at the leading brewery in India, but was in for a surprise as she discovered there were no jobs for women in the brewing industry. By that time, her father had become a consultant and had been asked to commission a brewery — Jupiter Breweries — in Calcutta. Kiran found it very exciting to work along with her father and successfully commissioned the brewery in record time.

But Kiran did not give up her dream of working at UB where her father worked all his life. She approached Vittal Mallya (Vijay Mallya's father and the promoter of United Breweries) for a role in one of his breweries in Bangalore but was turned down – because she was a woman. Vittal had no doubts about her educational excellence or her capabilitites but had a firm belief that a brewery was no place for a woman. He did not want her to be exposed to a male dominated workplace which had to often deal with labour unions and demonstrations.

Despite Vijay's generous endorsement of her skills and abilities, Vittal refused to give her the job at United Breweries, a company that her father had given his life for. She was very disappointed but determined to pursue her dreams of charting a course in brewing, if not in India then overseas.

As a woman professional, this experience made Kiran realize that in India there was no level playing field, there were several opportunities which were not available to women just because of their gender.

For some time Kiran continued to consult along with her father helping several brewaries in India to run their business, trouble shooting for them and aligning them with the best international practices of brewing. However, this is not what she wanted from life, her heart was set on being in the driving seat as the Master Brewer. She focussed on finding a job outside of India and very quickly landed a very interesting role at a brewery in Scotland.

However before she could make that move, she had a chance meeting in Delhi, with an Irish entrepreneur, Leslie Auchincloss, founder of the biotechnology company, Biocon Biochemicals. Leslie was in India looking for a partner to develop a papaya-based enzyme, Papain, for him. He came looking for Kiran on recommendations from Australia and persuaded her to give up her job in Scotland and replace it with a dream of being a biotechnologist entrepreneur in India.

Amidst apprehensions and with great persuasion from Leslie, Kiran accepted the challenge to be his Indian partner.

With no prior business background or access to capital, Kiran began her entrepreneurial journey. Biocon India was born in a makeshift office in a garage in Bangalore in 1978 with a small personal investment of Rs 10,000/- (less than 200 USD today). The young Kiran thus became the Managing Director of a biotech startup, which in the years to come would evolve into Asia's leading biopharmaceutical enterprise.

"I had a misson statement, Rs 10,000 and an office in our home garage in Bangalore. However I had no employees. At that time in India, there was little or no appreciation of enterprise and entrepreneurial talent, least of all for a woman peddling an unknown technology."

"So I put out a newspaper advertisement positioning Biocon India as a 'multinational company.' When candidates came, they were shocked to see me operating out of a garage. They then looked around for the MD as they assumed it was a man and that I was the 'secretary' and were somewhat crestfallen when I shared that I was indeed the Managing Director of the

Company. That's how we started, " she said.

With just two employees (former mechanics) Biocon India started making industrial enzymes for food and textile makers around the world in a 3,000 square feet shed nearby.

"I can distinctly recall that we did not even have a telephone in those days. Also, there was constant interruption of power supply, and we had little access to superor quality water and imported research equipment. Yet, I believed that we could focus on one step at a time and make things happen if we adopted a commonsensical and adaptable approach," said Kiran.

And adapt she did. Neither the infrastructural challenges nor the lack of funding support nor the negative reactions of others to her being a woman professional could deter Kiran. These adversities strengthened her resolve to pursue her goal with a vengeance.

"When I negotiated business, many of my suppliers would feel very uncomfortable dealing with a woman and suggested they would discuss prices with my 'manager'. It took a sustained effort on my part to educate these traditional people who were completely unfamiliar with dealing with women," she said.

Kiran turned this into an advantage. "These suppliers respected me much more once I negotiated good business for them and they saw their own businesses do better thanks to Biocon."

Kiran addressed the problem of funding for her start-up with the same sense of self-confidence and determination with which she had tackled the other problems. Legend has it that Kiran's first round of major funding came out of a chance meeting with a Senior Executive of Canara Bank (one of India's leading banks) at a wedding reception.

Besides her problem-solving abilities, Kiran also had one of the most important qualities of a business leader - foresight. She was able to see opportunities that others missed.

"I invested all of my savings to buy a 20 acre property in Bangalore in 1980s. At that time, friends joked about it and asked why I would want to buy a 20 acre property when I had such a small business. All I could tell them was that I had a big dream about the potential of this business and the difference we could make, and more importantly at that time this 20 acre property was within my reach," she added.

By 1983, Biocon India had progressed to making speciality enzymes for various industrial applications and had moved out of the garage into the Hosur Road office, which was on the outskirts of the city then and is now in the heart of the industrial hub, the Electronics City.

Over the next few years, Biocon had evolved into India's largest enzymes company. However, much later Kiran sold off the enzymes division to Novozymes for $115 million so that her company could focus exclusively on pharmaceuticals and healthcare.

"You have to keep evolving, you have to keep challenging the status quo, reinventing yourself and your business if you want to stay ahead," shared Kiran.

She had a much larger goal ahead of her, she wanted to leverage the company's expertise in fermentation technology to develop pharmaceuticals to find innovative soloutions for the chronic diseases which were posing a huge challenge for Indian patients who had little access to expensive treatment.

As the company's business grew further, there were ownership changes at the global level which compelled her to take complete ownership of Biocon, which happened in 1989.

In 1990, Kiran upgraded Biocon's in-house research program, based on a proprietary solid substrate fermentation technology from pilot to plant level, which received ISO certification the subsequent year. Leveraging this technology further by 1996 Kiran had entered the world of biopharmaceuticals with fermentation technology based statins, which was another first in India. In 2001, her efforts were rewarded in the form of USFDA approval for its fermentation plant for manufacturing Lovastatin.

Kiran's resolve to make a much larger difference to healthcare in India drew her to finding solutions for chronic diseases. Next on her radar was diabetes, which was on an increase in India. However, its treament was by and large inaccesible to most due to the high cost of treatment.

She therefore focussed on developing an affordable form of insulin in India using the innovative technology platform of Biocon. By 2004, Biocon had successfully introduced INSUGEN®, the new generation bio-insulin, manufactured in Asia's largest human insulin plant by Biocon. Biocon introduced INSUGEN at less than half the cost of the prevailing rates. This move compelled the innovator to also drop prices which enhanced access to insulin for a larger patient population.

Biocon is the world's first company to develop Pichia-based recombinant human insulin, which is today marketed in over 50 countries.

The same year Kiran decided to approach the capital markets. Biocon's IPO was oversubscribed 32 times and on its first day at the bourses closed with a market value of $1.11 billion. Till date, Biocon is the only biotech company to be listed on India's stock exchanges.

Taking her committment to affordable innovation forward Kiran collaborated with the Cuban Centre of Molecular Immunology to develop innovative antibodies for a host of autoimmune diseases, simultaneously Biocon also invested in building a world class biologics manufacturing facility for commerical production of biosimilar insulins and antibodies.

Sharing her expereince of those days Kiran said, "When I started Biocon, I was driven by the spirit to create a business that would leverage science for the benefit of society through affordable innovation. That has always been Biocon's raison d'être. We harnessed India's low-cost talent and innovation base and forged our way through the market through strategic research and marketing partnerships that helped us reach affordable therapies to the masses."

Today Biocon is Asia's leading bio-pharmaceutical company driven by innovation committed to develop affordable therapy options for chronic diseases like diabetes, cancer and several auto-immune conditions.

Over the years, Biocon as a company has made significant contributions to making healthcare affordable and accessible in India.

Biocon has to its credit two novel biologics delivered to Indian patients. The company launched India's first novel biologic BIOMAb EGFR®, a humanized anti-cancer antibody for the treatment of head & neck cancer, in 2006. It also launched ALZUMAb™, the second novel biologic to come out from its laboratories, for psoriasis in India in 2013. ALZUMAb™ is a 'first-in-class' humanized anti-CD6 monoclonal antibody with an excellent safety and efficacy profile. With promising preclinical and clinical efficacy data in other autoimmune diseases such as rheumatoid arthritis, psoriatic arthritis etc, Biocon is looking to take ALZUMAb™ to patients across the globe.

"One of my dreams as a company operating out of India has always been to demonstrate that the world must care for every person who needs medical drugs. It is my dream to see one of our drugs make a difference in not just India but across the world. Healthcare needs can only be met with affordable innovation. That has been the driving philosophy that has helped Biocon manufacture and market drugs cost-effectively," said Kiran.

Today, Biocon is India's largest biotech Company with a staff of over 7,000, and a business presence in over 85 countries. The company's consolidated sales stand at nearly half a billion dollars annually. In the next few years, Kiran sees her company becoming an even bigger global player. It has an aspiration of reaching US$ 1 billion in sales by 2018.

Kiran's pioneering efforts in biotechnology have brought her recognition both globally and from the Indian government.

These include the prestigious Padma Shri (1989) and the Padma Bhushan (2005) from the government of India, Nikkei Asia Prize for regional Growth, Wharton-Infosys Business Transformation Award, Ernst & Young Best Entrepreneur Award, among several others.

Recently, the U.S.-based Chemical Heritage Foundation conferred her with the 2014 Othmer Gold Medal for her multifaceted contributions to chemical and scientific heritage.

In late 2013, Indian technology giant Infosys announced that Kiran would be joining its board as an independent director. Kiran is one of just two women on the firm's male-dominated board. And in February 2014, the Indian Institute of Management, Bangalore appointed Kiran as the Chairperson of its Board of Governors. She is the first woman Chairperson of any IIM Board. Clearly, her role in shaping success for women is not done yet.

Kiran has not stopped thinking big. At 60, she continues to drive her Company and the Indian biotech industry forward. As the Chairperson of Karnataka Government's Vision Group on Biotechnology, she continues to be the torchbearer of this sector. She firmly believes that the Indian biotech sector has the potential to become a USD 100 billion sector by 2025.

Sharing her biggest dream Kiran said, "My vision is have our research programs like oral insulin or antibodies for cancer and auto-immune disorders transforming the approach to killer diseases. Affordable blockbuster drugs with the potential to change the lives of millions of patients around the world will truly stand testimony to our leadership. As a first-generation entrepreneur I am intensely conscious of the fact that I must do my bit for society, creating opportunities for others to grow. Making a difference in healthcare and education has always been my calling. My efforts are geared towards changing lives for the better by ensuring affordability and access through Biocon's biotherapies."

Leaders who have made the difference and steered their organizations to new horizons, have rarely been conformists. Spurred by the courage of conviction, they have the zeal to confront all odds. They are the entrepreneurial risk-takers and innovators and create their own opportunities. It is this spirit that enables them to stand apart.

Indian business has several examples of entrepreneurial leaders who have profitably delivered social good through innovation. Enterprise is a wonderful canvas to give free rein to one's innovative and creative instincts. Entrepreneurs can develop business models that add value and generate benefits for the organization and society through collaboration and cooperation. The most satisfying way to achieve this is to deliver products and services that benefit society.

Kiran is a living example of 'entrepreneurs par excellence' who has been driven to deliver transformational change.

In 2005, Kiran started the Biocon Foundation with a vision to provide marginalized communities access to healthcare services and educational opportunities.

Today, the Foundation runs 9 Arogya Raksha Primary Healthcare Clinics, which provide primary healthcare services to 75,000 patients a year. It is also actively involved in preventive health programs like oral cancer screening, early detection of cervical cancer and tackling child malnutrition. Moreover, the Foundation now prints and distributes about 100,000 'Chinnara Ganitha' maths work books annually among children in primary schools in eight districts of Karnataka.

"I have always been deeply concerned with the poor access to healthcare and education that challenges India's poor and rural population. I have therefore focused my efforts in these two areas," shared Kiran.

While Biocon Foundation looks after the philanthropic activities of her company, Kiran is also involved in a number of philanthropic activities in her personal capacity.

"My next phase of philanthropy has been focused on Cancer care. Cancer is an expensive and unaffordable disease to treat in India. I therefore decided to partner Dr. Devi Shetty, a renowned cardiac Surgeon who built a globally known affordable cardiac care model. My objective was to develop a similar model in affordable cancer care where economies of scale once again based on sheer numbers of cancer patients both in patients and out patients could help amortize the huge infrastructure costs that are required in Radiotherapy and Imaging Technologies for scanning," she shared.

The Mazumdar-Shaw Cancer Center, MSCC, was hence created in 2009 as the largest Cancer Center in this region as a 1400 bedded Cancer Hospital, which also has the largest Bone Marrow Transplant Unit in the country. Today it has already been recognized as a center of excellence for Head and Neck cancer in the country with the best diagnostic and treatment outcomes. Head and Neck cancers represent 30% of cancers in India, attributed to Tobacco consumption and afflict the lower strata of society. Accordingly Kiran has also initiated a large Tobacco Cessation program through Biocon Foundation which conducts a door to door education program using an innovative mobile technology based application that is used by the health workers to capture photographs of mouth lesions of patients, which are then transmitted to a team of Oncologists who remotely evaluate and suspicious looking lesions are then further investigated by the nearest tertiary care centers.

"Early detection has led to early treatment at lower cost and greatly enhanced outcomes. We are committed to scaling up this model of building an affordable cancer model based on early detection of head & neck and breast and cervical cancers in the first phase," shared Kiran.

Recently, Kiran has also established a world class Mazumdar Shaw Center for Translational Research (MSCTR) at MSCC that provides a platform for scientists at MSCTR and clinicians at MSCC to work very closely in advancing diagnostics and treatment for several life-threatening diseases like cancer.

Kiran is not resting on the social development initiatives she has taken so far but has extended her area of influence to civic issues in India. As a proud Bangalorean she believes good governance in the city is critical to restore Bangalore's lost glory and to transform the city into the most innovative city of Asia. Accordingly she has set up the Bangalore Political Action Committee (B.PAC) along with like minded prominent citizens of Bangalore, from different walks of life, all of them love Bangalore and are eager to bring in positive change.

Kiran is extremely passionate about her role with B.PAC.She shared, "Through B.PAC we are working towards mobilizing the educated middle class and the elite of the city to fully engage and work with political leaders to push for better policies and better governance with the aim of ensuring a better quality of life for the people of Bangalore."

B.PAC has been able to make a significant impact in a very short period of time. A 10 point comprehensive 'Agenda for Bangalore' has been communicated to the government and B.PAC team is working with the government and candidates of diverse political parties to ensure positive action in the direction of Agenda for Bangalore.

"More recently, we have introduced a unique civic leadership incubator program B.CLIP aimed at preparing political enthusiasts for better public service. Through a rigorous nine months training we are grooming select candidates for delivering better governance when chosen for a public career which is expected to translate into positive change on the ground. We aim to train atleast 100 people this year." added Kiran.

Kiran has very definitive opinions on being a woman leader.

"As a woman, I would also like to touch upon the sensitive subject of gender barriers that exist within our society. The bias against women only served to spur me on to greater efforts," narrated Kiran.

She added, "I was determined to be a role model for career oriented women in India. I wanted to prove that women should not be underestimated or denied opportunity just because of a social prejudice against women. To me it seemed quite logical that in a country so proud of its scientific prowess women should also take their place. After all there were plenty of women scientists sitting at home!" shared Kiran.

It is no surprise then that, according to recent reports, 40% of the workplace in India is occupied by women in the corporate world today. Though the presence of women may not be uniform across all sectors, what is encouraging to see is that almost 10% senior management positions are held by women.

"Women are excelling and succeeding just as their male counterparts in India's corporate sector. Six of the top 10 Banks in India are headed by women today," shared Kiran.

In Kiran's view women are naturally blessed with special attributes like compassion, sensitivity, the ability to multi-task and the capacity to solve problems with a clear head. She believes women are good team players and as leaders are more democratic.

"I am pleased to see that women are being well accepted in the urban workplace. However, we do know that society needs to do a lot more and the most critical of these is the change of mindset. We must work towards a safe environment for women and this can only stem from mutual respect between men and women. It is well recognized that a progressive society is an egalitarian society especially when it comes to gender equality." Kiran narrated.

*Kiran shared some of the learnings she believes helped her think big and create new opportunities and become a shining example for women in India as well as globally.*

- *Use courage and perseverance to build credibility:*
  As a first-generation entrepreneur, I am intensely mindful of the fact that credibility builds success. Building credibility is not easy and requires the courage of your conviction and perseverance of your efforts to overcome the disappointments and failures that are intrinsic to realizing one's potential.

  I remember how difficult it was to overcome the credibility challenges I faced in my early entrepreneurial years. Banks did not want to offer me credit, people were unwilling to be recruited and companies did not wish to do business with me all because I was a 25 year old woman who was trying to sell products based on a novel  technology called Biotechnology! But that did not deter me, in fact it inculcated a spirit of challenge and a deep sense of purpose that pushed me to my goals. It is this sense of determination that spurs you to overcome failure. Remember failure is temporary but giving up is final.

- *Adapt constantly. Be flexible:*
  You must adapt or your business will finally become redundant. It was emotionally difficult to move out of the enzymes business as that was what we started with. However we knew the market for enzymes was limited and that global patient needs would be best met through biopharmaceuticals. That flexibility helped us stay ahead.

- *Be prepared to take risks to shape your dreams:*
  Sometimes to win big you have to take a (calculated) risk e.g., my decision to buy that 20 acre piece of property in Bangalore!

- *Be ethical and do not be swayed by unrealistic aspirations:*
  Do not pursue a "hook or by crook" mentality to success. Earn the right to your success and riches by doing things in an ethical way. Even though it may seem far more challenging to do it right, it is much more satisfying and profitable over the long term. Your business partners will respect you more and competition will learn to fear and respect you too.

- *Invest some of what you make back into the community:*
  When you have a profitable organization, it is your reponsibility to

give back to the community that supported you. The success of your organization and the community you operate in is always interconnected.

- *Think big and do big:*
  There are incredible opportunities out there today, way beyond when I started my career. Anybody can become an entrepreneur if they are willing to commit to it. I think glass ceilings are in people's minds. The glass ceiling is a transparent ceiling, so it's up to you to either hallucinate that it is there or to think that it is not there. Break it.

When she started Biocon in 1978, Kiran had to strive to establish her credibility as a 25-year-old woman entrepreneur fuelled more by drive and vision than by business experience. However, it was this very drive and vision that helped her set up her business and grow Biocon into what it is today.

Born in Kyoto, Japan from the time she was a little girl, **Eriko Sakurai, President, Japan/Korea region Dow Corning** had tremendous passion for whatever she did. She focused not just on thinking big but also on energetically putting in the work to accomplish that dream.

Eriko was born in Japan to a University professor Dad and a resilient housewife Mum. Though of modest means, they encouraged Eriko to dream about a life she wanted and to work towards it.

"My parents were the first ones who made me believe that I could have all kinds of opportunities in the future. They made me aware of my strengths and encouraged me to challenge myself," shared Eriko.

As the eldest of three children, Eriko realized quickly that she was expected to be a good role model for her younger siblings. So she put in the work needed to excel at her studies.

"As early back as high school I had the dream to go abroad and study. In the 1980s it was uncommon for Japanese women to study abroad and start working in the USA. I knew that my parents also needed to support my younger siblings as well, so I studied hard and in 1983 I secured a scholarship from the Japanese government. I left Japan in 1984 to study Psychology at the graduate school of UCLA (University of California, Los Angeles)," said Eriko.

Eriko was encouraged all the way by her parents who reassured her that "If you fail you can simply return home to Japan and start over."

Success was on the 23-year-old Eriko's mind however. Landing in Los Angeles in August 1984, she was in completely unfamiliar territory. But she quickly adjusted to life in the USA, undaunted by the challenges of language and the style of classes.

"Even though I studied English hard in Japan, the real language has different nuances. And the small graduate school classes and seminars required active discussions and debates, not just listening and taking notes," shared Eriko.

So Eriko came up with a simple means of improving her English skills.

"The dormitory for graduate school students was already full so I searched for a shared room with an American woman professional. I thought it was one of the quick ways to learn better English. I also shared the research laboratory at school with other Americans, so that I could have more real discussions on our research subjects," shared Eriko.

*"Thinking big means you should be confident but not arrogant. I also learned that knowledge and leadership are not necessarily the same. Knowledge is tangible and leadership is intangible. I learned that even if you have the most knowledge about something that doesn't entitle you to lead."*

**Eriko Sakurai, President, Japan/Korea region, Dow Corning.**

Outside of school, Eriko threw herself wholeheartedly in the community, and enjoyed the local activities such as dance classes, and the Christmas chorus to learn American culture.

One particular professor at graduate school in the USA also inspired Eriko. Dr. Eran Zaidel, an expert in Neuropsychology and Neuroscience supported and sponsored her research project.

"Dr. Zaidel was not only intelligent but also a very warm-hearted person. He always welcomed me whenever I visited his office and we talked a lot. He shared that if I just repeated what others did, I wasn't adding any value. He encouraged me to think differently and share the ideas and reminded me that there were no stupid ideas," added Eriko.

"Encouraged by Dr. Zaidel, I began to get more creative in my thinking and started sharing my opinions. I started to feel comfortable to share my ideas with others. In general, it is tough to think out of the box in Japan so I rapidly embraced my professor's teachings," shared Eriko.

Eriko successfully got her Masters degree and shortly thereafter secured a marketing role with Dow Corning in Michigan.

It was likely the toughest challenge of her career.

Eriko quickly realized that she needed to learn business fundamentals as all the other new sales and marketing employees had business degrees.

Eriko began to attend every single onboarding training Dow Corning provided, and also started to take executive MBA classes at a local University in the evenings.

Two months after joining Eriko received her first position as the back up marketer for skin care marketing as the existing marketer (Cathy) at the time went out on maternity leave.

"I suddenly became responsible for marketing strategy and implementation, including pricing decisions, promotion materials and so on. My manager was the general manager for the entire personal, household care group, including S&T and product line, so that I could not ask him the minute details of the job," she shared.

Instead, Eriko decided to visit Cathy at her home and get some tips.

"Cathy had just delivered her baby boy and while she nursed her baby she patiently answered every single question I had ranging from specific customer insights as well as background on price recommendations," said Eriko.

Eriko also saw firsthand how a mother could also be a business professional at the same time.

Eriko delivered strong results in that first assignment. As a result, in 1989 with just two years of working experience under her belt in the US, Dow Corning offered Eriko a position in Japan as a marketing specialist in beauty care.

"At the time the Company decided to place the Marketing organization in Japan and I was the only Japanese they had who had worked in Marketing. I was so excited to move back and put my degree to use in Japan," commented Eriko.

But going back to Japan to work was a huge culture shock to Eriko.

"Japan and the USA were even more different at that time as far as work cultures went. And Dow Corning had not integrated the Asian operations into the global organization fully yet at the time. It was before the 1999 law change of equal treatment. While Japanese law suggested that women were to be treated equally, it was clear that the Japanese entity was not treating women as professionals," said Eriko.

Eriko highlighted how this meant that there were no performance reviews or career plans at the time. That did not stop her from pursuing her aspirations though.

"I quickly realized that I could not change the whole country instantly, and fighting would not bring me anything. I instead decided to focus on my goals and deliver outstanding results in that assignment," she shared.

Eriko did exactly that and used her marketing savvy to highlight the product benefits of Dow Corning's beauty care products in a highly compelling way. That would prove to be the beginning of using silicones in many beauty care products and their marketing in Japan.

"In the same year (1989) Eriko got married and had her first baby in 1990.

She continued to make progress at work and in that year managed to achieve aggressive financial targets with a broad range of new products, and completed the capital project of a local manufacturing site, which became the critical facility through which Dow Corning established a strong market position in Japan.

By the time Eriko had her second child in 1992 she knew that she would have to do something differently to balance out her responsibilities to the family and the work. So she went back to her management and talked to them. Dow Corning came back with a unique proposal – to work a three-day a week schedule.

"Dow Corning was so supportive. They understood my situation and proactively helped," shared Eriko.

But the dreamer in Eriko couldn't quite sit still. Settling into a three day a week schedule quickly and as the children grew Eriko knew that she would have to push herself to stay relevant in the career stakes.

In 1993 Eriko decided to go back to being a student on top of her day job. She enrolled in the Doctorate program on Information Sciences at Tohoku University, Japan.

"While my flexible working hours were a huge help, managing a working schedule, family and a PhD were a huge challenge. I planned meticulously to be well organized with my time. I prepared well for the odd times when unexpected circumstances developed, so the general principle I followed for work and for study was to always set an earlier deadline for submitting any work or assignment. That way I always had a buffer of 1-2 days. That came in very handy when for example one of the kids suddenly developed a fever or something unexpected as growing up kids always do," she shared.

"I also realized that I could not do it all alone. So I developed multiple layers of support both at work and at home. My husband, my friends, my close associates at work, all played a key role in this process. I learned to take help from them and also offer help when they needed it," she added.

In 1997, after her son started elementary school, Dow Corning asked her to resume a full week schedule! She continued to have challenging positions since then with increasing scope of business impact and team management.

In 1999 she faced a new challenge as the Asian area-marketing manager for the Construction Division, which was new to her.

"I had to manage a mostly male and multinational team, the majority of members having much longer experiences than me and they were mostly older than me, which is fundamentally against the Asian concept of seniority. Additionally I had no technical experience in the construction field.

Eriko responded to the challenge by focusing on the fundamentals of the work. She spent significant time understanding the construction business and its dynamics, and also the key members of the team and their cultures. She learned that to be a boss didn't necessarily mean that she had to be "bossy".

"I worked hard at building trust with my direct reports. There were no short cuts. I continued to take leadership in solving the issues for the team, customers, and had effective communication with each team member. My background in Psychology and human brain science and organizational behavior proved to be a huge asset," she shared.

Over the next few months, Eriko's efforts paid off. Her company recognized not just the results her team was delivering but also her individual contribution as a leader. Best of all her team became advocates for her leadership.

"We established new growth after being stagnant for the previous decade and business results started to come in. We secured the signature construction projects such as Thai Airport, Taiwan 101 Building, Korean world cup stadiums and so on," shared Eriko.

This first management challenge gave her the confidence "Thinking big means you should be confident but not arrogant. I also learned that knowledge and leadership are not necessarily the same. Knowledge is tangible and leadership is intangible. I learned that even if you have the most knowledge about something that doesn't entitle you to lead," she shared.

Eriko added,"The other thing that was different about this time was my ability to focus much more at work on developing a highly diverse, capable team. In the past as a student it was all up to me. I controlled the input and I controlled the outcome. Yet here as a working mum and studying as well, I knew that my work team would have to be incredibly efficient and supportive and it was in my best interests to not only attract the finest talent, but also to develop and grow the right members of my team."

"Most managers have a natural tendency to attract people like themselves onto the team, as most human beings subconsciously move towards their comfort zones. As a manager I realized that if I were to realize all the dreams I had to be a great global executive, then I would have to hire people different from me, and sometimes even more talented than me."

Soon her ability of being able to lead by attracting diverse talent got the attention of her management. In 2007, she became the first Asian leader at Dow Corning to lead the global business unit as Global Industry Executive Director. It was the smallest Business Unit with specialized lubricants.

But in similar fashion to her stint in the construction business, she established a diverse team and delivered strong financial growth. After two years, in 2009, this group was integrated into the one of the biggest Business Units, called the Automotive, Appliance, Assembly and Maintenance unit. Eriko was promoted to Business Vice President of this global business unit to lead.

As a believer of diverse talents, she appointed key talents regardless of their nationalities into the critical positions. Also she developed a strong pipeline of younger talent and worked with HR to create special three-month exchange programs, as the expat programs were limited in numbers. By doing this she was able to take young Chinese marketers to the USA, young Japanese talent to Germany and young German talent to China in the first year itself!

In 2009 she was appointed Chairman and CEO of Dow Corning and Toray Co., Ltd.(Dow Corning's joint venture in Japan with Toray Industries Inc.)

In 2011, Eriko was appointed as the President of the Japan and Korea regions.

Eriko believes that the challenges women face today, especially in Japan are many, but not unsurmountable.

"The first one is the acceptance of women leaders. This is especially true in Japan where it is difficult for traditional Japanese men to accept women as their bosses," shared Eriko.

Japan is the country with the lowest number of women executives among 45 nations according to GMI Ratings' 2013 Women on Boards Survey.

"The second challenge is women themselves in Japan. In many cases, we limit ourselves. Women hesitate to go through the door, even if the door is open for them. Being humble is good, but one must be confident at the same time, the two are not opposed.

Work family balance is another great challenge and last but not least collaboration and cooperation with men. I learned that fighting men doesn't bring solutions. Rather one must try to influence wherever one can. I have tried to do this both at home and in the workplace," she added.

"One of my key passions today is to give back to society and also help develop more women leaders. I often talk to women in business regardless of generation and also occasionally talk at universities in Japan and Korea. I believe that they do not think big, and I remind them that every single one of them has potential. I tell them that I am not a special person from a special family. That I just focused on a few things that led me to success and that they could do it too."

Eriko listed a few of the things she focused on in thinking big.

- *Know your strengths and focus on them:*
  Too often I hear women say what they can't do. Because of my psychology background I was forced to focus on my strengths working in the chemical industry – my ability to understand human behavior and to build strong teams.

- *Build active supporters and advocates:*
  Do not waste time on complaining on what's wrong about a system or situation. Instead focus your energies on doing something better and bigger.

- *Constantly transform yourself:*
  Darwin's theory of evolution has shown us that it is not necessarily the strongest that survive, but the ones who are ready to change. Expect you will have challenges and be prepared to change yourself.

- *Take on new challenges:*
  Embrace new experiences even though they may initially seem over powering. If the door is open, go through it. New challenges will always grow you.

- *Try to be happy:*
  Life is busy. Often I am so busy that I get very few of my scheduled tasks done. I feel frustrated. Be happy with what you have accomplished.

- *Invest in building other women leaders:*
  I always wish to contribute to make the work a better place. That is very important for my job satisfaction. I invest a lot of capacity to build the next generation of women leaders, and enjoy coaching and mentoring, as I believe people are the most important asset.

Eriko acknowledges the huge role that Dow Corning has played in her career success.

"At every stage, the company believed in me, and my ability, sometimes when it was difficult for me to believe in myself," she added softly.

Today, Eriko is still closely connected to both her parents who are retired but very active in the community. Her mother is playing an active role in rehabilitating the community in Tohoku, Japan, the area that was affected by a massive earthquake and tsunami in 2011. Her mother is doing that through raising funds for the arts and music and exposing children in the affected area of Sendai to the arts. Her son is 23 and daughter 21.

"Life has changed so much for me. I owe much of it to my ability to think big and then work towards my dreams. I owe a lot to my parents, my professors, and my colleagues and of course Dow Corning," she shared.

I asked Eriko what she believed was the biggest dream she has achieved so far as a woman leader.

She replied without pause:

"I continued my career while having a happy family. I have so many people (both men and women across the world) who have helped me, supported me and also count on me. Finally, I was able to deliver some great results for my Company. I'm happy," she concluded.

Eriko Sakurai is indeed a great example of thinking big and then putting in the actual effort of pursuing her dreams.

In 2014 I had the great opportunity to interact with a leader who personifies the ability to think big and who started her first enterprise on the back of moving to New York with just 150 US Dollars in her pocket. Yet today she is one of the most successful women in the world and shares her time between New York, Shanghai and Beijing.

Meet **Yue-Sai Kan** - the **Chinese American Emmy-winning television host** and **producer, successful entrepreneur, style icon and humanitarian.** Yue-Sai is also the author of eight books. People magazine called her 'the most famous woman in China" and Time magazine dubbed her "the Queen of the Middle Kingdom." Yue-Sai is the first and only living American featured on a government issued Chinese postage stamp.

Yue-Sai was born in Southern China, before the founding of the People's Republic of China and grew up in Hong Kong. Her parents immigrated to Hong Kong at the time of the Cultural Revolution in China. Her father Kan Wing-Lin was a revered traditional Chinese painter and calligrapher. He was also a champion swimmer, singer and musician.

*"I'm clueless about the challenges of being a woman professional. It's probably because I have spent all of my life just trying to be the best at whatever I did. Being a woman is only a problem if you are not willing to believe that you are the CEO of your own life. If you want to succeed big, you have to create your own opportunities, you have to do big."*

*Yue-Sai Kan, Emmy award winning TV host and producer, entrepreneur, style icon and humanitarian.*

"My search for excellence started when I was a little girl as I watched my father who was a complete perfectionist. Sometimes he would paint for hours. Then at literally the last stroke he would decide that the painting was not good enough and would scrap it and start all over," shared Yue-Sai.

Yue-Sai shared that from her father she learned perfectionism, to be eternally curious and to explore various things.

But it was her mother who taught Yue-Sai the financial instinct that would be so important to her years later. With four children to care for, her mother was constantly watching the finances of the household and even collaborated with friends to start a full fledged "savings club" wherein they pooled resources to make the most savings for their families.

"I didn't come from a rich family, yet we never felt poor. My parents prioritized our expenditure. So when I asked if I could have a piano at age 14, my mum though initially shocked, got me the best tutor possible, a Russian instructor. We had a piano at home before we had a Television. My mother would rather invest in that than buy us candy. It was my mum who taught me how to manage money," shared Yue-Sai.

Yue-Sai shared that she also learned dignity, honor, a work ethic and love for family from her parents.

"Years later, when my mum passed, my father's health got to the point where he was in a wheel chair. Yet, he always arrived in his tie and coat, as sharply dressed as ever," she reminisced.

At 14, an eager Yue-Sai went to her mother and shared that she wanted to go to the USA to study one day. Her mother was surprised by this request, but supportive. With her mother's help Yue-Sai studied for, applied and successfully secured two scholarships to study in the USA. She finally chose Hawaii as a location to study and moved there in 1966 to pursue a degree in music at Brigham Young University.

While studying as a piano major, Yue-Sai was nominated by the student body to participate in a beauty pageant sponsored by the local Chinese Chamber of Commerce, and was awarded second runner up.

"It was completely coincidental. I was 19 at the time. And a beauty pageant was the last thing on my mind at the time. But that one experience changed me. It showed me the power of make-up, of cosmetics. It shaped everything in my life from then on," commented Yue-Sai.

"As part of my duties of winning at this pageant, I travelled around the world as an ambassador, and my eyes opened to the huge opportunities for success that exist around us everyday. I realized I could make my own unique way. This small beginning was also my initiation into the world of beauty and fashion," she continued.

In 1972, Yue-Sai moved to New York with 150 dollars in her pocket to visit the city she had heard so much about. She fell in love with the city and stayed on in New York despite the obvious hardships of being there with no financial support.

Shortly thereafter by sheer dint of hard work, Yue-Sai formed a small television production company called Yue-Sai Kan Productions. Her first major TV production was the weekly series called 'Looking East – the pioneering effort that would introduce Asian culture to a curious and receptive American audience. It won critical acclaim and received a host of awards. The series was on air 12 years, including the last two years on the Discovery Channel. As a result of 'Looking East' Yue-Sai was often referred to as "the first TV journalist to bridge the East and the West."

"I decided to do 'Looking East' because nobody even cared about Asia at the time. It was a pioneering effort that was ripe for the market," shared Yue-Sai.

In 1984, PBS invited Yue-Sai to host the first live broadcast of a television program from China on the occasion of the 35th Anniversary of the People's Republic of China. This was a co-production between PBS and China's CCTV network.

"I said yes despite the difficulty in doing the show. I was given only 48 hours to prepare for the broadcast," mused Yue-Sai.

Overnight, Yue-Sai shot to prominence in China. Through this one show, the Chinese Government got to know of Yue-Sai and a month later offered her a new TV series on CCTV called 'One World.'

"The government was intent on leveraging television to educate the masses. One World showcased world cultures – 21 countries in all, each a six part series, to over 300 million viewers around the world every week," she continued.

One World was the first ever TV series produced in China by a Chinese American and made Yue-Sai a household name. The scripts were even used as teaching aids in China. With broadcasts in both China and the USA, Yue-Sai quickly became the most watched woman in the world.

'What was most amazing was the Chinese Government invited a foreigner to do this show, did not censor the series at all and gave me wide latitude in producing the best show possible,' commented an excited Yue-Sai.

"There were huge challenges. I received no payment to host the show. So I had to work through every single aspect of One World. I had to bring in sponsors, I had to work on production, and I had to work on logistics. I was putting in endless hours of work to make things happen. I would sometimes have to record a voiceover in a restroom in one country (since there was no other available quiet space) and send the voiceover back to the US or China. It was so hectic that we started to have two production crews. One with me on location and the other already doing an advance pre-shoot in the next location," shared Yue-Sai.

"The other challenge was the fact that my Chinese was not the best, but instead of this becoming a weakness for the show, fans across China and the USA started copying my accent," she shared.

Yue-Sai's legions of fans even started replicating the famous "Yue-Sai hairstyle."

As part of One World Yue-Sai interviewed Kings and Queens, Prime Ministers and heads of state across the 21 countries across four years.

In rapid succession she produced hits like the ABC documentary "China Walls and Bridges", which received an Emmy award in 1989, and "Journey through a Changing China", which was syndicated across the country, and was recognized in the United States Congressional Record, which called Yue-Sai a "citizen ambassador".

Her popular series 'Mini Dragons' and 'Doing Business in Asia', which Yue-Sai produced and hosted was broadcast on PBS, and fed the West's growing appetite for information on the East. A corporate version of the series was created and thousands of copies were sold to corporations and university business schools throughout the World for many years.

"Through the years, I failed to even recognize any challenges I faced as a woman professional simply because I was always too busy trying to be the best irrespective of gender," shared Yue-Sai.

In 1989 the Tiananmen incident had a dramatic impact on investment in China. Western businesses were hesitant to continue to invest and had started to pull back from the country. In 1990 Yue-Sai travelled to China and met with the Vice Premier.

"He looked at me and said 'Yue-Sai, you are very famous in China and also well known in the USA. We need famous Chinese Americans like you to do business in China. Would you consider starting a business here?'" shared Yue-Sai.

"I had just got married, and going back to the impact of my beauty pageant experience in Hawaii all those years back, I decided to get into the cosmetics business," she added.

"At the time people thought I was crazy. Few Chinese women used make up at all at the time. So how could I sell cosmetics in a country that used no make-up? But I knew Chinese women would change and would rapidly embrace this habit. I wanted to use my fame as a means of touching and improving the lives of women across China. I wanted Chinese women to be proud of their unique identity and beauty. I also wanted to demonstrate that Chinese products could be of high quality. As a former beauty pageant winner and with my work in TV I also understood the beauty and fashion business well enough. So I went and created the first unique Cosmetics brand for Chinese women," she shared.

In 1992, Yue-Sai launched Yue-Sai Cosmetics.

By 2003, Yue-Sai Cosmetics was registering revenues of close to 50 million dollars. Forbes magazine reported, 'Yue-Sai is changing the face of the Middle Kingdom, one lipstick at a time', The company was sold to L'Oréal, in 2004. Yue-Sai stayed with the Company as Honorary Vice Chairman of L'Oréal China.

Today, more than 90% of the Chinese population recognizes the brand.

"Yue-Sai Cosmetics is still thriving in China 22 years after its launch. It is the only beauty brand that has lasted so long in what is now a highly competitive landscape," added Yue-Sai.

Yue-Sai continued to produce a variety of television shows. In 2006 she set about with the aim to influence Chinese awareness about the latest international lifestyle via her popular series 'Yue-Sai's World' and 'Yue-Sai's Expo' on which she interviewed various North American and European celebrities and politicians. These include Robert de Niro, Quincy Jones, Halle Berry, Usher, Suze Orman and Queen Noor. Yue Sai has filmed in more than 25 counties, created thousands of programs, and been seen all over the globe.

In 2006, that influence resulted in the Shanghai International Film Festival bringing Yue-Sai on board as Chairman of the Invitation Committee of the festival. Yue-Sai's personal intervention secured the attendance of many A-list stars and truly catapulted the Shanghai International Film Festival to another level.

'Thinking big means doing big. To continue to progress and grow you must be open to new influences and constantly challenge the boundaries of your own potential. If I look back, I can honestly say I started with that one beauty pageant and kept exploring, kept innovating at every turn. I kept adapting my image and expanding my influence and business to what was most needed at the time," she shared.

Over the years Yue-Sai has continued to reinvent herself. In 2000 Yue-Sai also designed and produced a line of Asian female dolls known as the Yue-Sai WaWa , each with distinctive Asian features, accessories and educational facts, to help Asian children develop confidence, knowledge and pride in their heritage as well as educate children of all heritages about Asian cultures.

"I realized there was a unique gap in the market when a friend called me and asked me for a China doll to take back to the US. I soon realized that every single doll made in China at the time had blonde hair and blue eyes. So I created a whole range of beautiful dolls with uniquely Asian features,"

Yue-Sai has also demonstrated her prowess as an author. She has already written 8 best-selling books in China, including 'How to be a Beautiful, healthy and Successful Modern Woman', "Yue-Sai's guide to Asian Beauty" and "Etiquette for the modern Chinese". "The Chinese Gentleman" and "The Complete Chinese Woman" served as virtual training manuals for volunteers at the 2008 Beijing Olympics and the 2010 Shanghai World Expo. In 2009 she published "Exquisite Spaces, 25 Top Interior Designers of the

World", a coffee table book featuring design philosophies and tips from world-class designers, and their works. Her latest publication is "Life Is a Competition" aimed at promoting young women's all-round development.

The 'most famous woman in China' has not forgotten to give back.

Yue-Sai has been involved in charitable work for several years. She has built schools, libraries and awarded scholarships to outstanding but underprivileged students across China.

In 2002 UNICEF named her, alongside other international leaders and celebrities, as its first Global Chinese "Say Yes" ambassador. As part of her work with the China Soong Ching Ling Foundation (one of China's biggest charitable organizations committed to improving the health of women and children), Yue-Sai raised over RMB 10 million through the 2010 annual Foundation charity event to support 12 hospitals in remote regions of China.

Yue-Sai has also not forgotten the beauty pageant heritage that stemmed her initial success and gave her the opportunity to travel and see the world of beauty. Since 2011, she has served as the National Director of Miss Universe China. In that year itself Sue-Yai pulled in major corporate sponsors and celebrities and made the event a huge success. The winner of the 2011 pageant went on secure the fourth runner up position (out of 89 countries) in the Miss Universe global pageant held in Brazil.

"The basic objective of the pageant is to create a positive image of Chinese women and also support the community via education and charity so we use the slogan 'Celebrating Chinese women'," shared Yue-Sai.

In honor of the efforts of Yue-Sai, the China Soong Ching Ling Foundation established the China Beauty Charity Fund, which will support women and children in all aspects of their lives, particularly in health and education. The first official function of the Charity Fund was held in 2012 and was attended by 1,000 VIPs from Shanghai and distinguished guests from around the world.

Yue-Sai is modest about her great success.

She shared the top five things she does to continue to "Think big and do big".

- *Be clear about your decision making process:*
  I ask myself three fundamental questions –first, do I have a special talent

or skill to achieve my goal; second, am I passionate about the goal I am taking on and finally, is what I am attempting to do going to be good for a wide base of people. As an entrepreneur if what you do is good for other people, success will follow.

- *Aspire to be the BEST at what you do:*
  To do this you have to start from the place "My life and my destiny is in my hands. I am not a victim of someone else's action. I must choose to do things".

- *Do not let money distract you from succeeding big:*
  Start from the point of "I want to do something really great" and focus relentlessly on delivering a great product or a great service. Money should be the outcome of your great work and not the cause.

- *Learn constantly:*
  You can't get better if you don't learn from everybody and anybody.

- *Success takes work:*
  Focus on developing a work ethic that people can trust.

At the close of our conversation Yue-Sai brushed aside once again my question on challenges she faced as a woman. "That may be the case in the corporate world, but as an entrepreneur today there is little that women cannot do. I have girl friends who are leading in all kinds of business – construction, stone, automobiles. Being a woman is only a problem if you are not willing to believe that you are the CEO of your own life. If you want to succeed big, you have to create your own opportunities, you have to do big," concluded Yue-Sai.

# Chapter 6

TAKE
# RESPONSIBILITY
FOR YOUR OWN
## SUCCESS.
## SPEAK UP

For this chapter I spoke to three of the most assertive and accountable professionals I have ever known. *Leanne Cutts, President & Managing Director Japan at Mondelēz International; Anna Whitlam, CEO, Anna Whitlam People;* and *Pat Martin, first ever woman leader of the American Advertising Federation.* Studies suggest that the top 10% of the worlds most successful individuals have significantly higher accountability than the rest. They succeed because they take responsibility for their lives and operate with the paradigm of being the CEO of their lives.

From as far back as I can remember, I have always wanted to be a global leader - the one out front who makes the final decision and leads the team. The goal of the team has to matter i.e. the roles I have chosen are generally those that matter most to the company - they are strategically significant to the company, and they also allow me to leave a legacy. I've lived in seven countries, worked with over 20 countries, and travelled through over 40. I believe that in life anything is possible," shared **Leanne Cutts,** President & Managing Director Japan at Mondelēz International.

Leanne says that she realized at a very early age that the "anything is possible" depended on how much responsibility she took for her actions.

> *"I am always going to be assertive in not just having a 'seat at the table' but also a point of view in the discussion."*
>
> **Leanne Cutts,**
> *President & Managing Director Japan at Mondelēz International.*

This thinking was shaped by her parents who were both self-made. Her father was a tradesman, not well off. Her mother was raised in poor circumstances in inner city Sydney, leaving school at 15. When she was seven, her father secured a challenging role in Papua New Guinea and that one move changed Leanne's life forever. Both parents had a strong religious background (Protestant) and believed that their hard work would lead to a better life for Leanne and her siblings.

And it did.

While her father ran a coffee plantation, and Mum worked at the local hospital, little Leanne realized how loved she actually was. It gave her the confidence to be eternally curious and to be outspoken about what she wanted.

"Thanks to the love and security I received from my parents I grew up believing I could do anything I wanted and I would always have their support. I became fearless in the choices I made." said Leanne.

Leanne shared that her principle of "taking responsibility for her own success" was also influenced positively by her being part of a global girls' church group called 'The Girls' Brigade' when she was a teenager.

"Similar to the scouts but with a strong Protestant faith base, it was a huge influence on developing my leadership skills early. From the age of 14 I was leading a group of smaller girls on a weekly basis, developing sport, art and craft programs. This was supported by regular formal training by adult leaders (often teachers themselves) and feedback – not unlike the corporate world! The group also gave me an appreciation that in a team everyone has a role to play," shared Leanne.

At 16, Leanne had already started to serve several hours a week as an assistant at a children's home for the mentally disabled as part of her commitment to community service.

"It helped me become good at personal organization – between home chores, homework and the Girls' Brigade, I needed to take personal responsibility for my own organization and get things done," continued Leanne.

This service to the community ultimately earned Leanne the Duke of Edinburgh award.

At school, Leanne became versatile in the art of communication by being part of the school debating team.

"This helped me face fear on a regular basis! One of the most memorable campaigns was when I was 17. This particular competition was impromptu, where we had one hour to prepare and then go straight into the debate, always in front of a crowd. That experience taught me that you don't have to have 100% of the information to go into battle," she added.

"As a leader it is important to allow your people to make choices and debate without fear," she added.

So at 18, Leanne was well equipped to travel to the UK as Rotary exchange student. One year later she returned to the University in Sydney where she received her degree in Economics and History.

In 1988, Leanne joined global giant Unilever as the only intern in the Marketing department without a marketing background.

"At the time I had no idea what marketing was about. But Unilever was a fantastic training ground, and I had an open mind. I quickly fell in love with marketing and the ability to make things happen. I was also enjoying the high of finally being able to compete in something that I truly loved. Ironically, all through my childhood I was told by many that I was hopeless in sports. But here I was, being highly competitive and rewarded for it. I had found my voice." she shared.

Leanne quickly learned however that the corporate world was a little different from the Girls' Brigade.

"The first challenge I faced as a woman was the assumption made by management that the career path for a woman is different to that of a man. That I didn't want to go as far or as fast as a man, that I was not willing to move as quickly into new roles. This was evidenced in being asked to take on multiple similar roles to 'prove' one more time ('just do one more season to consolidate your experience Leanne!') that I had the capability to do a bigger job.

That prompted Leanne to be more outspoken about her long-term goals and desires, especially with her Managers.

"I knew I had to learn the Unilever business inside out if I wanted to be really successful. So I put my hand up and asked for an assignment in sales. I also indicated that I wanted to be on a General Management track. I knew I wanted to make broad contributions to the business and it was the 'line' jobs which held the most potential to make contributions," shared Leanne.

But working in sales, a male dominated function was not easy. As part of the sales team Leanne had to execute on a wide range of activities including customer complaints, customer needs and collect on bad debts and equipment.

"It was tough work. I recall several very tough customer complaints, including one customer that simply said he 'did not want to deal with a woman'. I stood my ground and assertively explained that I was the most competent to help. My manager supported my stance. I also recall many early mornings standing outside in the freezing cold waiting for the owner of a Mom and Pop storeowner to arrive so that I could re-possess our freezer equipment from the store. Other times it took me up to 10 visits to a bad customer to get one particularly bad debt paid up," commented Leanne.

Despite the challenges, Leanne learned the art of persuasively communicating her aspirations to her management. In 1992 she moved back to Marketing to run the 'take home' ice cream division. As part of her work here, Leanne was involved with a number of successful brand launches, including the blockbuster Magnum (ice cream).

In 1994, Leanne married Fernando and started to rethink the future.

She commented, "Our marriage marked a new step on my career journey. I decided to once again take responsibility for my own success and explore opportunities outside of Unilever. A great opportunity came in the shape of SmithKline Beecham, the healthcare company that finally merged with Glaxo in 2000 to form GlaxoSmithKline (GSK), one of the world's premier pharmaceutical companies."

"I knew that if I wanted to keep moving in the direction of my goal, this move would be good for me. I joined as marketing Manager for SKB. It was challenging however to break into the 'boys network' at the new company," she recalled.

"First, it was the smokers, then it was golf, then it was often the men's restrooms! What did I do? Choose projects and roles that were strategically significant for the company, and got noticed – said 'yes' to additional projects and work. So I offered to be part of the buy-back team in Australia to bring back some key brands from Reckitts to SKB. I knew it was the right move in terms of career growth as SKB had recently bought back a lot of brands that had been sold / licensed to Reckitt & Colman (which later became Reckitt Benckiser). By being on the buy back team I was in the heat of the action immediately after joining the company," shared Leanne.

I first led the analgesics marketing team, specifically Panadol, the leading pain relief brand in Australia. We built share in both adult and children's (the latter to over 80% for the first time). Following the successful buy-back of the Nutritional brands Lucozade, Ribena & Horlicks, I then moved on to relaunching the portfolio, and rolling out the global pipeline. Apart from building sales and share for these brands, a special achievement for the relaunch was clearly the signing of Lara Croft as 'spokesperson' for Lucozade, and the basis for a broad communication platform," said Leanne.

While the contract with Lara was initially only for Australia and New Zealand, Leanne was determined to leverage Lara in other markets as well.

"At a subsequent global meeting with my colleagues I persuaded them that there was a huge global opportunity for Lucozade. The biggest markets were by far the UK and Ireland – they were keen to find a new communication idea after years of one-offs. I then negotiated the global contract with the game owners, and became the key contact for the next four years. With the new communication in UK and Ireland, Lucozade grew double digits for the first time in several years. Personally, this one campaign gave me excellent exposure to many different functions, including global functions," commented Leanne.

"If women want to make progress in the corporate world, they must put their hands up for projects and roles that are strategically significant to the company and get noticed by Management as a result," added Leanne, underlining the logic of her actions.

In 1995, Leanne realized that to realize her dream of becoming a General Manager faster, she would have to equip herself with another piece of education – a MBA. After consulting with her managers, she secured the Company's support to do her EMBA at the Australian Graduate school of Management at the University of New South Wales.

At the start of the three-year course, 300 people were enrolled. By the end of year two, just a 100 of the participants stuck on to get the full degree. Of the 100 that finished, Leanne was one of just three women students in the course.

In 1999, Leanne was offered a role in either Melbourne or London. She chose the role in London as it was a global strategic role, and it also required working closely with local businesses, striving to establish the best models that could work across multiple markets.

In June 2001, Leanne and Fernando's daughter was born in London.

"Immediately I faced the challenge about my career future. What did I do? I was extremely explicit and precise on my aspirations and was clear that I would move anywhere in the world to advance my career. I was also very clear on timing of return from maternity leave and was also willing to travel on a regular basis," shared Leanne.

In Jan 2003, Leanne faced her toughest moment of truth in terms of her resolve to continue to grow in her career. On the table was a role in India. Leanne had worked for a short while with the India team on iconic brand Horlicks yet had no idea what work in India was like on the ground.

"I realized that if I wanted to really get exposure to a multi faceted assignment in terms of challenges, India would be a great learning ground. So I went back to my manager and shared simply that if the Company needed me in India I was willing to go there and help for a couple of years. It was consistent with my message over the years to my managers of 'I will go anywhere."

When she arrived in Delhi, the situation on Horlicks was grim.

"This iconic £100m brand was in volume decline when I arrived in Delhi in March 2003. I delivered a brand relaunch in 137 days from start to finish. With the support of the General Manager in India and other functional heads on the local management team, I established the burning platform – Horlicks must be turned around into volume growth – it was the future of the entire local entity. The relaunch involved every function, from R&D, supply, manufacturing, sales, with marketing as the project lead," shared Leanne.

She added, "I invited a group of critical thinkers from different functions within and outside the GSK network, to develop the 'essence' of the Horlicks brand and re-ignite passion for the brand. We summarized the essence as 'pleasurable nourishment'. This relaunch successfully convinced the mother whilst also engaging the child. One year later, with the brand back on a growth path, I then took clinical work from R&D and turned a very dry set of statistics into an entire series of claims and communication that brought alive the benefits of Horlicks: "now clinically proven to make your child taller, stronger, sharper". This work consolidated the relaunch momentum and accelerated the growth rate."

Leanne also aggressively rebuilt the marketing capability bringing back key Indian talent from the United States and Europe, and aggressively recruited locally from other leading companies. She also introduced global marketing standards and training programs, new grading and career development plans.

As a result the innovation program on Horlicks was revitalized, from zero to a rolling five-year vision board in place, with a Project Management Board and key metrics were well established.

"When I left in 2006, brand sales were growing +10%. Four years later, in 2010, annual portfolio sales had doubled, and Horlicks is still growing in double digits," shared Leanne.

The time in India was not without its challenges.

"I learnt in India that you have to be flexible and willing and able to manage complexity and ambiguity. There is so much opportunity, and in a sense so much distraction so you need to focus your resources and energy on what matters most," she shared.

"It was also not easy in the beginning to live there with a very young child. So I was forced to learn to trust others and accept their support – you need others around you to help navigate everyday life. Professional and personal boundaries are also quite blurred and this was a learning experience for both Fernando and me. I learned how to build a really supportive personal team – friends, my husband, my extended family. Especially my husband. I was aligned with him very early on that we would stay mobile and willing to move internationally at least till I was a General Manager," she added.

Leanne and Fernando turned that familiarity and blurring of personal and professional boundaries to their advantage and formed very close friendships with both locals and expats.

"By moving to India, I truly became a global citizen – that was India's gift to us," added Leanne.

Impressed with Leanne's commitment and results, the Company moved her in 2006 to Hong Kong in her first General Manager role for Hong Kong and

Korea. She was subsequently promoted to VP & GM for North Asia in June 2008.

This role marked Leanne's entry into the top echelons of the Company's management - the International leadership Team (ILT) of GSK, the only female GM on the ILT.

"For most of my five years as GM at GSK, I was the only female GM on the International team, and one of 2-3 female leaders on the team (in other supporting roles). At global meetings, there were a handful of female GMs from other regions. It's still rare. I would say that both Unilever and GSK have very strong diversity plans and I always felt supported in my aspirations (GSK now has a female Consumer Healthcare CEO, for example). But it's hard to build the pipeline, for all the reasons/challenges we've discussed. For women to become GM's, especially in MNCs, they have to be mobile, they have to be willing to take risks, they need sponsors, they need good feedback to develop as leaders.

Once I became GM, the challenges I faced were similar to men - it was continually important to build and leverage my internal and external networks. You have to spend time doing this, building relationships that you can call on for support and counsel as needed. And you have to deliver – there is no substitute for a good track record. And you need to make those achievements visible to senior management, in an appropriate way. Visibility is incredibly important – people need to know you and support you so that you are in the consideration set for bigger roles.

When I was in HK, I began learning about options for moving one of our key categories into China, I joined CEO forums, British Chamber of Commerce, built broad networks, all of which helped me break into key 'boys networks' and set myself up for success," added Leanne.

Leanne delivered strong business growth of consecutive double-digit growth across the region between 2006 and 2010.

In June 2011 Leanne realized it was time to move on from GSK.

She moved to yet another challenge – at Kraft (today known as Mondelēz).

"I faced another crossroads. I loved being a multi-market GM, but I wanted to do this on a larger scale. I had been with GSK for many years but I needed a fresh challenge in my career. So I kept an eye open. At this time, Kraft approached me to join them. I had met some Kraft people in the region and been impressed. Irene Rosenfeld was particularly inspiring as a CEO, especially after the Cadbury acquisition in 2010, and so was Pradeep Pant, the then Asia Pacific President. Their energy and enthusiasm for building a 'snacking powerhouse' was infectious. So in July 2011 I joined Kraft in a regional marketing role (based in Singapore) as part of Pradeep's Asia Pacific Leadership Team. This was a great introduction to all the markets as it catapulted me straight into the challenges & opportunities of all the different markets and I was able to tap into the global network immediately," she shared.

Leanne continued, "My aspirations remained the same – to build a strong businesses and leave a legacy. Less than two years later, Pradeep asked me to run the Japan business and now my family and I live in another great world city – Tokyo."

I asked Leanne to explain the few things she did to consistently support her ability of taking responsibility for her own success.

She decoded the DNA.

- *I start with the word 'yes' vs. the word 'no':*
  The optimism out of saying yes is an important part of my self-realization. It triggers my internal motivator.

- *I always ask myself "what is the worst that can happen":*
  And if that scenario is something I can deal with, I'll speak up and go for it.

- *Being responsible for my own success means I focus on what I can uniquely bring to the table:*
  I see so many young people today who worry about everything else except what value they bring to the table.

- *I have an open mind:*
  It is so important for a woman in career to get the breadth of experiences needed to keep moving ahead. I have taken advantage of every single opportunity – even something as simple as making sure I attend every

single training I can – whether its on presentation skills, communication, team building or listening skills

- *I have always focused on having a great support team both at work and outside:*
  I have focused on developing a 'support team/support strategies', both internally through training, coaching, mentoring, and also externally, from family and friends who encourage you to keep striving, are sounding boards, and also keep you honest! My husband and family (especially my mother now, since my father passed away) have been such a great support. There is no way I could have developed my ambition without their ongoing day-to-day support, and I do think it has been critical to my success.

Today, Leanne is determined to continue her lifelong journey as a global leader. She is finding more time to focus on her health and fitness and has recently taken up long distance running. She reads voraciously and spends as much time as she can with Fernando and her little girl, playing card games, which she believes, are great for learning strategy.

"I have always believed that my role as a global business leader can enable me to leave the world a slightly better place because of my efforts. I realized that, like it or not, I became a role model for other women in business – really as soon as I stepped into my first leadership roles. I have become a mentor or sponsor to a number of women. But I have also deliberately requested to be a mentor to young male key talent – they need to see women in senior roles as normal," shared Leanne.

"I believe I can persevere despite obstacles and take responsibility for my own success. I am always going to be assertive in not just having a 'seat at the table' but also a point of view in the discussion," concluded Leanne.

In October 2012 the Australian Financial Review named **Anna Whitlam** as one of Australia's 100 Women of Influence. She was one of six finalists in the Business Entrepreneur category. Anna is also a director on the Big Brothers Big Sisters Australia board, and has held non-executive director positions on a number of not-for-profit boards including VACRO (Victorian Association For The Care & Resettlement of Offenders). Anna is today one of the world's best-regarded leaders in people strategy and search as **CEO** of her own Company **Anna Whitlam People.**

Yet few people would imagine that at the age of 13 Anna was not yet able to read or write.

"I am the middle one of three girls. My older sister and I were both born in Papua New Guinea. When I was two years old we left to live in Australia, because the country was becoming lawless and my parents decided it was too dangerous to remain. We went to live in Canberra," shared Anna.

Then when she was five years old Anna's father left the family to make a new life for himself in the Philippines. The only contact Anna and her two sisters had with him after that was to visit him in Manila every once and a while.

*"People are who they are because of who they choose to be,."*
**Anna Whitlam, CEO, Anna Whitlam People.**

"We had no relatives apart from my grandparents who relocated to Canberra from Darwin to support my mother to look after us. We spent our primary school years at an independent private school which was based upon the Summerhill School in England, created by A S Neil. The aim of the school was to promote self-confidence, tolerance and consideration in children by giving them space to be themselves. There was a structured timetable though there was no formal curriculum. We had free access to art, woodwork and drama as well as a comprehensive outdoor program including camping, mountain climbing, caving, rock climbing, skiing, and snorkelling," added Anna.

During her early years at school Anna was unable to read or write. This was not considered to be a problem at first. But her teachers became concerned when she showed little improvement in her middle primary years. She always had a lot to say, but struggled to articulate herself or formulate her sentences on paper.

Finally Anna's mother had both Anna and her older sister to be professionally diagnosed. Anna was deemed to be severely dyslectic and her sister moderately so. So once a week Anna was taken out of school to attend a learning session at specialist clinic. In spite of this, Anna was still unable to read or write at the age of 13. The clinic advised that any exercises involving "balance" would be beneficial. Her progress was very slow. "I became very self-conscious and felt like the other kids regarded me as a 'great big dumb kid'" she shared.

Concurrently, Anna's mother was struggling to bring up her three girls alone. She was working full time and continuing post-graduate studies part time. Horse riding was a recommended balancing exercise for dyslexic children so Anna's mother put together enough money to buy both Anna and her older sister a horse each. As a consequence, the main focus of family activities over the next decade involved equestrian activities.

Anna took great pride in her horse, and had many different horses over the years – some very wilful and challenging. But with her determination to succeed, Anna overcame her fears and mastered their behaviour. She joined pony club and attended every equestrian show and competition possible. She spent most of her early mornings raking out muck from the stables where her horse was kept. Before shows she would be up at 3.00am down at the stables grooming, plaiting and preparing her horse. This discipline taught Anna a strong work ethic.

But Anna still blamed her old school in part for her inability to read and write. When she entered secondary school she wanted to change schools. To increase the household finances, Anna's mother had taken a job which required frequent overseas travel. During these periods the sisters would stay with their grandparents. Despite the best attempts of Anna's grandfather to tutor her in spelling and grammar, Anna made little progress.

Finally Anna's mother decided that boarding school would be the best option for the two older girls and a co-educational boarding school was selected. The school had stables and ran a Horse Mastership course and allowed students to bring their own horses. Several weeks later two vacancies became available and both girls and their horses commenced at that school.

Anna continued with her horse right through to the end of year 12. She enjoyed her horse activities, which included attending local shows and cross-country events as part of the school's equestrian team. However, Anna's difficulties with reading and writing continued and she was frequently at the bottom of her class. She remembers being bullied often and became quite reserved and insecure as a result.

Then in her last years at high school Anna's English teacher took a great interest in her and provided her with extra tutoring after school. During this period Anna's skills started to improve.

During Anna's first year at boarding school, her youngest sister became very ill with childhood diabetes. As a result, her sister's entry to boarding school was postponed and their mother decided it was no longer possible to continue travelling overseas for work, so she sought a managerial position with a company, with headquarters located in country NSW, about two hours drive from the school. This would mean the girls could become weekly boarders. With a diabetic child in the family a lot of lifestyle changes needed to be made. Anna needed to learn how to care for her sister in a crisis, how to avoid comas and how to deal with a coma. She also needed to learn about nutrition and dietary requirements. When her youngest sister did finally go to boarding school Anna had to take on responsibility for advising teachers and care staff how to manage a diabetic crisis.

Anna completed her schooling as a weekly boarder. At the end of year 12 she sat for the NSW Higher School Certificate, with a disappointing result. She failed to gain entry to University.

"I was bitterly disappointed and decided that before making decisions about my future, I would go overseas on a student exchange. I researched the information myself and decided to join the AFS Student Exchange Program, which had an active branch close to the town in which our family was now living. I wanted to go to Japan as I had studied Japanese in primary school but I was told I was too tall and would not successfully fit into a Japanese household because I would likely be considerably taller than all male members of the household. Instead AFS arranged a placement for me to Torino in northern Italy, to stay with a family whose male members coincidentally, were all considerably shorter than me," shared Anna.

Unfortunately the experience proved to be extremely challenging for Anna. Her host family made no secret of the fact that they had no desire to host a student. They only did so because they believed it would improve their own daughter's chance of going to the USA on the exchange program. Torino was bitterly cold when Anna arrived – she left home on a 37-degree day and arrived to minus 17 degrees. Her host family did not greet her on arrival – they were away for a few days. Anna was left in a large empty house with a housekeeper.

Anna said, "The expectation for AFS host families is that their student will be treated as one of the family. My host family, who were very wealthy, treated me more like a servant. They did not pay for me or include me in family outings. At the age of 17, I was left to fend for myself, negotiate my visa etc. and was completely ignored by my host 'sister' at school.

At home, I had a servant's room in the attic and was drafted into cooking the family's evening meal, which I was very happy to do as I enjoyed cooking. On one occasion I was able to go with them to their apartment in the Alps to ski, but I did not have the money to pay for ski lifts and access to the runs. To solve this the host family arranged a job for me with friends of theirs, caring for their small children, cooking the evening meal for children and parents, and cleaning their apartment. To make matters worse no one from the host family spoke English." But Anna used that as an opportunity to learn Italian.

With the treatment that she received, Anna could legitimately request a transfer to another host family or alternatively terminate the exchange contract and return home. She chose to stay on with her host family – she was determined to stick it out and make an impact on them.

"My experience in Italy and then returning to Australia, taught me that sometimes you may not follow the path you expected to, but there is always a better way ahead of you if are willing to give things a go, and be willing to accept responsibility for decisions you make," shared Anna.

Returning to Australia in 1990, Anna felt she could achieve almost anything. By then Anna's mother had decided there was no future for any of her daughters in a small country town and had obtained a new job in Melbourne.

Anna returned home just in time to help with the process of moving. Anna purchased a new horse and picked up a job at a Donut King outlet to support her equestrian activities.

"My first car was a 1978 Honda Civic which my mother purchased for $2000 from the local service station for me to commute to the stables each day. The car had one small fault – the fuses would blow at random leaving me without lights, blinkers etc. at any time. I became adept at learning how to change fuses. A box of spare fuses and a torch became essential equipment which I needed to use frequently on the freeway after dark," added Anna.

Anna had not forgotten her aspiration to secure a Business degree. She applied and after several interviews, where she literally had to beg to gain entry, she was accepted to the Business program at Victoria University in Melbourne. For the first time in her life she passed with flying colours. Her grandfather gave her a Canon Word Processor to help with assignments. Once she started using this with the spell and grammar check her marks improved markedly.

"I slowly began to realise I really could do anything if I set my mind to it. I continued to work towards my picture of success in my mind and my effort was awarded with almost straight high distinctions and several University prizes," added Anna.

Anna's two sisters ridiculed her for thinking that she could achieve much more. She ignored the criticism and continued to work towards her goals.

"If we have the same basic opportunities in life, then the choices we make along the way define who we become. And yes, the ability to take a chance on myself has become my main path to achievement and success," shared Anna.

In 1992 Anna started a role as a marketing intern at Tourism Victoria while finishing up her business degree, in addition to taking on a marketing major at Monash University. Immediately after getting her degree she was offered a position running the events and promotions at Southgate, Melbourne's first arts and leisure precinct. She also soon offered a great opportunity to run the experience brands as part of the marketing function at Fosters, Carlton United Breweries.

"I was the only senior female member of the brand team. The work was good, and so were the people. There was just one little problem. I wanted to be better, and to make a bigger difference than what the constraints of a corporation enabled me to do. Simply put, it was not enough to me to be average. I wanted to be extraordinary. I felt that we could do so much more and didn't feel the environment wanted or encouraged excellence."

Anna took the risk of leaving a very comfortable, well-paid role at Fosters to join an industry wherein she had zero experience – executive recruitment.

"I accepted a recruitment role at Morgan and Banks - one of the key executive recruitment firms in Australia at the time specialising in the industry disciplines I had experience in, marketing and communications. I believed that this role was very much complimentary to my three key passions – helping people, solving problems and using my industry related experience and networks. Yet after three years of working for the company I realised that I was not able to deliver the level of quality I aspired to," shared Anna.

In April 2003 with a huge home mortgage and very little savings, Anna resigned from her role and started working on the development of her own company, Market U. With a single computer and a loan of $10,000 from her Mum.

"For the first few weeks I focused on creating a clear vision of what I wanted Market U to look like. The core values of the company, the unique services we would offer, our USP, the aspired company culture etc. The entire company framework was captured in a series of folders which would guide the growth and operation of the business," she added.

While all of the large recruitment firms focused on broad recruitment across a variety of disciplines, Anna decided to step off the beaten path and focus on fewer areas of work, and those that we had worked in and already had established networks in. In essence she had established Australia's first executive recruitment and search firm specialising in the disciplines of Corporate Affairs, Communications and Marketing.

In a little over four years, Anna built Market U into a successful, award winning company. She had a team of 15 staff across Melbourne and Sydney and Market U was frequently recognised as one of Australia's fastest growing start-ups, ranking high on the BRW Fast 100 list in 2007. Regularly cited as one of Australia's top female entrepreneurs, Anna was named as a finalist in two categories of the 2007 Telstra Business Women's Awards.

"I also started a lot of thought leadership activity to build my own personal brand over and above that required for a recruitment company. I focused on adding value. People began to slowly appreciate the advice and value-add Market U was providing," added Anna.

By 2007 Market U began to get the attention of the large players. In January 2008, Anna was approached to sell, and sold Market U to a global management-consulting firm in London, WD Scott. She retained equity in Market U and joined their Board. But Anna was not happy. Eager to start a family, she instead found herself trapped in a lifestyle of too much travel and excessive late night meetings.

In late 2008 Anna had reached a point where she knew she had to change her strategy if her desire to start a family was ever to be realised. She had met her husband in 2003, and got married in 2007. Sadly her first pregnancy ended badly with her losing her child well into her pregnancy.

"That was a real wake up call for me. It became clear to me then that for a working woman, it is possible to have everything in life, just not at the same time. I knew I had to take a risk and do something different, something better. I also knew I wanted to continue trying to start a family" she shared.

In August 2009 Anna's daughter Arabella was born. Yet it was not an easy time. Arabella was unwell for the first 12 months of her life, which was a result of various allergies and food intolerances.

"I had no choice but to slow down and focus on my child," shared Anna.

In April 2010 Anna took the biggest risk of her career to date. As the main breadwinner, and with her seven month old baby, Anna resigned from her executive role at WD Scott, and her role as Chairperson at Market U and set out to do something completely on her own again. In June 2010, Anna founded Anna Whitlam People.

"Given my restraint of trade following the sale and my departure from

Market U, I needed to think laterally to generate an income so started structure and OD consulting within my functional areas of specialisation, corporate affairs, communications and marketing. Business slowly but surely began to grow, and then started booming again.

In November 2011 Anna's son Orlando was born. Simultaneously, she had secured a new office space in Melbourne CBD, and had recruited a small team to support work for clients such as Telstra, Commonwealth Bank and Qantas.

"I've accepted that as a woman, you can have everything, just not at the same time. You have to pace yourself. There will be times when you can push hard on your career. And other times when you have to take a pause in career and go slow. Accepting this has been one of my biggest challenges to date. I now appreciate, your ability to balance life and work is the key to long-term success," Anna added.

"My husband then decided that he would step back from his successful career as a restauranteur to take care of the kids day to day so I could get back to full-time work. He sold his businesses and led the negotiation and fit-out of my new business premises. By January 2012 I was full throttle again!" she added.

I asked Anna to share the key elements which she believes has helped her to take responsibility for her own success and transform herself from that 13 year old who could not read or write to one of Australia's most successful women.

"There are a few elements," she shared.

- *Always consider the big picture first:*
  I have always looked at the big picture. I look at the worst-case scenario in any situation. If I can deal with it, I take the plunge.
- *Don't' worry about things beyond your control:*
  Interest rates on a mortgage for example are something you just can't control.
- *Visualize the best-case scenario and keep that picture in front of yourself constantly:*
  I keep telling myself there is no other option.

- *Develop a strong work ethic:*
  I got mine from my mum.

- *Last of all, look after your personal health and fitness:*
  I stick to a strict exercise regime. Fitness has definitely enhanced my capacity to work hard, manage stress and feel good.

"Looking back, I think that if I had not been willing to take and move out of my comfort zone and take responsibility for my own success, I would not be, I would not be enjoying any of this success. I could have easily convinced myself to stay in that role at Fosters, or not start Market U, or not risk it all to set up Anna Whitlam People. Then at times like that, I think of my Mum. She brought us three girls (all under 5) up on her own. With nothing to fall back on except her own mind and will. She worked full-time, studied part-time to ensure she could provide for us.

Today Anna Whitlam People are leaders in retained executive search, organisational design and talent management expressly for the disciplines of corporate affairs, communications and marketing. With offices in Melbourne and Sydney and extensive networks and alliances in Asia, UK, UAE and the USA, Anna Whitlam People have national, regional and global reach.

For Anna, self-discovery and learning never ends. She has also recently completed executive training in Competitive Strategy at INSEAD in Singapore, and best practice Professional Service Firm leadership at Harvard in Boston. all in anticipation of taking even more risks that enable success.

"People are who they are because of who they choose to be," she said softly as we concluded our discussion.

Anna has come a long way from the 13 year old that could not read or write.


**P**at Martin is 85. She calls herself "the oldest volunteer in America in advertising and I still love it."

When I interviewed Pat Martin for this book, I was amazed by the eloquent and assertive manner in which Pat communicated. Pat sounded so incredibly youthful! As we spoke, it felt I was speaking to a CEO who was still at the peak of her career.

Pat grew up in a large family. Her father had two brothers, five sisters and their families.

"When I was six years old, my Mum told me. "I don't know if you are going to be smart. But I do expect you to be well behaved and to speak your mind! My mum and sister were big influences in my life," she shared.

A graduate of the College of New Rochelle where she is a member of the president's Circle; Pat also graduated from Marymount High School and St Walburga's Grammar School. She has always attributed her success to 16 years with the nuns and the Jesuits who served as a surrogate Father as her own Father died when she was four.

"One advantage of going to all girls schools is that you know that you can do it all yourself, because there is never any guy around to do it for you," she quipped during our interview.

Father Leo Fey who served at Guam and elsewhere in the South Pacific during World War II and Mother Loyola, a Marymount nun, specially influenced Pat.

*"Speaking up and being visible is critical for young women to succeed especially in a man's world. Throughout my career, I kept myself visible, and spoke up for what I believed in. I have rarely taken no for an answer."*

**Pat Martin, *first-ever woman leader of the American Advertising Federation.***

"Mother Loyola had a PHD in Shakespeare and I became her devoted follower and to this day I read and reread him. My love for English literature came from the three years I had Mother Loyola as a teacher. During her years I wrote volumes of poetry. It also shaped my skill of speaking up and expressing an assertive point of view," shared Pat.

"Mother Loyola had always taught at the college level so she began with our high school group reading the first chapter of 'A Tale of Two Cities'. The next chapter was 'Five Years Later'. Our weekend assignment was to fill in those five years in the style of Dickens. I worked till 2 and 3 in the morning all weekend but I finished it. It seemed many parents had called to complain (not mine) and of all the pupils she asked me if I thought it was too much. Because I loved doing it I said no –why they elected me class president after that I will never know. She read mine aloud in class," shared Pat.

She with; "I have always loved to write. In high school I had four close friends and I wrote a book about all of us grown up and brought a chapter to lunch every day. In college I wrote a weekly radio play for Props and Paint (our drama group) that a local station WFAS presented every Friday evening," shared Pat.

By the time she finished her College of New Rochelle in the 1950's Pat was adept at making her voice heard. But the challenges in her work in the corporate sector were extreme.

"I started in the 50's when women were non existent in business. Women were wives, nurses, secretaries but not at all a factor in business. I had the additional handicap of a wonderful education that did nothing to prepare for the world of business," shared Pat.

Pat was a writer and one day saw an advertisement for copywriter/proofreader at Warner Lambert.

"I applied for the job. I had graduated in June and a friend and I were trying to break into the (then) new TV world. We actually had two 15-minute programs on local (there was no national TV at the time) TV and a radio program on Fordham's station. Fordham is a University in New York run by the Jesuits. Murph, my friend went on to a quiz show and eventual marriage and I went to Warner Lambert," shared Pat.

Pat shared that she "got her first job through luck!"

"I was interviewed by the president of the pharmaceutical division who was the son of the Chairman. Ten minutes in to the interview he called his secretary and asked where his previous hire had gone to college. It turned out to be my college as well! He said the previous hire was great and so I was hired!" shared Pat.

"But after that stroke of good luck, making my way to success was a big challenge. As a woman I was invisible though I had a genius IQ and graduated cum laude," added Pat.

Pat believes that speaking up and taking responsibility for her own success has been a key contributor to her success.

"Speaking up and being visible is critical for young women to succeed especially in a man's world. Men in those days often thought of women as 'someone there to help them.' "That has changed," she added.

"Throughout my career, I kept myself visible, and spoke up for what I believed in. I have rarely taken no for an answer." she added.

One such instance was in the mid fifties when just out of college Pat worked for the International Silk Association who was presenting a weeklong International Silk meeting in New York.

"The man in charge of our small group was hyper-charged and my first assignment was to write a promo in French as that was the official language of the association," shared Pat.

Pat had barely studied French for two to three years. Despite that she managed to write up a great promo. It was a huge success."

"Today I know very little French but can still read it," she quips.

Pat also showed her ability to proactively shape her success through another important task – getting the famed designer Dali to do the creative for the association's event.

"After some considerable effort, I convinced Dali's wife that it was a good idea and Dali agreed to do the creative. The creative was used for the entire event and even used for a special commemorative scarf. I never met Dali but his wife was a good businesswoman. I still have my scarf," added Pat.

A couple of years later when she was invited to her first meeting at the Association of National Advertisers (ANA), the pre-eminent industry association of the largest advertisers in the US, in San Francisco and showed up at the reception desk of the important event, the receptionist turned to her, pointed over to a side section and said "the wives side is over there."

Pat Martin told the lady in no uncertain terms "I'm not a "wife". I have been invited to this meeting as a representative".

Pat was in fact one of the first women ever to be invited as a representative to a meeting of the ANA.

Pat's big moment of truth came when she was in her early thirties and at Warner Lambert.

"One of my managers called me in to his office and asked me for advice on who a particularly important post should go to. He knew I knew all of the staff really well. He asked me for a response by the coming Monday. I walked out of his office, then took an about turn, went back in and said. "I think I am the best person for the job."

"His shocked response was: "But you will have to manage many men."

Pat added; "He had never ever considered me for the role. If I had not spoken my mind, he would never have even had the opportunity to see what I could do."

That Monday her manager gave Pat the job. She went on to do a fabulous job in that role.

Years later the same Manager moved to Revlon, and Pat was one of the first people he asked to go with him.

Over the years Pat climbed the ladder at Warner Lambert from a junior copywriter to Director of Marketing Support and head of the in-house agency, Lambert & Feasley.

Pat commented; "Over the years I consistently put my hand up to help people across functions on top of my regular role. I met most of the members of my division and I tried to be helpful in many jobs other than those for which I was hired."

One of the beneficiaries of Pat's ability to put her hand up for work was one of her mentors- the lady who had initially helped her get her role at Warner Lambert.

Shared Pat; "The lady who had helped me get my initial role at Warner Lambert was made Manager of Labeling (a big job in the pharmaceutical division at the time) when her boss was assigned to Europe. On several occasions having made myself familiar with all the government labeling regulations, I provided her guidance that saved her from significant crises and she became my biggest advocate!"

During the course of her tenure with Warner Lambert, the Company acquired several Companies and increased staff and Pat moved slowly upward.

Pat was instrumental in many innovations such as integrating marketing into sales meetings and having creatives travel with the detail men to see how their materials worked.

She was also there when women were admitted to the sales force and helped smooth their way. Seeing her ever-ready desire to help and volunteer for work, Pat was finally asked by the President of one of the divisions, to handle all his promotion and advertising budgets for what was the most profitable division albeit not the largest at the time.

She also was closely involved with the purchase of Texas Pharmacal, one of whose products is still a best seller, Lubriderm.

"Women face many challenges today that are quite different from when I started work. First, they believe the media that women have really made it. There is still a long way to go. Second, most women today try to be superwoman and as a result get swamped by the over scheduling. Third, women struggle to keep up or ahead of technological advancements. Finally, family requirements are still so much more for women than for men," she shared.

Pat shared some of her tips for that would enable women even today to speak up and take responsibility for their own success.

- *Be prepared:*
  I kept learning about every single product. And every other department relentlessly. I was always honest with myself first and clear about my own coordinates and about what I wanted to say. I also took the time to

be intimately aware of the feelings and sentiments of others. I learned about all the people I interacted with and what they did.

- *Make friends wherever you go by being helpful:*
Everyone is so busy today more than ever before. If you can offer a helping hand to someone who needs it, it pays off in the long run. For many years I did budget planning for Product Managers who were not mathematically inclined. So I got to know the Finance department well. Because of this, I developed a friendship with two CPAs who shared an office. Fast forward 10 years and one became a division President and subsequently a President of another major corporation where I did freelance work post my retirement from Warner Lambert.

- *Do not be afraid to speak up:*
I got my first really big promotion as I mentioned earlier because I spoke up. It had not even occurred to my manager at the time to consider me for the role. If you don't express an opinion, you can't be counted.

- *Join business organizations in your field:*
I was member (and President) of Advertising Women of New York, was the first woman chair of the American Advertising Federation, member of the ANA," she shared.

- *Taking responsibility for your own success is also about "showing up" and getting involved:*
You cannot be around just when it is convenient.

Over a career spanning over 34 years Pat never missed a day at the Office other the usual public holidays. "Except for the time I had to have my appendix removed," she quipped.

"I have been so blessed. I've ensured that through my proactiveness I was always given work that I loved to do. I got involved, helped out and kept an open mind to everything and anything that came my way," concluded Pat.

In 1982 Pat was invited to lead the American Advertising Federation. She was the first ever woman to hold this prestigious post.

In 1991 Pat retired from Warner Lambert and opened her own consultancy.

"I ran that for 10 years and it was friends and contacts that made it a success. I must especially remember the Wall Street Journal and Bernie Flanagan and Jim Sullivan who made me more money than Warner-Lambert. And the joy of getting personal awards for my radio commercials and actually writing for a living was immense," she shared.

Pat today continues to mentor women in the advertising industry.

"I have always loved to work!! Here I am 85 – the oldest volunteer in America in advertising and I still love it. Though I am single, I have an enormous family with all the people I worked with or work with now whom I love and respect. I am constantly surprised when someone calls from years back just to say hello," concluded Pat.

# Chapter 7

# FIND AND LEVERAGE
# GREAT MENTORS

*71% of Fortune 500 Companies now have formal mentoring programs with the benefits of mentoring widely understood and appreciated by the vast majority of professionals. Mentoring has changed significantly over the years from a one to one relationship to a one to many (mentees can now choose to have multiple mentors in current day practice). I sought the insights of three top mentors in completely different fields – **Gail Klintworth,** Chief Sustainability Officer, Unilever Plc; **Jue Yao,** violinist extraordinaire and Founder and Director of Yao Jue Music Academy; and **Kristen English,** Global Coach, Consultant and Facilitator.*

Gail Klintworth has a unique and noble role. As Chief Sustainability Officer for Unilever plc. she leads a diverse team of professionals to bring to life Unilever's purpose – "To make sustainable living common place." It is a purpose in which Gail is personally vested. Gail joined Unilever in 1984 and prior to her current role she held a series of increasingly significant roles leading to CEO and Chairman of Unilever South Africa and then to Executive Vice President Global Savory at Unilever. Gail was one of the first woman executives in Unilever to lead a major global business.

One of Gail's key success principles has been to accelerate her learning and development via the leverage of great mentors. These mentors have been from business in the role of more senior leaders, but from much broader sources too.

Gail commented, "I have never thought of a mentor as a person who could secure my career progression, I have always thought of a mentor as a person who knows more because they have been there before, and so I can learn from their experience...not only in business."

"In the workplace there are several challenges that women have to face. First, dealing with the cultural norm in many countries where work cultures are predominantly male dominated, second - carrying the feeling of being responsible for relationships, family, parents and kids as well as career and third – having the desire to be well rounded individuals – who want to serve in the community beyond the workplace. So indeed, one of the best ways to negotiate all of these challenges is to learn and leverage great mentors at every stage of our developmental journeys," said Gail.

*"The initial chemistry or respect between mentor and mentee is very important. The mentee must truly believe that the mentor can help and be willing to be fully transparent and authentic. The real gift of mentorship is if you can get to the point where you feel safe enough to share your deepest fears and desires (work related of course), and those are received, empathized, decoded...and then you move forward."*

**Gail Klintworth,** Chief Sustainability Officer, Unilever Plc.

Gail grew up in South Africa. Her Dad was a factory operator who latterly worked in the chemical engineering field of water management. Her mum a housewife, who truly impacted the way Gail looked at life.

"I had a mum who believed I could do anything, and also showed me I could learn from anyone. I also had a teacher, Sheryl Wise, when I was 14. I had no idea what the word mentor even meant at that age. But I recall very clearly on one occasion that I handed in an assignment, which was very forward thinking for my age. She appreciated it so much. And started coaching me and giving me small tips that helped me learn faster. Like my Mum, she believed I could achieve great things," shared Gail.

Gail went on to study at Rhodes University between 1980-81 and in 1984 finished her Bachelor of Arts in Industrial Psychology and Languages from University of Witwatersrand. She has recently commenced formal study in Sustainability Leadership, once more, through the University of Cambridge.

"For me mentors came in many forms throughout my career both formal and informal. Mentors have helped me navigate challenging environments, decode cultural signals or unspoken signs in unfamiliar surroundings or simply heighten my business sense. A good example is my lecturer in Industrial Relations Steve Bluen who was extremely attuned to political environments and when I had decided that I was not able to deliver the change I desired after studying journalism, in the political context of South Africa at the time, I moved into the corporate world and his mentorship helped guide me into that," added Gail.

One of the key early mentors in Gail's career journey was Doug Baillie, who used to lead Unilever's business in South Africa and has since continued a global career and is currently Chief Human Resources Officer for Unilever globally.

"It was 1997 and I was on the verge of being appointed as the Category Director for Home Care, Unilever South Africa. I had no idea at the time that I was pregnant with my second child. Then when I found out, I started having major apprehensions about taking the job, fearing that I would not be able to make the commitment to succeeding in that role. But, I wanted it, so I came up with a proposal on how I could manage a short time off after my baby was born and a clear plan of how I would work once I returned to work …to retain sufficient flexibility whilst delivering the results. Doug encouraged me, and even when I was not sure, he talked me through the options and the impact it could have on my career and subsequently my life. As a consequence with my determination and his support and guidance, I accepted the role," shared Gail.

Gail not only did the job, but with Doug's ongoing mentorship and guidance, she did it with great success.

The challenge of continuing to build the largest segment of Unilever's business in Africa at the time was not a soft option and she was able to build each brand and the overall profitability of the laundry and household care category to the highest ever share and brand equity. However, probably more challenging at the time was taking a role on the executive team as the only woman, and one with a small baby at that. Today Gail does not remember too much about it being difficult to manage the logistical challenges.

"The fact that Doug believed in me, always treated me equally in the executive team, constantly reassured me that he was more interested in output versus how I managed my time, and in a gentle way made sure that my voice was heard…these were immeasurable contributions to me retaining my confidence and determination to navigate my role as the first pregnant senior executive in FMCG in South Africa," shared Gail.

In 2001, Gail's responsibilities were broadened and she was appointed Global Brands Director, Unilever HPC (Home and Personal Care) Global Division.

"This was my real first global assignment. The differences in culture across the breadth of this business were huge. I struggled to understand some of the nuances and reached out to one of our most experienced International executives at the time for help – Keki Dadiseth. Keki was the former Chairman of one of Unilever's most powerful subsidiaries – Hindustan Lever in India, and had been working with Unilever since 1973. He knew the people, cultures and organization dynamics. Most of all he knew the Home and Personal Care business globally. Over the next few months he helped me to keep my calm as I navigated the complex and matrixed structure of the global organization," shared Gail.

Gail believes that much of what Keki shared with her helped her become a more flexible, culturally aware and effective global executive.

"Keki's advice was critical in helping me establish an extremely diverse brand as one of our fastest growing global brands, Surf, by elevating processes and mechanisms to a global level. In the process, we successfully established Surf as a brand that brought brightness into peoples lives versus just being an everyday detergent brand," Gail shared excitedly.

She added, "Not only did this brand become one of the fastest growing in the Unilever world, but we managed to build a common Challenger Brand proposition, with engagement of people from countries across the Philippines, Brazil, South Africa, the USA and the UK."

Keki's major influence was once again being a background supporter, which gave Gail the confidence to challenge some established norms and practices in the business.

Gail added, "As so often, with mentoring relationships, it was not the professional or operational support I needed most from Keki at that time, but the unspoken moral support. When I needed help with a particularly difficult situation where a senior leader was being offensive and undermining, potentially because I had a different style and values, he helped me to keep perspective as we discussed the influence of different cultures. I was able to retain my self-confidence and proceed with what I believed to be right for the business, and to avoid sacrificing my own value system.

In 2004, Gail was appointed Chairman and CEO of Unilever South Africa. In this role she was personally responsible for merging a number of different business units into one cohesive unit and delivering strong business growth despite the many changes including merging the distribution systems of three different entities into one.

"At the time, one of the key challenges was also integrating three very different IT systems supporting the different entities. I could not have done that without 'air cover' from my mentors who helped support the changes," commented Gail.

Gail related how, during one very unsettling time when the new IT platform was taking time to come on-stream and was affecting business results, one of her informal mentors, Harish Manwani...then head of Africa and Asia and now COO of Unilever, gave her some very specific advice about self-managing.

"You might want to fix everything at once, but you need to relax and only personally catch the balls that are critical to resolve this situation. You need to allow the rest of the balls to pass you and allow others to catch them," shared Harish.

During Gail's time as CEO in South Africa, she was able to provide mentoring for many individuals, applying some of her own learning in mentorship relationships. Since there was a very specific need at the time to raise the representation of Black South Africans and women to more senior levels in the organization, Gail targeted a number of highly talented individuals and provided them with both opportunities and confidence building to help them advance in their careers. Over the six years Gail spent in the role, Black South African representation at management levels advanced from less than 30% to over 50% and women representation advanced from 27% to 58%. And what was most rewarding: the business went from strength to strength.

Gail recounted two of the key mentoring contributions she is very proud of.

The first was an extremely talented Supply Chain Engineer whom Gail encouraged to move into a Category Leadership/Marketing role in order to prepare him for General Management.

"Thabo was rather apprehensive since he had no marketing or sales experience and a great deal of this role involved these activities, but I had faith in him that, with the right support, he could flourish. He went on to lead us to victory in one of the most competitive challenges we had yet experienced in the laundry business. My role here was to act as a sounding board and guide, and I am delighted that Thabo latterly went on to become CEO of the Unilever business in Nigeria," shared Gail.

"The second contribution was a talented group of wonderful women across the business...Kathy, Masingita, Mosidi, Claire, Sue, Ilse, Ursula, Natasha, Trudi, Xoliswa, Angela, Antoinette, and so many more, I can't list all of their names, with whom I shared wonderful personal and business time.

We discussed, individually, and together how best to build the business and manage our families. And I am pleased to say that they are all thriving, with beautiful children and partners, and continuing to pursue great careers both in Unilever and in other businesses," added Gail.

Gail is insistent however on making it clear that these mentoring relationships were mutual: "I learnt so much from each of the people with whom I became close, in that they felt safe enough to give me direct feedback and I trusted them because I know that they also cared for me..so I listened. I also learnt by watching them in their joys and challenges and that helped me to be a better leader overall," she added.

After spending six years in her CEO role in South Africa, returned to London to head up the Savory Division as Executive Vice President.

"By this time I had developed deep relationships with people around the Company globally. This certainly helped in a role where once again the task was to deliver a strategy and vision for a business unit and brands, which others were dependent on to drive their own success. I was quite clear about how to build a more successful Savory business since we had one of the world's strongest in South Africa, but convincing others... particularly in established Western markets, was not that simple. I had less input via mentorship in this role, which I really missed, but I did reach out to colleagues and some reached out to me. I remember Antoine De Saint-Affrique, who is now President of our Foods Business, who introduced me to a colleague he had known that led a very successful savory business in Austria...that meeting was really good since it confirmed my instincts on the need for global leverage but how important it was to retain local tastes (strangely a concept that was being challenged as we were becoming more global). During my time in Savory, I led the creation of a single packaging identity and architecture for the brand which is now implemented in 180 markets. ; the rolling out of a single customer platform for in store retail growth which has proved successful in all markets; the roll-out of top innovations on baking bags and jelly pot bouillon, across the world, to create 100m € big hit deliveries, and the creation of a global team, from a diverse set of regional and local groups, all focussed on delivering one vision and competing and collaborating to deliver to this vision," shared Gail.

She added, "However, the greatest success for me personally in that role was creating a global brand vision for Knorr (soup/stock) linked to sustainable sourcing and agriculture. This has been a real breakthrough for the company. One of the big challenges businesses face is that consumers don't believe industrial products are good for them. So for Knorr for example we committed to getting the tomatoes sustainably sourced, working directly with farmers in Europe, the US and Greater Asia," shared Gail. The repositioning of the Knorr brand globally on a 'dedicated to flavour' platform, with sustainable sourcing as a key reason to believe is improving brand equity and the brand has gained share in 80% of the markets where it operates."

In March 2012 Gail was appointed as Chief Sustainability Officer for Unilever Plc. In this role she is the key leader responsible for strategizing and executing on Unilever's sustainable living plan – a ten year journey towards sustainable growth by improving health and well being, reducing environmental impact and enhancing livelihoods.

"This role has been very different but also very exciting. It has helped me unlock a true passion of mine – building a sustainability focused business. In my current role, I have needed to reach out to mentors in the broader sustainability world and whilst the relationships are informal, I count myself to be fortunate to have a network of people such as Sir Jonathan Porrit of Forum for the Future, Jeremy Oppenheim of McKinsey, Paul Gilding of the Carbon Trust; Nick Craig - founder of Authentic Leadership, Malini Mehra of the Centre for Social Markets, Helio Mattar of Akatu, the faculty at the Cambridge Programme for Sustainability Leadership and my many peers in similar roles in other organizations as wise guides," enthused Gail.

"These individuals and groups provide me with a sounding board and encouragement, in an interesting situation where the change one is driving is quite uncertain and certainly not in line with the current successful norm. They are keeping me motivated with their constant emphasis on the truth, based in science and a slightly longer term focus, sharing of own challenges, and faith in me and my leadership," added Gail.

Gail continued, "Interestingly, so much of the role of a CSO is in fact rooted in mentoring. Most of what I am doing, other than defining where and how

Unilever can make our greatest impact, is having conversations with people within and without the business to bring new insights, share examples from other industries and build confidence to go against the norm. So much of what we are actually trying to do is create a new model of doing business in a way that is truly sustainable and can add value to all stakeholders without destroying the very social and environmental resources that gives the economic system life."

"In this role I am fortunate enough to also have access to a formal mentor – the well renowned Lord Terence Burns, former Chief Economic Advisor and Permanent Secretary to HM Treasury. This is part of a formal mentorship program for women leaders in the UK to be groomed and grown in the British business environment so that they might be better prepared for more senior a roles Lord Burns is currently the Chairman of Santander UK and a Non-Executive Director of Pearson Group Plc. I have an opportunity to learn from his extensive range of experiences and apply some of that to my work, but once again so much of what we discuss is to do with me personally and how my personal balance and confidence are holding up in this change leadership role," laughed Gail.

I asked Gail how she had been able to consistently leverage good mentors to improve her business success.

She responded.

- *First be self-aware of the challenges you face:*
  Where you feel most certain and most vulnerable. This is the first step before seeking or accepting mentorship.

- *Take responsibility for your own progress and don't blame anyone:*
  In the times I've been in very challenging situations, I have, after some blaming and self-flagellation, crept out of a divisive mindset to look for a solution. I've always tried to put myself in the other party's shoes and used that as a starting point before seeking help. Sometimes, the solution may not be what you wish to hear…but at least you are dealing with it and discussing it.

- *You need to trust your mentor:*
  So the initial chemistry or respect between mentor and mentee is very important. The mentee must truly believe that the mentor can help

and be willing to be fully transparent and authentic. The real gift of mentorship is if you can get to the point where you feel safe enough to share your deepest fears and desires (work related of course), and those are received, empathized, decoded…and then you move forward.

A good mentee understands that this is not about getting the next job: But leveraging a mentor means being able to enroll the person to groom you over the longer term and move you forward in your career and your life.

- *Fifth, mentors need to see "return" on their investment in you and believe that you will pay that forward.*

  If there is any manner in which you can reverse mentor your mentor in areas that are new to him or her that would be very helpful. This reverse mentoring does not need to be calculated and formal. I have had mentees who understand this and send me a poem or movie clip or quote that is so right in my, and our journey that is MAGIC. In my experience a good relationship I have had with a mentee has often delivered at least as much, if not more, to me.

- *Do not think of your mentor network as only those who are in senior or influential positions.*

  Some of my greatest support and 'mentoring' has come from my peers, people who worked for me and most significantly my family and friends. If you consider the term 'Mentor', which means 'one who imparts wisdom to and shares knowledge with a less experienced colleague,' and if you are someone like me who wishes to be successful in a career but also in broader life, there will be many people who fit that bill. I have specifically noted business mentors thus far since that was the focus of this 'article', but there are many more true mentors whom I will cite if asked 'whom do I thank for my success to date?' There's my husband and two sons. Then there is my sister, Elaine Midgley, a business entrepreneur who used to own an aluminum trading company 'Gammid Trading' which has since been sold to Alusaf. She has been my mainstay female mentor… always believing in me. My girls friends outside of work: Ingrid, Megan, Corinne, Marie, Gail, Clarah…who care for me as a woman and want me to succeed as a human being, not only as a business person

- *Finally be grateful for all of the support you are getting and pay it forward:*

There is always someone who can benefit from you reaching out…you will experience great joy from knowing that you have provided some support and the universe will repay you with support in abundance."

A lover of nature, gardening, philosophy and meditation, Gail has been married for 30 years to Keith, a medical specialist and head of Clinical Risk for Pru-Health in the UK. She is constantly reverse mentored by her sons Christopher and Kimball.

"My husband and my two sons are probably my three most significant mentors," concluded a smiling Gail.

What started at the age of four, as being tutored by her father to play the violin has become the cornerstone of **Jue Yao's** success. Jue is one of Asia's top violinists. She attributes much of her success to the many mentors she has been blessed with starting with her first one – her father, Yao Di who was a conductor for the Shanghai Film orchestra.

"I was born towards the end of the cultural revolution in Shanghai, China. My father who was a conductor and violinist was therefore not allowed to formally teach his students. But he continued to teach me. Over the years the practice sessions stretched on for hours. And when I did not practice properly, my father would often make me kneel for 30 min stretches to teach me how to focus. I resented it then, but today I am so grateful for that discipline he instilled in me," says Jue Yao.

Guided by her dad's disciplinarian ways, Jue continued to practice the violin. Most days the practice session lasted for several hours. So long that Jue claims she often tampered with the clock to cut short her practice sessions. Yet her fathers undying encouragement and faith in her ability right down to rushing out to buy violin strings for her when she deliberately broke the strings to avoid practicing finally brought her around to committing to the violin.

By the time she was 11, Jue was already handpicked by the national recruitment program and sent off to boarding school, the Shanghai

Conservancy of Music. It was here that her love for the violin blossomed supported by the ongoing encouragement of her father.

"My father actually came across to practice with me every week! He also continued to teach me about life. He taught me focus and discipline. He taught me character. He taught me to 'give back'. But most important he showed me a simple way to better myself," says Jue.

> "Talk to and interact with as many successful people as possible. Learn from every single one of them. Even a short conversation affords you an opportunity to learn something new. Finally, if nothing else works recognize that you do not have to have a mentor in the flesh to be there with you at all times. I have learned quite a bit by just reading the books and autobiographies of great leaders. So if you want a mentor and cant get one, go buy their books."
>
> Jue Yao, violinist extraordinaire and Founder and Director of Yao Jue Music Academy.

Surrounded by influences both good and bad, Jue felt her father's advice ever present in her mind.

"If you can accumulate all of the good parts of your friends to yourself, you will be a better person," said Jue's father.

Surrounded by students in a simple dormitory from age 11 also taught Jue to adapt quickly to people from different backgrounds and mindsets. It also taught her to deal with different situations.

Then at age 16, destiny played a role in shaping Jue's success. Issac Stern, the famous Soviet born violinist (who played a major role in saving New York's famous Carnegie Hall) came to China to identify upcoming Chinese talent. Jue was one of the very few students who were asked to play for him. She performed the Handel Sonata and Stern was impressed. Stern also gave a master class, which Jue attended.

"I was so touched by Stern's passion for music. When Stern returned to San Francisco, he spoke to several important people in the music business. One of those person's was Milton Salkind of the San Francisco Conservatory of Music who was following up on a scholarship program that Stern had started for Chinese students. Salkind came to Beijing and Shanghai to select talented students and I was again selected by my school to perform. Subsequently I was sent to the USA on the exchange program between San Francisco and Shanghai which are sister cities," shared Jue.

At the San Francisco Conservancy of Music, Jue Yao was awarded a full scholarship to continue her studies with Zaven Melikian. Jue then graduated from the Julliard school of New York under the tutelage of Dorothy Delay.

Jue claims that Dorothy Delay was also one of her key mentors.

"She picked me, encouraged me, helped me way back in the early eighties. She taught me that that life and music are interconnected. Everything is connected," shared Jue.

Jue also discovered an expert mentor in Issac Stern.

"My goal when I went to the USA was very clear. I wanted to learn, to get better, to win competitions. Most of all I wanted to be a concert artist. I had a lot of passion and people saw that! They knew I wanted to be somebody. Every time I was in San Francisco, Issac Stern would select five students to play at friends' homes. He would meet each of us. So I always played my best every single time and demonstrated to him how committed I was to my music and to improving," she shared.

Jue added, "In Issac stern, I found the mentor that taught me a real love for music. While with my father, it was discipline that was the foundation of our relationship, with Mr. Stern, it was his true passion and love for music that changed my perception of what I was endeavoring for. With the move to the USA, I was not only able to deepen my musical skills, I was also able to open my mind to the world."

I asked Jue why Stern was agreeable to being her mentor to which she responded:

"I consistently stayed in touch with Stern. I kept him informed of my progress. Updated him on all that I had been learning. Made him aware that

I was doing my very best to get better in my music. By demonstrating my commitment I believe I earned his trust and mentorship," shared Jue.

The challenges of moving to the US as a student of music however were plentiful.

"The violin is a particularly complex instrument. You have to really concentrate and focus. It meant that often I had to use every bit of time I had, literally hours to practice versus spend time with my friends."

The other challenge for Jue was a culture completely alien to her upbringing.

"In China, we are not taught to be expressive. While in the USA, from a very early age, students are encouraged to speak up," she shared.

"Music takes a huge amount of effort. The added difficulty for a female violinist is the extensive travel required. This is so much a factor that once women have families, they need to give up their music so most of the professional violinists are younger women," shared Jue.

"But to me, music became my life. I was determined to break the stereotype. In music the definition of success is how long you can last. Stern also taught me how to balance multiple priorities...and this became critical to my longevity of my success. He often told me that true success is not measured by how well you do in one instance but how long you can consistently do well. I thought he was talking just about music at the time, but later I realized this lesson is also true of life in general," added Jue.

Jue credits Stern with helping her switch her mental focus between music and other priorities.

"This has been instrumental in my success. Being able to switch my mental concentration from one activity to another. From my music to business, for example," she shared.

In 1997, Jue moved back to Hong Kong after getting married.

This again threw up new opportunities.

In Hong Kong Jue finally realized one of her childhood dreams – to give back to young students what her mentors have given to her. In 2001 she established the Yao Jue Music Academy to give the best training in music learning to the younger generation and also support young local musicians and get them ready to represent Hong Kong on the world stage. Jue's school today has around 160 students.

In July 2013, as Founder, Artistic and Development Director, Jue embarked on an even more ambitious project –the Hong Kong String Orchestra - the first-ever professional string ensemble which offers training and international mentorship programmes to the music graduates of Hong Kong residents.

"We are a non-profit organization with the mission to support local young graduated musicians to pursue their dreams of joining professional orchestra and performing on stage. The basic objective of the program is to provide post-graduate training to recruited young local musicians by veteran orchestral members to hone their skills in music performance. While nurturing these talents we encourage them to contribute back to society by the joy of music appreciation to the lesser privileged through various community concerts," shared Jue.

"I am quite fortunate that the HK government subsidies a lot of the activities. The Chief Executive is our honorary patron. I am so tremendously excited to see my students grow into professional musicians," she added.

Jue's plans for 2014 included inviting top overseas artists from renowned orchestras to be instrumental coaches. Artists like David Ehrlich (violin), the founder of the Renaissance Music Academy of Virginia and the first violin of the famed Avanti quartet; Chang Li-Kuo (viola), Assistant principal violinist of the Chicago Symphony Orchestra and Qiang Tu (Cello), Cellist of the New York Philharmonic.

Jue highlights that one needs different mentors at different stages in life.

"Sometimes when you have a mentor, you don't appreciate the value till much later."

Jue claims that the biggest challenge she faces just like most women do is finding balance in life.

She shared some simple ways she has worked to find that balance, learning from her mentors.

"Abhor bad habits and eliminate unnecessary things. Make your interest your job if possible.

Be meticulous about arranging your schedules. Follow the schedule religiously. And always be on time.

Do things quickly. Do not procrastinate. Finally, believe in your dream and yourself. Don't give up," shared Jue.

She also shared her top few tips on best leveraging mentors.

- *Talk to your mentors:*
  As often as you can.

- *Talk to and interact with as many successful people as possible:*
  Learn from every single one of them. Even a short conversation affords you an opportunity to learn something new. Women in particular must learn everyday.

- *Look for opportunities to upgrade your skills:*
  Do this constantly and meticulously.

- *Seek out mentors proactively to help your journey:*
  It doesn't matter if some do not agree to help. What matters is that some do.

- *Finally, if nothing else works, recognize that you do not have to have a mentor in the flesh to be there with you at all times:*

"I have learned quite a bit by just reading the books and autobiographies of great leaders. So if you want a mentor and cant get one, go buy their books. The amazing thing today is that thanks to the Internet, you can learn peoples bad and good habits, their strengths and weaknesses all online!" shared Jue.

Jue has clearly leveraged her mentors' wisdom and her own ability to succeed. Critics worldwide recognized her for her performances across the United States, Asia and Europe. She was awarded the "Outstanding violinist 2002" by Rado and "The Most successful woman" award by JESSICA magazine in 2005.

Jue today is happily settled in Hong Kong with two daughters.

She believes that her success is an accumulation of all the knowledge and support she received from her mentors.

And often she finds herself giving her daughters the same advice her first mentor, her father gave her.

"If you can accumulate all of the good parts of your friends to yourself, you will be a very successful person."

Over in sunny Singapore **Kristen English** has over 24 years of experience working with international organizations in the fields of executive coaching, global leadership, strategic diversity and inclusion initiatives, leadership team development, organization design, work-life balance and more. Kristen is on the faculty for ThomasLeland and Duke CE's leadership practice. She is also the **Co-founder** of **FlexLife.**

While originally from the US, Kristen has lived overseas for the past 19 years, in China, Indonesia and currently Singapore. Kristen has lived, worked or travelled in over 70 countries on 6 continents.

Kristen attributes much of her success to the contributions her mentors made to her development in the early years of her career.

"I grew up in Lansing, Michigan. My Mother was a teacher, and my father was a teacher who became an entrepreneur, starting his own business when I was three years old. My parents grew up poor and, through education and hard work, escaped poverty to become middle class. Family, education, hard work, financial responsibility and self-reliance were the values they worked hardest to teach my brother and sister and I," shared Kristen.

*"Great mentors are great encouragers - both when things are going well and when they are not. You need a portfolio of mentors to build a successful career."*

**Kristen English,** *Global Coach, Consultant and Co-founder of FlexLife.*

She continued, "I loved school and enjoyed challenging myself with the hardest classes. I decided to study Chemical Engineering because I was told that it was the hardest major. After a few years of study, I knew that I wouldn't be an Engineer for my whole career, so I sought out companies that would allow me to move around through different functions, if I wanted. Also, I knew that I wanted to work abroad, so it had to be an international company. P&G was the perfect fit. I joined them in 1991 after internships at Johnson & Johnson, General Motors and P&G."

At P&G Kristen realized early on that finding success for herself meant defining what success meant to her.

"I think this was the first step in my development – being able to define what my objective was or what success meant to me," shared Kristen.

At P&G Kristen also discovered the power of mentorship.

"From my very first annual review, under career aspirations, I told my boss that I wanted to go abroad. I also told everyone I met in any company-networking situation. Most of them would chuckle and say, "maybe, someday..." My attitude was that there is no guarantee, but you won't get it if you don't ask, so I kept asking.

And then I met Jim Thompson, my first mentor. Jim was the guru of Total Quality and Statistics at P&G," commented Kristen.

She continued, "Jim facilitated the statistical process control course during my first six months with the company, 23 years ago. I was so inspired that I took every course he taught. He believed in diversity and he believed in me. He could see my passion for the work. When the opportunity came up to become a facilitator for one of his programs, I volunteered, even though I had to do it in addition to my regular job. He guided me to become a facilitator, a skill that is invaluable in my business today and invited me to go co-train with him in Hong Kong and India. He helped me to get exposure to Asia," shared Kristen.

In 1995, that exposure lead to Kristen being offered a role in China with P&G, after just four years with the Company. P&G was making a huge push in China, and people remembered her consistent request to work abroad.

"Today everyone knows that China experience is great for your career. Back then, nobody wanted to go. I jumped at the chance. I was given a huge role for my level of experience - Recruiting, Training and Development Manager.

It could have been an Associate Director job, but nobody at that level would go. I was a newly promoted second level manager. Just like in my school days, I wanted the biggest challenge there was. But the move would never have happened without Jim's mentorship," clarified Kristen.

China was still largely an unknown culture to Kristen. It was rife with challenges for the uninitiated.

"It was not easy when I got to China. Kelly Lewis, a long-time China Marketing leader, was assigned as my mentor when I first arrived there. She helped me understand organization politics from her perspective and to understand Chinese culture. I remember a time when things were not going well. An internal customer was unhappy with the support I was providing; I had given feedback in the wrong way, culturally, to my staff; and a program I delivered had been a total flop. It was a Friday night, and I called Kelly and told her all about it, how I felt like a failure. She talked me through each situation to identify the learning, and then helped me to see the bigger picture. She built my confidence back up so I could go back Monday morning and start again, better than before," shared Kristen.

Kristen continued, "Great mentors are great encouragers - both when things are going well and when they are not. You need a portfolio of mentors to build a successful career. Some mentors will give advice on your industry or function. Others will help you navigate the politics of a new organization; or guide you as you follow in the same path that they have taken; or advise you on how to keep your career on track when you face a personal crisis. They can be older or younger (though usually older), male or female (best to have both), and the mentoring may go on for many years or a short period of time - maybe even just one meeting."

Over the next three years Kristen led her staff to dramatically increase the corporate training available to all of P&G China's employees (from 12 programs per year to 200 per year); and to create systems to effectively manage the large recruiting needs (200 managers per year and 100 administrative/technical employees per year). The accomplishment she is proudest of from her China years are the many employees she developed who still play a leading role in P&G's business today.

In 1998 Kristen was offered the next opportunity – an assignment in another relatively unknown market at the time – Indonesia.

"I was supposed to be the Human Resources Manager for a new plant start-up, but President Suharto stepped down, chaos ensued, and the company decided to postpone the plant indefinitely. Instead, I became the Organization Effectiveness manager for P&G Indonesia, where I had many great experiences with Change Management and Organization Assessment and Design," shared Kristen.

"After 10 years with P&G, I decided it was time to move on. I wasn't sure exactly what I wanted to do, but I knew I wanted to try working for myself. I took some time off to travel, visit family and friends and think about what would be next for my career," shared Kristen.

"Some mentors have a long lasting impact. For example, Moheet Nagrath, who had been my manager in China, and who went on to become the head of HR for all of P&G, stayed in touch with me. When I started my cross-cultural consulting and training practice, he introduced me to an organization in the company that had that need, and he gave me advice on how to make sure what I was offering would meet their need. It was still up to me to get the business, but he made the introduction. The program we designed was deployed globally and contributed to P&G's special award by DiversityInc for Top Company for Global Cultural Competence in 2010."

"I started my business in the US, but quickly missed Asia, so I moved the business to Singapore in 2003. I don't have any full-time employees, but I work with many different partners who are leaders in their fields so we can all bring the latest ideas to our clients. I have the great pleasure of working with people from all over the world, in different industries and functions. I am never bored! I enjoy working with global leaders and companies to help them develop their leadership, teams and organizations," commented Kristen.

Kristen offered a few simple tips on how to find great mentors and be a good mentor oneself.

- *Search actively for the right mentors:*
  As Sheryl Sandberg says, the best mentor/mentee relationships are

when there is a natural rapport. I highly recommend Chapter 5 of Lean In, "Are You My Mentor?". A lot of the formal mentor assignments for newcomers in China didn't work out. It worked for Kelly and I because we had that natural affinity. You can't force it. Chemistry and trust is very important. While natural affinity is important, you do have to get out there in situations where you can find potential mentors, e.g. industry events, professional networking associations, volunteering, etc. I met Jim because I volunteered to become a course facilitator.

- *As a mentor, you are going to give advice:*

  However, don't forget that good listening and coaching/questioning skills are still really important.

  Make sure you don't let your own issues and emotions get in the way of seeing your mentee's situation with perspective.

- *As a mentee, respect your mentor's time:*

  Don't come to complain or rant about how unfair it all is or how unhappy you are - save that for your girlfriends. Come to your sessions with clear challenges and questions to discuss. Take action on what you've agreed to and report back on how it worked.

- *PIE – Performance, Image, Exposure:*

  To truly get ahead in your career, you must have all three. Good performance will get you noticed, but it's not enough to move up. A mentor is invaluable in helping you craft your image and get the right exposure opportunities.

- *Look out for ways to help your Mentor and give back:*

  Introductions to helpful people or teaching her about a new technology, etc.

- *Find a portfolio of mentors:*

  You won't ever find one person who will meet all of your mentoring needs, so you need a portfolio of mentors.

"Today I am fortunate to be coach, consultant and facilitator to some of the world's most influential organizations including BNP Paribas, BCG, Novartis, Procter & Gamble, SC Johnson, Genpact, American Express, Infosys, Parexel and many more. They benefit from the investment of time that my mentors made in me," concluded Kristen.

# Chapter 8

# FOCUS ON
# THE POSITIVE VS NEGATIVE.
# NEVER GIVE UP

There are several studies to underline the power of positive thinking. One famous such study was done by Barbara Fredrickson - a positive psychology researcher at the University of North Carolina. Fredrickson's research showed that when people experience positive emotions like joy, contentment and love, they see more possibilities in life. This is turn allows human beings to build new skills and resources that can provide value in other areas of their lives. I spoke to three professionals *Dominique Reiniche, former Chairman, Europe, The Coca-Cola Company*; *Valerie Khan, Executive Director of Group Development Pakistan, Chairperson of the Acid Survivors Foundation of Pakistan;* and *Ella Stewart, Chief Executive Officer, BBDO Russia Group* to discover how they have used this unique attribute to fast track their success.

Since 2003, **Dominique Reiniche** has consistently been classified as one of Fortune Magazine's Top 50 most powerful women in business. She went from 40th place in 2006 to 16th place in 2012, becoming the first French woman to reach such a high ranking. She also figures among the 10 most influential European Women according to The Financial Times.

> *"I learned early on in my career, the power of saying YES. Say yes first! I don't mean you have to say yes to everything but be open-minded. Listen and try to bring people to your point of view. Yes is a better word than No. Always focus on people strengths vs. their negative energies. Conflict is better resolved if you start from a positive place, and influence versus confront."*
>
> **Dominique Reiniche,** *former Chairman, Europe, The Coca-Cola Company.*

Dominique has been **Chairman, Europe of The Coca-Cola** Company since January 2013.She was previously President of Coca-Cola Europe, overseeing 28 countries in the European economic zone. Previous roles were with global giants P&G and Kraft. Her career reads like a continuous path of success. As the tune of going to print, with 'Break the ceiling, touch the sky' Dominique had just moved to a new career opportunity.

Dominique believes that her path to success was not without severe challenges.

She shared: "I faced several challenges in my career which I believe women face even today. These include - Lack of leadership culture, training and education: For women, even in the most advanced countries and cultures this still exists. Work – life balance is very tough. Those who say the contrary are not being sincere. When you are trying to balance work, partner relationship, children, you need a huge amount of energy and self-awareness. Because there are so few women in top roles, there is a tendency for women to behave like men. There have been so many challenges on the way to the top."

Dominique shared candidly that her success is largely due to a simple leadership principle – Focusing on the positive and never giving up.

She shared; "I learned early on in my career, the power of saying yes.

Say yes first! I don't mean you have to say yes to everything but be open-minded. Listen and try to bring people to your point of view. Yes is a better word than No."

"Women need to be very resilient. For hundreds of years women have lived in the private versus the public space. They must recognize that they will likely have setbacks and more obstacles versus men in their careers, but must never lose the mindset of "never give up," shared Dominique.

Dominique was born in Lyon, south east of France to Jo and Bernard. She spent most of her life in Paris.

"I travelled a lot in my childhood since my father liked foreign languages, etymology and both loved travelling during holidays: so I was very motivated to study a lot of languages like Latin, Greek, English, German and understand different cultures," she shared.

Dominique continued, "My parents taught me the sense of effort and work in order to succeed: they have always encouraged me to make efforts and told me that nothing is impossible. If you try hard enough, nothing is impossible. I got this positive mindset, this openness to the others and to the world during my childhood thanks to my parents. That is probably why my first Company I worked for was an international Company where I found that mindset."

"My mentors have been many – My father was my first mentor. He invested a lot of time and effort into my career. I am the eldest in the family so wanted to make him happy. I was also deeply inspired by my teachers and bosses. "I know how to listen to good advice. I like larger than life heroes such as Amelia Earhart, Hélène Bouchet or Jacqueline Auriol: they were the first aviation pioneers showing courage and modernity. At that time there were no inspiring model in politics or economics. Later I was inspired by two female writers and reporters in the 50's and 70 's, Simone de Beauvoir and Françoise Giroud. Boldness, and anti-conformism are the values that I have learnt from those heroes," shared Dominique.

In 1978, Dominique finished her MBA from the ESSEC Business School in Paris, France.

It was the second year that graduated young women attended High Business Schools.

"We felt like pioneers with a 15 % proportion of females within these first mixed chairs but there was no particular discrimination neither negative or positive. As young women, we were more than welcomed by our males colleagues," added Dominique.

"Despite all the good progress that women have made to date, they still bump into glass ceilings and glass walls. The glass walls come into play where women are often parked in some support areas of the business versus P&L roles that directly drive the bottom-line. I call these the glass walls," shared Dominique.

In 1978 she joined Procter & Gamble, for whom she worked for eight years based in Paris and quickly started working on European projects.

"I remember that I was one of the first women who participated in the traditional field sales training at that time. Another young man recently hired was also part of this induction program and was selected to achieve this internship in the Rhône- Alpes Region for the summer as I was assigned to the same Region in winter. The Management tested my resilience as well as my ability to drive in that mountainous area, in tough climate conditions.

Moreover, my manager thought appropriate to give me, from his standpoint a valuable advice, i.e. 'not to wear purple stockings' 'as customers are used to men, not women,'" she shared.

In 1986 Dominique joined Kraft-Jacob Suchard (now known as Mondelēz). A couple of years into her role there, she was placed in a critical position working for a Company that had been acquired by Kraft.

"At the time I had been hired by the General Manager of the chocolate business to be part of the newly created Executive Committee in order to turn around the chocolate business in France. But within a year, the GM disappeared and a new leader appeared who had never worked with women before. This manager found no pleasure in working with me, and in fact I later found out was working silently against me, and had even encouraged a few headhunters to connect with me and lure me away from my then role and leave the company," shared Dominique.

But Dominique resisted!

"It was a traumatic time. I simply told myself to focus on the positive. I decided to acknowledge this was a challenging circumstance and decided to work on influencing this General Manager via his right hand man in Sales. I was at that time working in Marketing. I also decided I would be far more conscious and diplomatic about which battles I picked with the GM. Finally, I also determined that I would be super efficient in my work with him," she added.

"Always focus on people strengths vs. their negative energies. Conflict is better resolved if you start from a positive place, and influence versus confront. Confrontation should be a last resort. It takes time to win people over so one must commit. You must make the best efforts to get people around the table to reach consensus versus fighting each other," shared Dominique.

In six to nine months, Dominique's GM came around and began to appreciate her work.

"Over time this GM became my best advocate. This allowed me to expand my responsibilities from just marketing to product development, strategy and also being part of the integration team of the new acquired 'Côte d'Or' brand.

In April 1992, when I moved to Coke, this same GM made the most touching speech at my farewell. He recognized the great work I had done with him and had tears in his eyes at the end of his speech. That moment was such a victory for me. I realized that through my hard work I had not only won this persons mind but also his heart. Till today he and I are still in touch," she added.

Dominique has been equally resilient and positive in managing her work family balance. She is a French citizen, and has an English spouse. She has one daughter and two stepdaughters.

"One of the most striking lessons I received came surprisingly from my four year old daughter. One evening coming back home after a tough and tiring working day as I just opened the door and entered the living room, she put both hands on her hips, she looked at me right in the eyes and said as solemnly as she could 'Mum, you have a great job, but when you are at home, it is to take care of your child!"

Dominique added, "She helped me realize – fortunately very early – that I needed to shift my mind towards my family as soon as I was driving back home, in order to stay fully focused on their needs and wishes. From this time on, I realized that although women have to balance a lot of activities and duties, they have to focus on each of them at the appropriate timing, instead of trying to execute all of them simultaneously. This guided me throughout my career: when you are doing something, you need to have a full awareness of what you are doing, even if it is a brief and short activity."

In 2005 Dominique's trademark resilience and positive attitude was further tested when she was appointed as President of UNESDA (The Union of European Soft Drinks Associations).

Alarmed by the increase in obesity rates across Europe, the soft drinks industry was facing severe challenges from concerned parents, nutritionists and Government authorities.) Undeterred, Dominique in her role of President, Europe of the Coca-Cola Company, listened to the voice of the consumer, and on behalf of The Coca-Cola Company, she encouraged other Food and Beverage Companies to make voluntary commitments to battle the obesity epidemic. Dominique led the industry to liaise more with the EU authorities, to communicate more broadly the choice of drinks it offers, as well as to adopt a self-regulatory code on not marketing to children and not selling in primary schools. The Coca-Cola Company played its role of leader by example.

"What was amazing was that we managed to lower our caloric content by 10% while still growing the business. Clearly our consumers were appreciating our approach. In addition, the UNESDA approach was re applied by several other companies working with associations in other parts of the world, including the World Health Organization (WHO). That is the beauty of working for a leading and responsible Company like The Coca-Cola Company," added Dominique.

"I learned yet again from that experience that it's best to see the glass as half full versus half empty. Because if you are persistent and convincing, the glass will fill up anyway," shared Dominique.

Dominique today sits on the Boards of some of the World's leading Companies such as AXA (The No. 1 Insurance Global Brand) and PSA-Peugeot–Citroën (one of the most historically important car manufacturers in Europe).

She has a keen interest in cinema and architecture and loves skiing and swimming.

"I enjoy everything that makes your leisure time interesting and dynamic. I don't like competing during my leisure time; competition is enough in business and leisure is more about changing gears and relaxing," added Dominique.

While at Coca-Cola, Dominique was one of the major ambassadors in Europe of the 5 by 20 program launched in 2009 by Muhtar Kent, CEO and Chairman of The Coca-Cola Company. Dominique has been very active in sitting on the Board of the Women Leadership Council aiming at identifying, coaching, developing networking for young female talents.

Dominique is often invited as a keynote speaker at Conferences sharing experience and learnings. She takes questions and give practical tips on how to make women's' lives easier.

"For example, everywhere I have been in a managing position, I banned any meeting early in the morning or too late in the evening. I have always promoted flexibility together with availability."

"I have always believed that despite the challenges, women are being increasingly recognized for their successes. I spend a lot of time coaching young professionals. One of the things I continue to reiterate to them is that execution is strategy. The fact is that strategy is 20 % and 80% is spent in executing the plan. Execution is from A to Z not just up to P or R. Even the brightest minds are of no use if execution is flawed. I also encourage young women to be real, to be themselves, to be bold. To work and collaborate with their colleagues because team is much stronger than individual. Being tough on themselves and their time utilization," shared Dominique.

"But finally, the biggest enabler to one's own success is one's attitude and resilience. The ability to take any circumstance and get the best out of it. To most often be able to say "yes"! concluded Dominique.

Dominque's top five tips for consistently staying positive:

- *Say YES. Say yes first:*
  Be open-minded, listen and try and bring people over to your point of view.

- *Be very resilient:*
  Women will likely have more setbacks versus men in their careers, but women must never lose the mindset of "never give up."

- *Focus on people's positive strength versus their negative energies with:*
  Always see the glass half full versus half empty.

- *Stay fully focused in the moment:*
  At work, be fully present. When with family be similarly so.

- *Enjoy quality leisure time when you can:*
  Do something you love.

D eep in the bustle of Islamabad, I have a very special young fan. Noor-Eva Salammbo Khan. She is 13 years old, adores reading and her dream is to become a human rights lawyer and change the world. She is constantly asking her Mum when 'Break the ceiling, touch the sky' would be out.

Little Noor-Eva takes after her Mum **Valerie Khan** who lives in one of the most dangerous parts of the world, works daily with acid attack survivors, street children and children victims of Child Sexual Abuse (CSA) / Commercial Sexual Exploitation of Children (CSEC) and has witnessed multiple bomb attacks, yet she believes in the cause she is fighting for and reiterates that she is a born fighter.

Meet **Valerie Khan**, Executive Director of Group Development Pakistan, and **Chairperson of the Acid Survivors Foundation of Pakistan,** living in Islamabad.

"I am a fighter. I never give up. Anyone who knows me will use that word to describe me. Because I was taught and believe that when you fight for the right cause, God will not let you down and positive energy will always surround you. One must focus on its role, its potential, and its strengths - and use that as fuel to tackle obstacles," shared Valerie.

Valerie comes from a family of 'fighters for a cause.'

Her maternal great grandfather fought the Germans in World War One. Then her paternal grandfather, barely out of his teens fought in the resistance against the Nazis in the Second World War.

"So I grew up with a legacy of fighting for human rights in the face of tyranny. Since the time I was a child, I knew I had a goal-a role to play, a responsibility as a citizen to help in creating a better society, a better world," shared Valerie.

> *"There will always be challenge in a career. There will be attempts of being taken advantage of; there could even be violence. What is important is that you focus on the positive and never stop believing you can do it."*
>
> **Valerie Khan,** *Executive Director of Group Development Pakistan, Chairperson of the Acid Survivors Foundation of Pakistan.*

Valerie began volunteering at the age of 11 and discovered that her role of fighting for a cause could be very satisfying.

"I continued to read books from enlightened French philosophers such as Voltaire, Diderot and Rousseau. I gained a deep respect for all human beings through these readings," added Valerie.

Valerie also shared that she was fortunate in a sense to understand socio-economic conditions that were very diverse thanks to the differing backgrounds of her parents.

"My dad is quite traditional and comes from a background of very modest means, and has seen poverty close up. My Mum on the other hand comes from a very affluent background. This diversity of background has been very useful to me in life as I can relate to rich and poor alike," shared Valerie.

"On my fathers' side, there have always been simple, dedicated, hard-working men and women in the family. My grand father was a volunteer firefighter and on my mother's side, more military intellectuals, fighting for a more humanistic society," she added.

"I was 11 when my parents got divorced, and had to witness my Mum having to raise the three of us kids alone," shared Valerie.

That was the start of Valerie's battle with adversity.

She took it in her stride.

"Sitting in the vehicle that was taking us back to Paris, where my Mum originated from, I told myself over and over that whatever happened in my life, I would be resilient. I would focus on the positive and never give up."

In 1984, at the age of 11, when she was living back in Paris, Valerie was attending a Catholic school. She was very nervous to join a new school right after her parent's divorce, but she was welcomed by the class who told her she would like it at the school and that they would take good care of her. Indeed they did.

"I was actually surrounded and welcome by the entire class. Within this school, we were all encouraged to develop social projects, which I did with a few friends, to help vulnerable children. We organized baking turns on a weekly basis and we used to sell this bakery and the money collected would enable us to prepare support packages for those children (mostly books, clothes and a few sweets). The bakery routine really went well, and children used to come to us for snacks and we managed to raise decent money," shared Valerie.

"The project and the frequency of the bake sale had been allowed by the school administration but one day Sister Dominique decided to 'stop the activity on moral grounds' without informing any of us children," she added.

Valerie's classmates came and explained to her "She (Sister Dominique) is not letting us do it."

Valerie took one hour of "free study" before the break and went to knock at Sister Dominique's door to talk to her.

But Sister Dominique looked at Valerie coldly and said "I am in class I am busy, I cannot talk to you right now."

Valerie responded; "I understand, sorry for disturbing you Sister, I will wait for you outside until you are available. The doors were glass ones and for the whole hour, she could see me standing and waiting, not moving away. Then when the bell rang, she came to me, trying not to become angry."

Valerie explained to Sister Dominique; "We respect your perception of our project Sister. But you see, when we bake and sell, our priority is not to "eat and feel contented". Our priority is to create a business that can serve more vulnerable ones and that can make a difference. While we sell, we talk and we explain to other children and sometimes parents even, why it is important to help others and how we are doing it. This is what you want isn't it? You want us to share values and you want us to establish a solidarity network. Well this is what we are doing. Furthermore, we were allowed to start this project and it is nothing but fair that we should be allowed to finish it and achieve the planned results, which was to support 1000 support packages for vulnerable children."

There was a moment of silence, as Sister Dominique and Valerie looked each other in the eye.

Then Sister Dominique sighed and said, "Ok you can do it."

"Thank you sister, you will not regret it," added Valerie.

Valerie and her friends continued the project, and achieved the goal of 1000 packages delivered to the more vulnerable children!

A year later, Valerie moved with her family and changed to a good government public high school in Bois Colombes, a small town next to Paris.

"I was extremely depressed to have to change school. The first day I arrived, I was dressed in a navy blue coat, jeans, white shirt, with navy blue jumper, shoes and white socks. All the students looked at me while I was waiting in the middle of the class: I looked too posh, felt ridiculous, humiliated, lost, waiting for the teacher to decide to notice me and allow me to join my seat. She was writing on the black board and was obviously focusing on punishing me for my appearance…After 20 long minutes, she turned to me and said 'well, why are you standing here? Go and sit there, and start your math exercises," said Valerie.

Valerie obeyed, concentrated very hard on not letting a teardrop fall and did her exercises and totally failed.

"I showed her my assignment five minutes before the class ended and when she looked at the terrible work, she looked at me and declared 'well if this is the way you work, we are not going to be friends young lady…" Since then, I became terrible in Maths," added Valerie.

When the time of the equivalent of her French O'levels came Valerie secured 100% in French Literature and failed in Maths yet again.

"The coordinator called me and asked me how I could "mock people this way".

"If you get 100% in literature there is no way you can be so bad in Maths," she shared.

Valerie cried this time.

Then two years later while she was attending A section (French Literature, languages and philosophy), her Maths teacher came and looking at her assignment told Valerie, "You know young lady, even the best linguists and writers are good in Maths!!! You will do nothing with your life, you will end up a nobody."

Valerie had had enough.

"This time, I decided it would be the last time I would tolerate humiliation coupled with stupidity, so I smiled, looked at him and answered 'Oh really??? Best writers are also good in maths? Well, then I may have serious chances of becoming someone then, if ever I decide to."

The whole class burst into laughter and the maths teacher finished the course with no further comment.

"I passed my baccalaureate with good marks, and went on with my life, the work that I love and I am happy to say, I never wanted to be 'someone' but rather to be a good one, I was just happy with whatever change I could be part of, what difference I could always make: as a teacher and as an activist, as a development professional.... But I never forgot how raising your voice against what is wrong was essential and how victimization could be countered, even in a simple form such as this," she shared.

Then in 1992, while working as a sales assistant on a student part time job (they recruit linguists for this as customers come from all over the world) for EURODISNEY, Valerie met and fell in her love with her husband Faqir Mohammad.

"I looked at him, and as I got to know him I realized he was so spirited and intellectual. Like a "noble warrior," she shared.

After knowing Mohammad for four years, in 1996 his Mother passed away. He went back to Pakistan for the burial rites and on his return proposed to Valerie.

"My family was not concerned about me marrying a Pakistani. They were concerned about me living in Pakistan," she shared.

But move she did. And took up a role as teacher and pedagogical coordinator.

Several years later, the security situation worsened in Pakistan and one day a bomb went off in the lane just next to her kids' school.

"I grabbed my baby and rushed to the school to pick up the rest of my children and brought them back home; we learnt to live with the fear of terrorism, and at some point you actually forget the fear, learn to live with uncertainties and not accept terror, not to be enslaved by it. You learn to look at the positive and try to make a difference where you can," added Valerie.

Valerie shared that staying positive and raising her voice has also enabled her to make a difference in day-to-day things in Pakistan.

"One day as I was driving with my children, I saw a police truck randomly picking up street children off the road. I blocked the truck and introduced myself as a local child rights activist and a concerned citizen; I asked the officer who seemed to be in charge, what he would do with the children and where he would take them. I knew, thanks to my job, how child protection was a challenge in Pakistan and especially in police custody. I requested him to give me his name so I could compliment his good work, and report their achievement to relevant authorities when I wrote to his superiors. But in reality I was just making sure that the police were in fact who they said they were and that they were pressurized to send children safely to the child protection cell in the relevant police station. After three days, I met the same children in the street; they knocked at my car window, I smiled, opened the window and they said, "Hey Baidgee (elder sister), the policemen were very nice this time, thank you! And they laughed," shared Valerie.

In 2005 Valerie started the biggest fight of her life. Something that would indeed change her life. She was visiting a beauty parlor in Lahore and came in contact with a lady who was a survivor of an acid attack. At the time Valerie had no idea what that meant. All she knew was that the persons face was disfigured. Subsequently she took up a role with an NGO working to help these acid attack survivors but within a few months discovered that money was being embezzled by the NGO and diverted for other activities.

"In the meantime, I was contacted by Acid Survivors Trust International. They urged me not to give up on my role to help these women and advised me to create a board and register our new NGO – Acid Survivors Foundation of Pakistan (ASF). They had the funds to support this initiative," commented Valerie.

She added; "In a year, we started the new organization in Islamabad. ASF provides comprehensive rehabilitation services to acid survivors, such as medical services, psychological and social counseling, legal and socio-economic assistance. We also conduct advocacy and lobbying campaigns. These services are provided by staff and volunteers as well as pro-bono doctors, specialists and lawyers."

"The challenges facing women are many in the corporate world, but in the social sector we are dealing with life itself! Many issues in our world have very many important learnings for women in business. The women we help as part of ASF for example face so many tough challenges – violence, lack of education and feudal/ tribal cultural systems. I have learned so much from these experiences working with them. I see so much positivity in the face of overwhelming adversity. I see courage, I see humility," added Valerie.

In 2009 Valerie met Nazeeraan.

Nazeeraan was attacked by one her close family members in 2009 and is blind and disfigured.

"This was probably one of the toughest cases I had ever came across: she was initially treated as a 'dead body' in the hospital she was admitted to but our field officer contacted us and said, if she has a chance we need to give it to her. So we did. We had her transferred to Islamabad for treatment and rehabilitation and she made it! She now lives in her own house with her two school going daughters, has set up her own business and is now an integrated community member in her family and in her village life," shared Valerie.

Valerie talked about how supporting Nazeeraan, to her, was also very much about learning, discovering and staying positive.

"How do you hold hands and for how along and when? I remember my first words to her: "Hello Nazeeraan, my name is Valerie, I am glad you came here, it means you are a very brave woman...How are you? How do you feel?" Valerie asked.

Amidst all the pain of her tortured body and suffering she was going through Nazeeraan replied, "I am fine, thank you."

Valerie asked her; "Nazeeraan, I hope you will be more comfortable in a few days, it will not be easy you know but we will be there for you. Are you ready to fight Nazeeraan?"

"Yes I am," came back the answer.

"And indeed she was. Indeed she fought. She fought the pain, she fought darkness and blindness, she fought desperation, she fought in court and obtained the custody of her two daughters', in her own way, after making her own decisions," shared Valerie.

Over the time of her recovery Valerie and her team helped all along providing key inputs to Nazeeraan. Valerie ensured that relevant resources would be available for her to be treated. She helped Nazeeran redesign her life with the support of her doctor who helped her to live being blind, with the help of her psychotherapist. Valerie helped Nazeeran discover that she was capable of so many things.

"We did French cooking lessons together, we sang, we went to see the policy makers and media with many civil society members and lawyers to ask for some adequate laws to be passed. She co-wrote her book Brûlée à l'acide, Burnt with Acid, Ed Flammarion and now has an endowment fund that will support her and her girls for a long time. She proved to her perpetrators and the world, that intelligence, strength and good will is stronger than hatred and violence. She is now protected by influential community members who are among our volunteers now. Safe and happy," added Valerie.

"Nazeeraan shows the world that acid may burn you – but it cannot burn you entirely. Your spirit and your will still make you exist as a woman. When the survivors themselves are so full of hope, how can we not follow their example?" shared Valerie.

Valerie urges women across the world to "never give up. And to always focus on the positive vs. the negative."

"There will always be challenge in a career. There will be attempts of being taken advantage of; there could even be violence. What is important is that you focus on the positive and never stop believing you can do it," she shared.

Throughout our discussion Valerie reiterated that "fighting for a cause" is a way of life for her.

"My fighting spirit which has fuelled me ever since my parents divorced, has been my great support over the years," she commented.

"For example, our advocacy program started with a presentation of the situation of acid violence in Pakistan to the Chief Justice of Pakistan in the supreme court: I was called to the bar. I was terrified, but thought, Okay this is the chance. Do not waste it. Convince him," Valerie added.

Valerie made her presentation in Urdu!

Immediately after, the Chief Justice directed the government to legislate on the matter. After two years of advocacy and lobbying against acid violence as one of the worst forms of gender based violence, this violence was made a crime against the state unanimously in Pakistan.

"This is a historic moment in the country," shared Valerie.

"Staying positive has helped me in my fight to advocate a new legal framework to be established in Pakistan in order to monitor and regulate the sale of acid and to punish perpetrators of acid attacks. It has helped me deal with the most inhumane acid attack cases. It has helped me work with feudal tribes and systems, it has helped me deal with corruption," shared Valerie.

Valerie shared that she believes that when you fight for what you believe in, you earn respect.

"It has helped me fit in very well into the Pashtun society (also known as ethnic Afghans or Pathans). They accepted me though I was a foreigner and never made me feel that way. They never asked me about my religion. They were silently supportive of my work. I love this about Pakistan and about Asia in general. When you are sad, people will give you a hand to pull you up."

The challenges and obstacles have come fast and swift in Valerie's line of work.

"One of the greatest barriers to our work is the funding pressure we face for our rehabilitation center. Pakistani philanthropists have had to face significant corruption from NGOs and don't know whom to support," she added.

Valerie continued "Apart from availing sufficient and adequate resources, one of the greatest barriers to our work now is the discriminatory power structures prevailing in the country: acid violence mostly targets the poor and women, it is also quite under-reported and policy makers are too slow to respond to problems that do not directly target them. Most policy makers belong to the elite. Additionally security is a big issue, here the fact of belonging to a big Pashtun tribe helps but also the non confrontational style and positive communication is fruitful: we are telling these people, "let us talk about it, let us see whether it serves our purpose as human beings or not. There is a problem, we need to find a solution and we can!"

"Despite ongoing progress and new legislation being passed, it is a daily struggle, unwavering determination and persistence that pays off. One needs to keep on speaking to media, keep on calling parliamentarians, keep on tracking data to prove what you are saying and conduct an evidence based advocacy. It is also about linking and talking to communities and LEAs (Law Enforcement agencies) to generate social support. I waited a whole hour in front of the glass door of my teacher to get a chance to talk to her and convince her, now with acid violence, women and child rights, I know that it is matter of several meetings, several achievements step by step and that instead of an hour I may have to wait for years in front of those glass doors, but I will, and eventually we will altogether eradicate acid violence and improve women and child rights in Pakistan, it is feasible," shared Valerie.

Another challenge, which Valerie has faced, is the political instability and frequent changes in the government, which makes coordination with Government officials difficult.

"High rates of illiteracy makes interaction with affected communities even more challenging. Also, our survivors are from around the country. This geographical spread often makes it difficult for us to reach them," shared Valerie.

Despite all these challenges Valerie has managed to build and lead a team of around 15 people in her organization and help hundreds of women in the last several years.

"As the chairperson of ASF one of my key roles is my ability to keep morale high and demonstrate very high positive energy personally. My inspiration lies in the women and survivors whose lives we are helping re build. Women like Nazeraan. She is blind, yet she has learned braille and is learning to sew. As I mentioned earlier she is proof that the acid can burn you, but it cannot burn you entirely. It cannot burn your spirit as a woman. So when our survivors have so much courage and positivity, how can I have less?" shared Valerie.

Valerie shared how her learnings could be adapted to the corporate world.

- *First, we focus on positive communication:*
  Do not attack people. Instead engage. Focus on solutions, versus just the

problem.

- *We work on the basis of facts:*
  We are technical. We do our homework. We are evidence based and outcome oriented. In short, people know us to be tough, ethical, loyal, hard working, credible and dedicated to deliver results and change.

- *We collaborate and do not waste time on politics:*
  We synergise and acknowledge collective efforts. This is the reason why civil society in Pakistan as well as the media are also very supportive to our work. This has created a tremendous solidarity.

- *We work across levels, including at a grassroots level:*
  We involve the survivors themselves who share their story and demand solidarity and justice: it is a human mirror that we are proposing to responsibility holders and vastly all people see their reflection in those women and therefore decide to help. This way we promote democracy: acid survivors sat in the senate while senators were voting for the first law related to acid violence to be passed. All the policy makers could see them, sitting silently yet powerfully demanding justice via their dignified presence only.

"We have also managed to get the first government led rehabilitation center for victims of acid violence - the only one in the region. So we know that our belief in dialogue, partnership and technical expertise is working!" added Valerie.

"So our motto is work hard, exchange politely and focus, but continue until you've made it! Stay positive and never give up. Because indeed, far more work is needed."

I asked Valerie when she intended giving up on her "fighting for a cause" and whether the constant struggle ever affected her positivity.

"NEVER," came back the simple but emphatic answer.

Valerie had a few more tips on "Never giving up" for women professionals

- *Never see success as an end stage:*
  Think of managing success vs. "achieving success." You are least likely to give up on anything when you think that way.

- *Always look for the silver lining:*
  If you don't see it at first, look again. There almost always is. When one door closes, 100 others open.
- *Make resilience a habit. Fight laziness:*
  Be patient. Learn new skills. As an educator my life was so different but as chairperson for this organization I have to manage an extensive workload and I must always be learning process oriented.
- *Stay hopeful:*
  There is so much misery in the world. And if we sit by and do nothing, how can things be better? Think of others more than you think of self.
- *Be thankful for what you have:*
  Take inspiration from others courage and struggles.
- *Be humble and collaborative:*
  You will always achieve more if you use several brains instead of one, if you are ready to listen to various perspectives before taking a final decision, and if you are ok with making mistakes: one learns from them.
- *Be strategic:*
  Choose and select carefully your mentors and your team; always do your homework before starting a fight even if it takes you more time, to achieve you need credibility and one must be informed/competent.
- *Be sincere and ethical:*
  This is the only way you will convince and influence and the only way you will be respected.

Ella Stewart was only seven when she faced her first test of resilience and learned the power of never giving up.

"I was learning how to dive at the local swimming pool. It was intimidating. There were several boys there at the swimming pool. Some much older and stronger. But I had set my sights on diving off the highest board. The boys were afraid. They would not dive off the high board and kept diving off the lower boards. Not me. I kept going back up to the high board and kept practicing relentlessly. Not once did I consider giving up. I knew if I put in the hard work, I would be able to do it," shared Ella.

Just a few days later, Ella was diving off the high board perfectly.

Ella Stewart was born on April 27th in Rostov-on-Don, Russia. She graduated from the faculty of International Economic Relations of the Russian Federation Government Financial University in Moscow.

She started her career in advertising in 1996 as Financial Director of BBDO Moscow. Earlier Ella worked for Ernst & Young, Mars, Kraft Jacobs Suchard.

> *"To me focusing on the positive means taking ownership of your work with a passion that your colleagues and bosses can see and understand."*
>
> **Ella Stewart,** *Chief Executive Officer, BBDO Russia Group.*

In 2000 Stewart became Co-President of BBDO Russia Group. Since 2003 she has been Chairman of the Board, Chief Executive Officer of BBDO Russian Group. In May 2005 Ella became Russia's first representative in the BBDO Worldwide network Board of Directors.

Ella believes that it is still a male-dominated professional world wherein there are many challenges.

"The main challenge is to be perceived as a professional and not just as a woman. Combining work and family, the constant feeling of guilt for time not spent with your child, the expectation of always being well groomed, the need to have a variety of interests, and to manage the vulnerability that comes with being a woman – these are all additional challenges which women must face head on," shared Ella.

"Personally, I faced two main challenges. First, when my son was little, I had the constant feeling that I was not spending enough time with him. The feeling of guilt is still there. Second, now, since my son has grown older, I am trying to develop and grow. I want to learn more about art, get to know other cultures, learn languages. There is a catastrophic lack of time for all of this. That is why the feeling of opportunities gone creates a feeling of time ticking away – which is scary. But one must continue to look for the silver linings and keep going," shared Ella.

Focusing on the positive and not giving up is something that Ella has cultivated over the years. From that early incident at the age of seven in the pool, she resolved that she would just stay focused on her goals in life and keep going.

"I never give up and lose sight of my goals. I consider this to be the key to my success," shared Ella.

At 20, pregnant with her son, Ella aspired to join the prestigious Moscow State Financial Academy. She wanted to get into the International Economic Relations course, one of the toughest. Perfect English was required, which Ella did not have at all! She was in fact competing with the children of well-to-do Russian diplomats for entrance to the course. Undaunted, Ella travelled three hours several times a week to an English tutors place for three months. In three months she mastered English through sheer dint of hard work.

"It was not easy. Heavily pregnant with my son, the daily travel for hours was tough, and the progress in my opinion was excruciatingly slow. But three months later I indeed did pass the test, and was granted admission to this prestigious course," she added.

When her son Ilya was born, Ella had to continue her studies and her work in parallel. In 1991 she was earning just about 150 dollars a month, yet the cost of a basic baby sitter for her boy as she went to work and study was by itself over 300 dollars a month.

"My mother who helped support me through those very difficult years often commented that it would be more cost effective for me to sit at home with Ilya versus go to work at all," added Ella.

But Stewart persisted. In 10 years she did an outstanding job of developing an agency, which initially consisted of only 50 people, to a group with over 1000 employees.

One such example of her positive attitude and grit was a project when she was just 23.

"I was part of a group of 4 professionals deputed to do an audit of an Uzbekistan bank. It is important to understand that Uzbekistan – is Central Asia, and a country with the mentality to match. Our group was to be headed by a French manager, who was simply unable to fly in. I refused to abandon the audit and took charge of our group of four. At night, I studied the case and in the morning I gave out tasks to my colleagues. In two weeks, when the head of our audit group was finally able to fly in, we had already completed almost half of the work," shared Stewart.

As the quality of her work impressed her bosses, her salary went to 300 dollars a month, then kept increasing slowly but surely. Within three years she was earning a salary of over 2000 dollars!

"To me focusing on the positive means taking ownership of your work with a passion that your colleagues and bosses can see and understand," shared Stewart.

In 1998, when the global financial crisis struck, Stewart was by then heading the BBDO operations in Russia.

"It was an incredibly difficult situation. I remember the Russian currency had dropped from seven rubles to a dollar to 16 rubles to a dollar in a single day! There was chaos in the market. People were losing their jobs all round. I was faced with some very tough choices. I did not want to let go of the business we had worked so hard to build, or the people who had built it. So despite the challenges of the environment we crafted a plan to let go of only a max of 10% of our people in a worst case scenario." shared Stewart.

Stewart came up with an unconventional plan that would help keep the team together.

"I convinced all of our staff that if each of us (starting with myself) took up to an 80% cut in salary, we could survive the crisis as a team. It was traumatic for all of us but we never gave up. We stuck together. As news spread that we were not cutting stuff all round like other businesses were, we attracted the best talent in the industry to work for us. Today, many of the people who were with us through the financial crisis of 1998 are still with the company in very senior positions. Most important of all, after that crisis, we have found it so much easier to deal with crisis situations over the last few years. We know exactly what to do. We survived because we saw the upside and never gave up on our work in Russia," shared Stewart.

BBDO today is one of the top agencies in the market.

As Ella's reputation for success grew, recognition came from not just within her company but also from the external world. In 2011 Ella was ranked one of the most professional managers in Russia for the 9th time in a row by Russian

Managers Association and one of the most prestigious Russian business newspapers "Kommersant". In the same year she was elected President of the Moscow International "Red Apple" Advertising and Marketing Festival.

"Today, I am so proud that I never gave up on my pursuit of studying English. That single commitment changed my life in a dramatic way. I feel satisfied today that I am in fact on the honors list for the Moscow state Financial Academy," shared Ella.

Ella credits her Mum with building in her persistence and "never say die" attitude.

"My Mum is truly a very beautiful woman. She is incredibly hard working. She and my Dad were divorced when I was five. Yet my Mum brought me up, supported her parents and then supported me in the early stages of my career. All on her own hard work! She is still very active, working on her own real estate business," added Ella.

"My Mum's attitude of never giving up has rubbed off on me and also on my son! At the young age of 26, Ilya has his own production Company. All done on his own steam with ZERO financial support from me. Having him is my greatest achievement in life," shared Ella.

Stewart claims her second greatest achievement is building BBDO from scratch in Russia.

"I am the only woman to head a large communications holding company in Russia. Yes, there are other agency heads. But no woman at the head of a large communications holding company in Russia, a country that has its own unique challenges."

Stewart closed with some advice for our readers.

She commented:

- *Never give up:*
  Whatever the hardships keep going.

- *Believe in yourself:*
  If you don't believe in yourself, who will.

- *Invest in your personal life:*
  Harmony and success come along only if you are happy in your personal life.

- *Trust and love people around you:*
  They will repay you for that many times over.

- *Be a good example that inspires people:*
  When it comes down to it, you must be the example that inspires your people. If they see you behaving in a resilient manner and tackling the toughest of challenges with creativity and integrity, they will rise to the occasion too.

# Chapter 9

# DELIVER RESULTS

Results matter if one wants to move up into the rarified atmosphere of upper management. Irrespective of the level, organizations rely more heavily and often reward more handsomely the employees that are contributing most. I connected with three of the world's most results driven leaders- **Miki Tsusaka,** *Senior Partner and Managing Director of The Boston Consulting Group (BCG);* **Chanda Kochhar,** *CEO, ICICI Bank;* and **Dina Howell,** *CEO, Saatchi & Saatchi X* to understand their unique tips on delivering results consistently and earning high credibility within and outside of their organizations.

**M**iki Tsusaka says that the greatest achievement of her life is being a happy and healthy mother of three children and the wife and best friend of her college sweetheart for 28 years.

These might not sound like the words of a corporate leader. But Miki—a senior partner and managing director of The Boston Consulting Group (BCG), based in Tokyo, Japan—is one of the most powerful women in business in Asia and has been listed as one of the industry's top 25 most influential consultants.

Miki is currently responsible for leading BGC's global marketing function, in addition to serving a wide range of clients internationally and sitting on the firm's Executive Committee. Prior to her current role, Miki founded and led BCG's global Marketing & Sales practice, which constitutes more than 10 percent of the firm's revenues, covering the topics of marketing, sales, pricing, and consumer insight across eight industry practices.

> *"To be credible, you must first have the results that will attract attention to your work. Once you secure that credibility, it becomes far easier to get great assignments, approach potential mentors, and ultimately aspire to bigger successes."*
>
> **Miki Tsusaka**, Senior Partner and Managing Director of The Boston Consulting Group (BCG).

For Miki, success has always been about delivering results, both at the workplace and at home. "My father was an executive with a trading company, and my mother was a stay-at-home mom, a graduate student, a teacher, a college lecturer, a private college dean, and now a high school dean. My maternal grandmother was also a huge influence as she started the school my mother currently runs. The standard of results expected from me and my sister was always very clear," shared Miki.

Miki learned just how high her mother's expectations were when she came home from school one day in the third grade with a high score on a test paper. "The test was about naming the prefectures in Japan. You had to name all 47 prefectures to get a perfect score. I named most of them correctly and ended up with a score of 95. When I got home, I shared what I thought was good news with my mom. She looked at me and asked, 'What happened to the other 5?'"

Her parents' emphasis on excellence was coupled with a tremendous amount of encouragement and support. "We didn't have a lot of money in those days," Miki recalled. "But I played classical piano all the way through school. One day, my parents took me to Woolworth's in Queens, New York, and showed me a toy piano. And I told them, 'No. I want a real piano.' So with their savings, they bought me a lovely upright piano when I was in kindergarten. My father challenged me that if I was ever able to play Beethoven's Pathetique Sonata, he would buy me a grand piano."

Miki added, "There was no option but to deliver results as part of my upbringing. My parents were firm but fair, and their guidance put me on the path to a great education. We were coached consistently on the need to give our best effort, to be humble, and to be respectful of everyone around us."

By 1984, Miki received her undergraduate degree from Harvard College in Government and East Asian Studies. That same year, she and her husband, Jun Tsusaka, moved to Tokyo, where Miki joined BCG. The couple returned to the United States to attend Harvard Business School together. Upon graduation, Miki continued her career with BCG in New York, while her husband opted for a career on Wall Street.

The values her parents instilled in her have served Miki well in her career. "Life as a consultant at BCG has always been about delivering results as a member of a team. It has remained a rewarding career for me as success bred success. But there were many challenges along the way that I had to overcome both as a woman and as a professional, which made me even better at my job," commented Miki.

For example, in the early days at BCG, delivering results was about not only doing great work for her clients but also being part of a young team that built out BCG's New York office from the dozen people of the early days to its current number of around 500. Miki assumed a number of management roles, including running internal people processes such as recruiting and career development.

"We had very few resources and little infrastructure, so we had to be creative in leaning on the entire staff to keep doing more than the base workload. It required long hours. But with every recruit, with every new floor we opened, with every new client, we were so excited about what we were building that the days and weeks went by in a flash," Miki shared. "These experiences under such challenging circumstances helped me build management skills at an early age, and I became recognized as someone who could be counted on to build out an office and perform a variety of line functions while serving clients."

Miki's experience running people processes and a business internally clearly helped on the client side. Consider Miki's five-year tenure running BCG's global postmerger integration (PMI) efforts, leading a team developing unique IP, tools, and approaches—then marketing this expertise to clients and, most important, applying these tools and techniques to real client situations. Miki worked directly on many successful global PMIs in the consumer goods, pharmaceuticals, and technology industries. Moreover, she helped her clients "beat the odds" of PMI failures, which typically fail to deliver positive outcomes two-thirds of the time. "These deals are once-in-a-lifetime big events for most companies, and being there at that critical juncture creates lasting impressions and impact. I am very grateful for such opportunities to create value for our clients in a real and material way," she shared.

Miki also points to her founding role as the global head of the relaunched Marketing & Sales practice. Although the practice began as an internal initiative, over the last seven years, Miki and her global team established the practice's external presence with clients. Emphasizing "fewer, bigger, better," she took a sequential but aggressive approach to developing the practice pillars of marketing, sales, pricing, and consumer insights. Synthesizing and building on client experiences, launching unique primary research, hiring a slate of external expert practitioners, and marketing and delivering the expertise to the client base were critical to ensuring the success of the practice.

Miki commented, "Much of the success was the result of mobilizing my peers and getting back to the people side of things. Getting people energized and excited to contribute to growing something new and different—often on top of the usual base load of client work—is no easy feat. But forming the right team of leaders and recruiting the right people to follow and amplify the message was, for me, the most important aspect of how I delivered on this mission."

Miki is quick to share that while her career looks quite smooth on the surface, life in the consulting profession is not without its ups and downs. "I remember that in 1994, in the midst of a highly challenging career and being a new mom, I was working nonstop for one client in the beauty industry and another in the health care industry with very different and intense problems. The time and energy demanded from these two clients was enormous. I finally hit the wall and in desperation turned to one of my mentors, Dr. Sandy Moose, who was then the head of the New York office," recalled Miki. "Sandy sat down with me and went through my calendar day by day. She highlighted some things that were obvious to her but not to me. She created 25 percent more space in my calendar by identifying opportunities to consolidate meetings, shorten meetings, eliminate meetings. And at the same time, she added back to the calendar time for my family, my friends, and myself. It was an eye opener for me."

Miki put that advice to good use. In 1995, she was promoted to partner at BCG—and Sandy Moose has remained one of Miki's primary mentors.

"Sandy is widely regarded as the most brilliant and perhaps first female consultant in our industry. In fact, when she was head of the New York office, the office composition was at one point 50 percent women. She taught me many life lessons, including clients coming first, the need to always deliver, respect for the individual, making time for friends and family, and investing in a good wardrobe. 'Looking good makes you feel good,' Sandy would say!"

Miki has confronted other professional challenges through the years, but she sought and received help from her mentors, friends, and even clients. She continued to work more or less full time through the birth of her three children—Mia, Ken, and Jo, who were born in the United States in 1992, 1995, and 2000, respectively—with the help of what Miki described as "the best nanny in the world."

In 2007, Miki's life took an unexpected turn when her husband was offered a position back in Japan. Having spent nearly 20 years in the United States,

Miki found that working in Japan was a very different experience. "Japanese culture, like many others, historically has assumed that the woman's job was to stay home and take care of the kids. You have to respect the culture and the choices each and every family makes. But in today's society, the choice is for the woman to make, especially if she has the financial freedom to chose to work or not," commented Miki.

Miki reflected on the 2013 gender gap rankings, recently released by the World Economic Forum, which placed Japan 105 out of the 136 countries surveyed: "So much has changed for women. And while Japan remains low on the global list, I am hopeful that this will—and has to—change. I look forward to doing my part here."

The key to Miki's ability to deliver results has been achieving work-life balance—what she calls "work-life blend" because the two parts don't compete for share of mind but are an integrated whole. "Behind most of the results that I have delivered during my career was my practiced ability to focus and manage my work and family together," shared Miki. "Like every other working mother, I believe that I don't spend enough time with my children. So I focused on little things that I could do for them that ensured we stayed connected and then helped me focus on my work more deliberately."

This included sending faxes to the kids from her business travels long before the advent of e-mail, setting clear priorities, getting home for occasions that were important to her children, soliciting help from her friends and family, and, perhaps most important of all, sharing responsibilities with her husband.

"The support I have received from my husband has been particularly critical. But I also had to work towards alignment with him and securing his support. We are grateful we can have everything we want in life—just not everything at the same time. We got this alignment right in the early days of our relationship when we decided to study at business school together, so I am indeed very fortunate," she added.

What is Miki's advice for women in the workplace? "I have been brought up to deliver results and keep my promises. Both are essential for young women to progress in the workplace. To be credible, you must first have the results that will attract attention to your work. Once you secure that credibility, it becomes far easier to get great assignments, approach potential mentors, and ultimately aspire to bigger successes."

Today Miki is passing on her ability to deliver results to others at work and in the community. She leads BCG's Women's Initiative in Asia as part of the firm's global mission to recruit and retain the best professional female talent. In addition, she is a member of the Japan Association of Corporate Executives, J-WIN (Japan Women's Innovation Network) Executive group, the Ministry of Education's National University Assessment Committee, the American Chamber of Commerce in Japan, and the American School in Japan's board.

"I am honored to have been able to help clients achieve their very best results and to have served a wide range of consumer-facing companies, including those in beauty and personal care, food and beverage, apparel and fashion, consumer electronics and durables, retail services, and media," Miki commented.

But some of Miki's happiest moments are when she finds the time to play the grand piano that her husband bought her when they had their first child to fulfill the promise her father made to her many years ago. It serves as a reminder of her fundamental life principle: deliver results.

Miki's top tips to deliver results:

- *Keep your promises:*
  To be credible, you must first demonstrate the results that will draw attention to your work.

- *Attract good mentors:*
  They will help you grow, and guide and challenge you.

- *Ask for challenging assignments:*
  They will pave the way to bigger successes.

- *Forge a strong alignment with your partner:*
  If you share responsibilities with your partner, you will expand your capacity and effectiveness.

- *Maintain your personal 'blend' between work and family with:*
  A balanced professional is a more effective professional.

**C**handa Kochhar is the first-ever woman **Managing Director and CEO of ICICI Bank,** one of India's most prestigious financial institutions. In 2013 Chanda was ranked fourth on Fortune Magazine's global list of top 50 women business leaders and also listed as the most powerful businesswoman in India (for the third consecutive year) by Fortune. Chanda has also featured for several years on Forbes list of the 100 most powerful women in business and was awarded the 'Retail Banker of the Year' 2004 by The Asian Banker. Apart from being on the Board of ICICI Bank and various group companies, she is a member of the Prime Minister's Council on Trade & Industry.

*"Grow through merit. Results are what matter."*

*Chanda Kochhar, first-ever woman Managing Director and CEO of ICICI Bank.*

Chanda was conferred with the Padma Bhushan, one of India's highest civilian honors, in 2011.

Tremendous achievements for a woman who has based her career success on a critical factor – Delivering results!

"I believe that women can and should grow only through merit and the results they deliver. Women should not think that they will be treated as second grade citizens and hence, will not be given opportunities. Likewise, they should never expect any special privileges or opportunities to be created for them because of their gender. For example, if they believe that they are as suitable as a man for any role, then they must be willing to do whatever it is the man could do to fulfill that role – travel, long hours of work, etc. If they demonstrate this in every role and deliver solid results in every assignment, success will come," she shared candidly.

Chanda leads by example. In 2013, a year when the Indian economy took a hit, Chanda led India's largest private bank to yet another profitable year. Chanda today oversees about USD 90 billion in assets (as on September 30, 2013), 3,507 branches and the Bank's operations in 19 countries. ICICI is considered one of India's greatest success stories, with over 25% year on year increase in standalone profit after tax for the last three years.

Chanda's focus on results results started as a child. Born in the beautiful city of Jodhpur, Rajasthan, India, she finished her schooling at St. Angela Sophia School and went on to complete her Bachelor of Arts degree from Jai Hind College, Mumbai. She then earned a Masters in Management Studies (Finance) from the Jamnalal Bajaj Institute of Management Studies, Mumbai and is also a Cost Accountant from the Institute of Cost and Works Accountants of India. Chanda excelled throughout her academic years.

In 1984, Chanda started her career as a Management Trainee with ICICI and over the next few years handled a number of increasingly important roles across all of the major functions in ICICI.

"When I joined ICICI 30 years ago, India was at a very different stage of development in terms of women succeeding in the workplace; so there definitely were challenges. The thing that was unique about ICICI even way back then was the culture based on merit. At ICICI there was no gender discrimination. So that meant women had the same opportunities as men, but that meant that they were expected to face the same level of challenge and hardship as any male employee. I was required to visit remote factories and plant sites, travel extensively just like what was expected of any male employee. It was tough, but you earned a certain amount of credibility and respect by demonstrating your commitment. I am proud to say that women employees at ICICI do not seek special benefits based on gender," shared Chanda.

Chanda demonstrated that commitment over and over again as the years passed. She was instrumental in establishing ICICI Bank during the 1990s, and subsequently headed the infrastructure finance and corporate banking business in ICICI Limited. In 2000, she took on the challenge of building the nascent retail business, with a strong focus on technology, innovation, process reengineering and expansion of distribution and scale. The Bank achieved a leadership position in this business.

During 2006-2007, she successfully led the Bank's corporate and international banking businesses during a period of heightened activity and global expansion by Indian companies. From 2007 to 2009, she was the Joint Managing Director & Chief Financial Officer during a critical period of rapid change in the global financial landscape.

In 2008 at the height of the global financial crisis, Chanda was at the helm of the efforts to bring stability to the banking operations at ICICI.

"It was one of the toughest times in my career. People automatically assumed that since ICICI has offices in multiple countries, we are a global bank, so if something goes wrong with the global economy, ICICI will be affected. I had to get into every detail. We set up a control room, and I had to work through very detailed plans with the team on how to communicate with employees, how to work to satisfy the small depositors who came to our branches, how to handle the larger investors, regulators and at the same time communicate with media. It was relentless, stressful work," shared Chanda.

Chanda successfully negotiated through those turbulent times keeping regulators, investors, the media and ICICI employees abreast and satisfied that ICICI was adequately equipped to weather the crisis.

And ICICI did weather that crisis.

By focusing multiple stakeholders on what mattered most - cost efficiency, credit quality, capital conservation and current/ savings account expansion, Chanda was able to turn the crisis into an opportunity for ICICI.

Within a year the bank had increased its capital adequacy, improved its share of current and savings account deficit and prevented slippages in non-performing assets.

In 2009, Chanda was elevated as Managing Director & CEO of ICICI Bank and is responsible for the Bank's diverse operations in India and overseas. She also chairs the boards of the Bank's principal subsidiaries, which include India's leading private sector life and general insurance companies.

Today, ICICI is India's largest privately owned bank with assets of over USD 90 billion and is rapidly spreading its footprint across the world.

"We have transformed from a development bank to a retail bank to best serve the interests of our rapidly expanding segment of customers across India and across the world. We are intent on creating and sustaining our growth over the long term," shared Chanda.

Chanda manages her career alongside her role as Mum to her daughter Aarti and son Arjun.

"As much as women would like to bucket their personal lives and the work life, it is not always possible. You just have to manage both. I find it challenging sometimes to stick to fixed hours at work. I carry work home all the time. Yet, at the same time, I think its perfectly fine to take a few minutes during your work day to check on the children, make sure they are home safe, etc.," shared Chanda.

Kochhar shared with me her top principles for delivering results.

- *Know the vision and direction of the organization:*
  Know the core fundamental principles that the organization believes in. Align your actions to these principles. This is perhaps the single most important enabler of success.

- *Prioritize minute by minute:*
  This is very important if you want to truly get to the top. For a woman this is the basic essential to be able to manage both career and family life.

- *Stay in touch with trends that affect your business:*
  This is one of the most important roles of the leader – to make sure you are in touch with reality and with broad trends. Today the need for speed is so great from leaders – often you need to get things done in 90 days, sometimes even less! Staying connected with what is happening in the world and what could impact you is a critical element.

- *Trust your gut:*
  There are several times when we get into analysis paralysis, because we keep asking for more and more information. In my experience the best decisions I have made are based on fact and instinct. You will never have 100% of the data, but you will have sufficient to make a decision in conjunction with what your gut is telling you.

- *Be a good listener. Then communicate:*
  Understand what people are saying inside and outside your organization. Take into account the viewpoints of all of your stakeholders. Then communicate your logic and rationale well to share with all why you are doing what you are doing, how it will benefit the organization and others over the medium to long term. I make regular visits to all our branches,

often unannounced, and hold regular employee meetings.

- *Keep learning for the future:*
  Never ever stop learning. When you make mistakes, course correct quickly, and don't ignore the problem.

- *Finally, excel at whatever level or role you are at in the organization:*
  At different stages of your career you will play different roles in an organization. Make sure you give your best at every level and every role so that people associate you with performance. Your aim should be to do the job better than others, at each level.

Chanda is confident that the status of women in the workplace in India and across the world will improve over the next few years.

"In reality, there has been a lot of progress in the last 30 years in the role women are playing in leadership in India. Many Indian operations are in fact going out of their way to attract and retain women talent. There is a long way to go yet for women, but clearly the attitudes towards women leading in the workplace has changed," shared Chanda.

Chanda is proud of the fact that under her direction ICICI is playing an important role in the empowerment of women in India.

"I am aware of the huge challenges facing women in the country, especially in the economically challenged sections of society. ICICI is working with 45,000 self help groups for women wherein we provide small loans, nurture these women, teach them how to consolidate their resources and create sustainable opportunities for themselves in their villages at the grassroots level. The most satisfying part of this program is that we see women growing in confidence once they are economically self-sufficient. They are then able to have a voice and identity in their communities, they can contribute to social development in their villages and districts," shared Chanda.

Chanda shared that she has witnessed how empowered women such as these, stand up for what is right at a grass root level on things that may appear small to developed cities but are life changing for small rural communities.

"I have seen these women fight for the proper setting up of wells for safe water in their villages or vote against the setting up of a liquor store next to a school in a village. They are active, aware of their social rights and are making a difference," she added.

The self-help groups already cover 600,000 rural women today. Chanda's dream is to extend that to 1 million women in the coming years.

Today, in addition to her responsibilities at the ICICI Group, Chanda is a member of the Prime Minister's Council on Trade & Industry, the Board of Trade, High-Level Committee on Financing Infrastructure, US-India CEO Forum and UK-India CEO Forum. She is a member of the boards of the Indian Council for Research on International Economic Relations, National Institute of Securities Markets, Institute of International Finance and International Monetary Conference. She was co-chair of the World Economic Forum's Annual Meeting in 2011.

Chanda values the time she gets with her family in the midst of her hectic schedule.

"After a hard day's work, I look forward to sitting down with my family, having a meal with them and simply spend the evening chatting about what's going on in our lives. I feel blessed that I have been successful in my career, but equally important is the fact that I can share this success with my family," concluded Chanda.

**D**ina Howell is Chief Executive Officer of Saatchi & Saatchi X, the most-awarded shopper-marketing network in the world. Saatchi & Saatchi X has been globally transforming how brands and retailers connect with shoppers since it's founding in 1997 and is the shopper-marketing agency for the worldwide Saatchi & Saatchi family of agencies.

A pioneer and architect of shopper marketing, Dina is a well-known international authority on the fastest growing segment in marketing today. As an industry expert, she is cited in the landmark study by Deloitte Consulting on Shopper Marketing; wrote the Foreword to Google's "ZMOT, the Zero Moment of Truth"; and is often quoted in business publications, such as The Wall Street Journal, The Economic Times, Shopper Marketing, and Ad Age.

Dina joined Saatchi & Saatchi X in 2010 after retiring from a 22-year career at Procter & Gamble. While at P&G, she served as Vice President Global Media and Brand Operations and led the establishment of shopper and retailer marketing within the company.

"I have always believed that to succeed it is fundamentally about delivering results and demonstrating a track record of performance, irrespective of gender," Dina shared. "Women and men are different: their perspectives are different, their points of relevance and foundations are different. Understanding the commonalities of women and men around the world is much more important than just focusing on their differences. To be successful, to have excellent results, you need to understand all shoppers."

> *"I have always believed that to succeed it is fundamentally about delivering results and demonstrating a track record of performance, irrespective of gender, Most of the worlds CEOs were promoted to their positions because they delivered results and remain in the C-suite because they continue to deliver results."*
>
> **Dina Howell,** *Chief Executive Officer, Saatchi & Saatchi X.*

"Most of the worlds CEOs were promoted to their positions because they delivered results and remain in the C-suite because they continue to deliver results. You must become an EXPERT on your subject. You get to the top by being competent, by being much better than most at something," she added.

Dina's focus on results started in her childhood.

"I think one of the biggest influences on my attitude and approach to life was my parent's unhappy marriage. To the world, they were a normal couple. But behind closed doors, tensions were very high. In a strange way, it taught me to block out distractions and hardship, staying focused on what I wanted to be and what I aspired to achieve," she commented. "I am the youngest of three children, so there was always sibling competition and I liked to win. I started playing a stock and bonds trading game with my family at the age of five, that we all still play today. I learned very early that no one in my family was going to let me win because I was five. If I wanted to win, I needed to earn it. So I studied hard and modified my strategies. Our family games have always been highly competitive, therefore most of our spouses choose not to participate as they describe them as oddly cut-throat."

Born in 1962, Dina spent her early years in New York. "My father's job required us to move quite a lot and I spent my junior high years in Kentucky before they finally moved to Ohio. I went to the University of Kentucky for a couple of years before meeting the love of my life, Duane, and moving back to Ohio. I graduated from college and got married all on the same day. Once it is clear which direction I am going to go, I just go do it.

I joined P&G in 1988, and that is where my inner drive to achieve and produce strong results was really tested. Everything in business is a competition; the best P&L, strongest growth in categories, largest brand volumes. Men are taught from an early age to keep score. You either win or lose. Women, traditionally, have been taught to be more relational – everyone needs to win."

Dina shared that in the late 1980s when she started work, there were few role models in terms of other successful women in the workplace so ensuring that she received time from role models was critically important to her development. Today, Dina mentors many women and men to help them succeed.

"It is never easy to show you are vulnerable, especially for a businesswoman at that time, but there were people who were willing to invest in me, for which I am grateful. It took a lot of courage to make that first ask for help. Many of these relationships and friendships are still close friends today. It also instilled in me an incredible desire to do whatever it takes to deliver the results to make these mentors proud that they had invested their time with me," shared Dina.

The other big challenge according to Dina is the reality that women have the children and are therefore forced at times to choose between a family or aggressive career growth, as often the times overlap. "Many leaders, male or female who have chosen not to have children, have difficulty believing you can be a great Mom and a great leader," she shared.

"After each of my two pregnancies, I went back to work after six weeks. You are still not ready after six weeks to return and it was a huge emotional challenge. But I managed it by calling on a support network of some family and close friends. Not going back to work was not a financial or personal option, so when faced with the challenges you have to find a suitable solution," she added.

"Shortly after our second child was born and I was given the opportunity to make a career defining move to work on the P&G Walmart team. My husband and I made the decision that he would stay home while I actively pursued my career. It was a radical and very unusual decision at the time for a man to be the homemaker, although it is much more common today. Because this decision was different from the norm, it was a society adjustment as well as a family adjustment for both of us.

Fortunately, due to Dina's leadership, it is much easier for women today, many of whom credit Dina for breaking through.

"There is no doubt that I would have probably dropped out of P&G without the support that Dina gave me during my pregnancies, and after," said Julie Walker, P&G Director of Business Development for Sam's Club. "She made it possible for me to do my job, have a family, and be successful at both."

Dina recalled; "When the opportunity came up to move to the Walmart team, there was a lot of discussion that this move could be a career killer. It was a very high profile assignment and the customer did not view marketing as important at that time. My job would be to create the demand for marketing across our business globally."

The P&G/Walmart assignment proved to be pivotal as Dina led the charge for how the CPG Industry worked with retailers, utilizing CPG marketing skills and expertise. P&G added $1 Billion in new sales, which were attributed to Dina and her marketing team during her seven-year tenure on the Walmart assignment.

Dina believes that delivering results is very important, but delivering results through nurturing relationships is even more powerful.

She shared, "In 2004, my boss Bob McDonald (former Chairman and CEO of P&G) shared with me "If we ever want something done, we know we can come to you, Dina. The problem is, you surround yourself only with people who deliver results and you sometimes struggle with people who don't deliver as fast or as completely as you want. You will need to learn how to get results out of all people in order to continue to grow your career further."

It was not feedback that was easy for Dina to hear, but she set her mind to the challenge.

"With the help of Wynn Baldock, a superb executive coach, I learned how to let myself be more vulnerable, share my softer and empathic side, which helped me become more approachable to people. In a few months the results started to show. A different kind of result to be sure. My direct reports began to flourish and it was a great learning experience for all of us. Shortly after that, I was promoted to Vice President Global Brand and Media Operations," commented Dina.

"Changing my behavior and cultivating a more inclusive leadership style while in the workplace was the most difficult thing I ever had to learn. But, it helped me continue to deliver results by taking my entire team along. The reality is that perception does matter. For a man, if you are aggressive and focused only on the goal, that's perceived as being a strong leader. If a woman behaves that exact way, she would be labeled a b----" shared Dina. "That's just the perception today that hopefully women are changing so our strong daughters won't deal with the same labeling."

Since moving to the agency side, Dina has continued to take the learnings and coaching from her executive coach to her new team.  Under her leadership, the agency has been honored with over 125 industry and client awards, including earning four times more Shopper Marketing Effie Awards than any other agency.  All in a short three years.

Dina had the following advice in terms of delivering results and exceeding the expectations of her bosses.

- *Understand your own personal brand and be as authentic as possible:* I have always been an extremely candid person and I have used this to provide constructive feedback over my career. The key was to be candid without being abrasive or rude. And, to know when and how to share your opinion and when to wait for a better time.

- *Be the best at what you do:*
  The person people know they have to "go to" on a particular topic. And then, deliver.
  Control your emotions and think before acting.

- *Any behavior or skill if taken too far becomes a weakness:*
  For example if you are a natural extrovert, you could be perceived as "over the top" or over friendly by a more sober set of peers. If you are far too bold, you be perceived as too aggressive. Moderate your actions based on your audience while retaining your focus on what you are trying to do.

- *Keep your promises on deadlines:*
  Nothing builds trust better than basic reliability. Your managers and peers should be able to believe that you will do exactly what you say you will do.

- *Don't brag, but do spend some time advocating and getting others to advocate your results:*
  A track record of success is built on the momentum delivering results.

- *Remember the people who helped you to get where you are:*
  Do not underestimate the power of a simple "thank you" to a boss, mentor or colleague who has invested in you.

- *And always remember to help other women up the ladder:*
  Advocate for them, mentor them, and lean in, and hopefully our daughters will have a more equitable business environment.

# Chapter 10

# GIVE
## AND
### TAKE SUPPORT

Research shows that collaboration increases efficiency and effectiveness. Flying in formation for example greatly boosts the efficiency and range of migrating birds. By working together, and taking turns at the front of the formation, it is estimated that each bird can reduce induced drag by 65% and as a result increase their range by 71%. Collaboration and giving and taking support is a prized quality in the business world as well. I spoke to **Lynne Anne Davis,** *President, Asia Pacific Fleishman Hillard;* **Cilla Snowball,** *Group Chairman* and *Group CEO, AMV BBDO;* and **Louise Beehag,** *Head of Executive Education, Lee Kuan Yew School of Public Policy.*

**L**ynne Anne Davis is President, Asia Pacific, FleishmanHillard. Based in Hong Kong, Lynne Anne oversees FleishmanHillard's Asia Pacific operations, encompassing 19 wholly owned offices in 10 countries.

Lynne Anne was born in Connecticut, USA. In her early years she was impressed by two important personalities in her life – her father Gerald Stevenson and her grandmother Vivian Bradford.

> *"In today's Corporate and social environment it is impossible for anyone to go it alone, no matter how gifted or hard working. Over the years I have benefitted so much from the support of others. And I attempt to pay it forward. That means repaying the many kindnesses I've received by doing good turns to others."*
>
> **Lynne Anne Davis,**
> President,
> FleishmanHillard Asia
> Pacific.

From her father, Lynne Anne developed her appetite for career adventures and the courage to move out of her comfort zone.

"He was the first of his family to attend college. Determined to provide more for his family than he had growing up, my father was extremely ambitious and therefore willing to move our family in order to take a better job and move up in his career. Our address was always changing, from Connecticut to Canada, Florida to England and back to the US even before I was six years old. His success taught me the value of hard work, being open to new challenges and taking risks," Lynne Anne softly shared.

"From my grandmother, I had an early impression of how many thrilling life choices lay at my feet. She was one of the first women to graduate from the well-respected University of Missouri School of Journalism, which also became my alma mater. She went on to be a newspaper columnist, a tap dance instructor, an in-store detective, a high school teacher and a genealogist. A mother of three, she was a circuit judge's wife and actively campaigned for my grandfather. What an incredibly full, rich life of experience and adventure she led. She never talked about challenges, only passions. She was a fascinating person," shared Lynne Anne.

But the biggest additional takeaway Lynne Anne had from these two towering personalities in her life was the ability to work collaboratively with others and to give and take support.

"In today's Corporate and social environment it is impossible for anyone to go it alone, no matter how gifted or hard working. Women face tremendous challenges in the work place still. A dearth of inspiring female role models, the fear of finding balance, the 'audacity' to aspire higher or to put their hands up to take the P&L reins," shared Lynne Anne.

Lynne Anne has faced several of her own challenges in career. But she has always managed to learn from her experiences.

In 1987 at her first job out of college, in an advertising agency, she made a major error distributing radio spots to stations across the Midwest U.S.

"Late that evening I was madly scrambling to stuff reels into envelopes and get them 'overnighted' (remember, this was the '80s – faxes existed, but no email). The head of the agency walked by and asked how I was doing. I blurted out a full confession about my stupid mistake and waited for the backlash. He simply asked if I was making it right. When I said yes, he smiled and replied, 'Fantastic! You're doing a great job'. This was one of my earliest lessons in considerate management. And the power of having people around you who would offer support versus unproductive and harsh criticism that unnecessarily dampens drive and enthusiasm," shared Lynne Anne.

In 1990, Lynne Anne joined FleishmanHillard as assistant account executive.

After working for several years in FleishmanHillard's global headquarters in the US, she craved change, and put her hand up for an international assignment.

That opportunity came in early 1997 when as a recently promoted vice-president, she was seconded to Hong Kong just in time to witness its historic change in sovereignty.

"My one-year assignment was to acclimate a small acquisition into our network and our culture, and build business. When the principal unexpectedly returned to the UK in late 1998, as many Europeans did when the Asian economic crisis hit, I was appointed GM of the Hong Kong office and its nine staff members. My ascent to GM, however, was not automatic. After an exhaustive search that came up empty, the decision was made to give me a chance. I was eager to accept the challenge and prove it was a safe bet," shared Lynne Anne.

Up to then, client service and strategic counseling were Lynne Anne's expertise, having come from a large well-managed team in a massive, well-established operation in the US.

"I had never run an office, never picked a team, never managed a large-scale budget, and never pitched business on a regular basis. All that changed overnight.

"Was I scared? Absolutely. More than anything, I felt the pressure of so many people counting on me – staff, clients, and headquarters. Survival skills kicked in. Our firm's culture had taught me that if you build the best place to work to attract the best people – respect and appreciate them wildly -- then the great clients and financial success will follow," she shared.

Lynne Anne reached out for help. Beth Boswell, a colleague parachuted in from the Toronto office to build an IT practice as the tech boom loomed on Asia's horizon.

"She became the left brain to my right, the yin to my yang, and one of the best thinkers and coaches in our business. Having diametrically opposing styles, we rarely saw eye to eye (even to this day!), which ensured every decision was punch tested and smarter for it. I learned yet again the power of taking support and giving it," laughed Lynne Anne.

After consistent and exhaustive efforts to pitch new business and bring onboard professionals passionate about being part of a longer-term success story, word of mouth spread on the FleishmanHillard team, and the positive recommendations and referrals from happy first clients such as Samantha English sparked more business. By the end of 2000, the Company was handling Asia tours of Fortune 50 CEOs, start-ups, product launches, M&A's and marquee clients. Revenues had more than tripled over three years.

FleishmanHillard was named Asia Pacific Consultancy of the Year in the 2000 Asia PR Awards.

In 2001, the dot-com downturn followed by 911 became the one-two punch that floored the Asian economy.

"Our business was not immune. From managing growth to managing costs, it turned into an instant MBA in leadership through the best and worst of times. And another example of how taking and giving support would be critical to the long term health of our business," shared Lynne Anne.

The company asked Lynne Anne to run the 10-office region.

She commented, "Our centers of excellence at that time were in Tokyo, Hong Kong and Singapore, but the rest of the region demanded greater consistency. More and more China was the common denominator for regional RFPs, so strengthening our leadership there was imperative. For years, the conventional thinking in our industry was that Westerners should oversee their China business, primarily because the client opportunities were multinational corporations turning to Asia to tap new markets. But instinctively I knew I needed help to find the best communications consultant in Beijing to run our Mainland China business, and that leader must be Chinese."

Lynne Anne did her research through industry press and talked to dozens of people to learn who was the very best.

"Then I found a mutual friend to make the 'shoulder tap' and connect with the top choice and prepared for my first meeting with a well-known marketing and public affairs expert who was running the largest global advertising business in Beijing at the time after building up its PR arm, Mr. Li Hong. I showed up at the breakfast café of Beijing's China World Hotel armed with a case for joining our firm around the hot buttons of his career aspirations. Long story short: in 2013, Li Hong celebrated 11 years with our firm as president of our China operations, having grown the business more than 16 times over, with impressive profitability. He leads with his head and his heart with unbridled passion for our business that has been absolutely game changing for Fleishman Hillard," she added.

Lynne Anne's ability to seek support as well as give it has been critical in expanding this local leadership model in nearly every market in which FleishmanHillard does business in Asia Pacific with 90% of the offices run by local nationals.

"In retrospect, probably my biggest challenge as a female professional was making the transition to working mother and especially when I had my first child," she reflected.

"Before getting married and having kids, I had all the time in the world for work and for me. From the moment the first baby arrived September 1, 2007, 'me' got pushed so far off my priority list that I couldn't find it," shared Lynne Anne.

She added, "Just before I delivered my first, we learned that our office had to move far east on Hong Kong Island, and depending on traffic -- about 30 minutes to an hour from our flat. My crazy travel schedule was getting more intense as our network continued to expand as the fastest growing part of FH worldwide. It was important to me to nurse my children as long as possible, far past the six weeks of maternity leave. I was distressed. What lay before me was a huge unknown," she added.

Then help came from an unexpected source.

Lynne Anne continued, "One evening, when I was in the 10th month of pregnancy -- you know, the one they don't tell you about - my neighbor came over, carrying a black briefcase. At the time, she was one of GE's top in-house attorneys and is Asia Pacific's foremost authority on FCPA compliance. Her geographic remit and travel schedule were almost identical to mine. She had just weaned her second son. Kelly Austin looked me straight in the eye and said: You can do this. I did. And so can you."

"That was no ordinary little black briefcase. In it was hidden a breast pump. It was, in fact, an Authentic Medela double electric Pump-In-Style Advanced model with 2-phase expression technology and a maximum comfort vacuum in an On-The-Go case (that they don't even make any more)," added Lynne Anne.

After returning to work and to travel, Lynne Anne's sons were nursed exclusively for more than six months, thanks to this unique bit of support from Kelly.

"In turn I passed on the incognito breast pump to a friend and former colleague who runs corporate communications for Disney Asia Pacific, Alannah Hall-Smith. That little black bag came with a message: You can do this. I did. So can you, and reassurance that a friend with this very breast pump had been down that road, and on that plane, in that passenger lounge rest room, even in the board room of our parent company offices on Madison Avenue!" shared Lynne Anne.

"Alannah nursed her daughter, then her son with it for many months. She then passed it on to an entrepreneur who set up her own business focusing on curating high-end children's toys. She passed it later to a media executive for a television cable channel. Each time it came with the same message.

"That mantra: 'You can do this. I did. So can you' is incredibly powerful and essential to encouraging women to take on challenges with confidence, and helping teach them it's possible to integrate more into already full lives. This 'sisterhood of the travelling breast pump' became the most unexpected icon for taking and giving support," added Lynne Anne.

Lynne Anne finds it easy to take support and give it. Her management style has always focused on building a culture based on kindness and respect and also "paying it forward".

"I am a firm believer that a culture built on kindness and respect is a growth driver, it's too under-rated and it brings out the best in everyone," she shared.

"Routine acts of graciousness and consideration add up and keep this reputation alive. Clients notice, too.

My colleague, Bill Black, in Washington, D.C., was at a launch event with a global Chinese client who mentioned how important it is for his company to build a strong corporate culture in North America. Bill chimed in about how we exported ours around the world. The client stopped him and said, "I know all about your culture. In fact, I am trying to emulate it." He whipped out his iPhone and began scrolling until he found what he was looking for. It was a picture he had taken of the poster in our office of our corporate philosophy. He showed it to his colleague and began reading the items approvingly. "See," he said, "it starts with people. Respect for the individual." He continued down the list, "Teamwork is everything, etc." His colleague nodded vigorously. As Bill said, "It was a very nice moment," shared Lynne Anne.

Lynne Anne added, "Giving and taking support also means one must mentor and pay it forward."

"After all, it's nearly impossible to think of a problem we could face in our line of work that others around us or across the network haven't encountered and conquered somewhere along the way," she added.

Lynne Anne also credits FleishmanHillard Chairman John Graham as someone who has influenced her leadership style of collaboration and giving and taking support and building a culture of respect and excellence.

"On the day before I left for Hong Kong in 1997, John met with me to offer advice and encouragement, and to make sure I felt prepared for the challenges ahead. As always, he stressed the importance of fostering a strong people-first culture and to let me know the firm had my back. As we have expanded in Asia Pacific, the collaborative culture and values inspired by John continue to be a positive driving force today," she shared.

"Over the years I have benefitted so much from the support of others. And I attempt to pay it forward. That means repaying the many kindnesses I've received by doing good turns to others," she added.

Lynne Anne shared how she had carefully cultivated the ability to give and take support over the results, which has played a big role in her success.

- *First, be open and transparent about your aspirations, the challenges you face and the help you need:*
  The concept of balance looks and feels different for everyone. This calls for open-minded employers initiating dialogues about how to adjust the right fit to retain their female stars, and ensure satisfaction all around. Likewise, women need to speak up and volunteer recommendations about what kind of flexibility they need in order to continue their careers and not only cope, but thrive. I am open about my children and

declaring why something at work may need to shift around them, be it a meeting, business trip or teleconference that overlaps with private time or a family obligation.

- *Second, be proactive about who you tap for help:*
  Create a list of people in your organization – your own "kitchen cabinet" -- who you know excel at certain things. Go to them for advice in those areas. A great example was when I moved to Hong Kong in 1997. I had never run an office before, but with support from a few specific colleagues I was able to borrow from their vast experience. A University of Virginia and Harvard study found that people with three mentors are more likely to get promoted than someone with one or two.

- *Do what you can to build a culture of respect, because that attracts and keeps high-performing women:*
  People ultimately make or break the culture of an organization, across levels, across hierarchy. At whatever level you are, remember to help build a considerate culture with high emotional intelligence that expects professional courtesy, shows appreciation and empathy, and rewards collaboration. A culture where women feel safe to speak their mind and take risks. Having women in leadership roles is an important element for a culture that brings out the best in all staff - both female and male.

- *Have the audacity to aspire higher:*
  If there is one thing women can learn from men, it's the temerity to think big, ask for more and keep shooting for the top. Ambitious men eye the alpha leadership role, plan the steps to get there, and then ask for the next challenge and the next to reach it. Often, hard-working women shine in a role expecting it to be noticed and wait to be asked to take the next step. Essentially, women unwittingly kick themselves out of the top jobs.

My message is to have the courage and confidence to set ambitious goals, to never underestimate ourselves and not allow others to either. For example, in business, more women advance to the highest levels of business through "staff" tracks, such as HR, marketing and accounting, than running the P&L operations. Yet, taking responsibility for overall financial results appears fraught with risk, but being accountable for generating profit and doing it successfully is the fastest route to credibility within the enterprise and opens up a new world of career options.

- *Finally, do your best to find a good boss!*
  I know this is easier said than done. But if you do have a choice, whom to work for, choose carefully. Male or female, a good boss is the ultimate game changer. Mine was Vice Chairman Bill Anderson. You can spot a good boss by their willingness to coach while giving you space to learn, their praise of your efforts to others, and their constant focus on removing your obstacles, encouraging you through one threshold then the next. They let you be yourself and try new things. They ask the right questions when you entertain a risk. When you blossom, they take unusual pride in your achievements. Behind every great leader was a great boss.

Today Lynne Anne continues to grow the FleishmanHillard brand in Asia.

Over the last five years, Lynne Anne has doubled revenues for Asia Pacific—a 10-country regional network of 19 offices in key markets like India, China, Japan and Australia— and increased profit a whopping 175 percent. Her teams handle a client base ranging from governmental ministries to large multinational corporations such as Procter & Gamble, HP, Philips Electronics and others.

But she is equally proud of another achievement.

"The gender balance of our top 25 leaders in Asia Pacific is equally split, female and male. Over half of our 19 offices are run by women, many of whom are working mothers," she says softly.

In 2013, Lynne Anne was named "Global Women's Champion" in the Women of Excellence Awards held by the National Association of Female Executives.

Looking back, Lynne Anne believes her decision to go abroad and move out of her comfort zone was the pivot point in her career. She encourages women to consider overseas assignments because they open up a green field of possibilities to try new things and apply what you know. Plus, she says, the female brand of team-building, communication and diplomacy plays well in cross-cultural situations. "The transfer to Asia allowed me to exercise leadership, learn and grow in all ways wonderful. Foreign experience is a gift that changes you deeply and brings out your best if you avidly embrace all it has to offer. Meaningful exposure to foreign cultures, policies, economies, consumer habits, and work styles is crucial to corporate advancement. Having a truly global frame of reference is a job requisite for any top post in a multinational company or business with cross-border ambitions."

Lynne Anne continues to experience adventure in Hong Kong with her husband Jackson and their two sons, Beecher and Vance.

I love the Madeleine Albright quote that says 'There is a special place in hell for women who don't help other women'. I think it's really important for women to help women if we are to succeed in getting more women into leadership roles. Until and unless there is a pipeline of enthused, informed women ready to share their wisdom with confidence, we won't shift the diversity numbers in the dramatic proportions we need to address real change," shared **Cilla Snowball, Group Chairman and Group CEO, AMV BBDO.** Cilla is one of the most powerful women in the advertising world, yet asking for help, and giving help has always been one of her key success drivers.

Cilla is the youngest of three children born in Staffordshire in the UK to a father who was a vicar and a mum who was a home economics teacher.

"I had a blissful early childhood, till the age of five when my parents got divorced. Divorce was very unusual in those days and it was hard for all of us. My Mum brought up my brother, sister and I on her own. We went from living in an idyllic, sprawling country vicarage to a tiny little semi detached house. We all 'grew up' fast. Everyone piled in to help from friends and family.

Being sent off to boarding school at 11 was the big break for me personally. At a boarding school, everyone is equal and where you come from and what's going on at home is invisible or secondary. You just get on with it. We were all able to throw ourselves into school life, make friends, play lots of sport, work hard and it was an incredible bonding and liberating experience, as well as giving me an early taste of independence and standing on my own two feet," shared Cilla.

She continued, "It's often said that there is education in adversity and it certainly applied to me. Once at school the focus became doing well, working hard, getting the most out of life and out of each other, amongst friends and from the teaching staff. I'm enormously grateful to the teachers who made me feel I was good at things, even when I patently wasn't."

One such teacher was Betty Wadely, Cilla's endlessly patient piano teacher.

"Betty sat with me for hours battling with Bach and Chopin, pushing me into terrifying piano exams, then sharing the joy of passing them and moving up a grade. I can still play some of those pieces now...all thanks to her...but what she unknowingly gave me was the confidence to believe in myself, to throw myself into trying things I thought I couldn't do, to have a go," shared Cilla.

Cilla described how her French teacher Pam Weston did the same.

*"In my career I've been helped by numerous women ahead, alongside and around me in the business world. Women who willingly shared their tips, mistakes, advice and wisdom to help me develop and to give me confidence. Who did so thoughtfully, selflessly and honorably. I really think it is important for women to help women if we are to succeed in getting more women into leadership roles."*

**Cilla Snowball.** *Group Chairman and Group CEO, AMV BBDO.*

"She was a French literature enthusiast and I caught that from her. I owe her a great deal too. She was a very quiet, unassuming woman, incredibly patient and kind and focused on extracting strengths rather than slamming weaknesses. So again, I flourished with her expert teaching, built my confidence and resolved to study French.

I was also given responsibility at school including being Head Girl in my final year. One of my school pals, recalls how terrified we were of the prefects in the prefect's room in our early years and how incredibly scary the prefects were towards us. My friend vividly remembers me saying at the time 'When we are prefects we're not going to be like them. We will be fair and kind.' I find that hilarious now, particularly since I can't remember either the fear or the retort, but looking back it's probably where I learned first learned about leadership, learning from bad leaders!" commented Cilla.

In 1981 Cilla graduated from Birmingham University with a BA Honors in French. As part of her studies in French, Cilla had to spend a year in France. Another defining experience, living and working in another country, far from home. Daunting at first, it proved to be another important career step, with Cilla immersing herself in her studies and doing part time teaching work.

"Best of all, one of my pupils was a superb cook and spent hours teaching me French cuisine, painstakingly writing out recipes for me, which I have kept to this day. By the time I returned to the UK in 1980 I was already very independent, a pretty decent cook, not to mention a few pounds heavier! But I had learned that I could stand on my own two feet, master new skills, earn a decent living.

My daughter Rosie will embark on her year abroad in September. She's studying French and Spanish so will go through the same experience. I have plenty of advice for her, as well as feeling mildly jealous of her for having this opportunity," shared Cilla.

At 21 Cilla started trying to get into the right job.

"I knew I wanted to do a job that was creative and was toying with either Marketing or Advertising. I thought Advertising would have more variety, so on that flimsy logic I chose Advertising and applied for traineeships," commented Cilla.

Her career began as a trainee with Allen Brady & Marsh, before moving to Ogilvy & Mather for nine years as an Account Manager, rising to Business Director during which time she married and had the first two of her three children.

She then joined AMV in 1992, initially as New Business Director. She has held senior management positions for the past fourteen years at AMV BBDO, the largest advertising and communications Group in the UK.

Named as one of the 100 Most Powerful Women in the UK by BBC Woman's Hour Cilla was also awarded a CBE for services to the advertising industry in January 2009.

"In my view you are never too young to be a role model or too old to need one. So we have to park our modesty and embrace the imperative to help other women as active not reluctant role models. Not at the expense of men, nor instead of men. We want to be equal to men but we don't want to be men! Plenty of my mentors and mentees are men. But for as long as there is such stark gender inequality in business, women have to recognize their responsibility to help other women," shared Cilla.

She continued, "In my career I've been helped by numerous women ahead, alongside and around me in the business world. Women who willingly shared their tips, mistakes, advice and wisdom to help me develop and to give me confidence. Who did so thoughtfully, selflessly and honorably."

One such person was Dianne Thompson, head of Camelot Lotteries in the UK.

'Dianne gave me invaluable advice as I was taking over as CEO of the agency. Her advice was to beware of 'nemesis and hubris,' getting too carried away by success or failure. Her philosophy was that when something bad happens, don't worry, something good will happen. And vice versa. She taught me to take the ups and downs of leadership in my stride, which has served me well. Dianne has been friend, client and role model for me," commented Cilla.

"Countless other women in business have helped me along the way. Carolyn McCall, CEO of easyJet and one of only four female CEOs in the FTSE 100 has provided friendship and support through countless tough periods as well as being a shining example of effective leadership as a working mother. Whether dealing with tough negotiations, building my Non Executive Director portfolio, Carolyn has always been on hand to help," she added.

"Dame Julia Cleverdon, former CEO of the charity Business in the Community (BITC), on whose board I served for six years, helped me see the benefit of giving back. Together with BITC and a local charity called the West London Mission, our agency raised £1.4million in 2001 to purchase a homelessness centre called Big House, still running successfully and saving lives to this day. Charity work is a big part of AMV BBDO's remit and my own and much of the impetus for both came from the indefatigable Julia Cleverdon," she shared.

Cilla now makes a huge effort to help other women in return.

She commented, "The number of women on boards is increasing in the UK but we still have too few women in leadership positions. In the UK advertising business, women lead only 22% of advertising agencies. This is up from 13.5% two years ago (Source: IPA Census) which is encouraging, but it's still not good enough or changing fast enough when we know that balanced boards are more effective in business than all male boards."

"In my own company, AMV BBDO we have a number of senior women in the top team, hopefully showing by our actions that you can do a big job and have a family. Proving that you can be a competent professional as well as a happy mother. And through mentoring support boost a wide range of women at all levels inside and outside our business - employees past and present, clients, students, school kids, aspiring non-executive applicants, we are all actively involved in giving support back," added Cilla.

Between and 1999 and 2000 Cilla chaired and as an Honorary Member still belongs to a network called Women in Advertising and Communications in London (WACL).

"We share wisdom, network contacts and train the next generation," she shared.

But Cilla's big success in giving back and supporting women is an alumni-mentoring programme at her university, the University of Birmingham, where she sat on the University Council.

Cilla commented, "I came up with a pretty obvious but apparently unique programme whereby university alumni mentor final year students and help them secure jobs. It's been a huge success and very rewarding on both sides. We have mentors in the arts, politics, retail, media and health fields who can offer invaluable help to their mentees, building their knowledge and confidence, both of which are so essential to develop at under graduate stage."

Among the high-profile mentors who agreed to take part are former chief medical officer Sir Liam Donaldson, former editor in chief of the Wall Street Journal, Baroness Patience Wheatcroft, actress Tamsin Greig and The Iron Lady director Phyllida Lloyd.

Cilla shared that the program is focused around coaching, supporting and challenging a final year student so that within six months of graduation they have found employment.

In the Birmingham programme, Cilla mentored Erin-Jane Golding, a final-year undergraduate in American and Canadian studies who wanted a career in media or advertising. Erin was returning from the USA and looked at the mentoring program and connected with Cilla. Over a period of 12 months, Cilla helped Erin make important decisions in terms of what direction to take with her career, how to look for jobs and how to maximize her time.

"Other than meeting once a month in as informal a place as the local pub, I have taken Erin with me to a number of networking events, invited her over to my own agency, and often just had her over to use our space," shared Cilla.

On graduation, Erin ended up with two handsome job offers, choosing a great marketing traineeship with Channel 4.

Cilla shared, "I will continue to look out for Erin and she knows she can always come to me for support and guidance."

She also sits on the Women's Business Council - an independent, working group advising the UK Government and business on how to maximize women's contribution to economic growth.

'I joined a team of male and female leaders from the recruitment, enterprise, retail, legal and pharmaceutical sectors, supported by the Government Equalities Office at DCMS,' shared Cilla.

Cilla's ability to give support is also reflected in the strong early success, which her own children are enjoying. One is a solicitor, the other is studying for a PHD in neuroscience and the third has followed in her early footsteps - she is studying French and Spanish.

Cilla commented, "I think many challenges women face today are the same as the challenges male professionals face - the challenge of doing a great job at work and a great job as a parent, the challenge of growing our businesses in a no or low growth economic environment, the challenge of making, managing, monetizing and measuring our creativity, the challenge of demonstrating our value and our values in all we do. And as women professionals, the challenge of being severely outnumbered in executive leadership roles."

She concluded, "Business is about relationships. Women around the world face so many challenges in their work and personal lives. The early years are so important. İ learned so much from those who supported me. I knew from a very early age that I could be far more successful if I asked for help when I needed it. İ made that a conscious habit over the years. Now it is my turn to give back."

Cilla's tips for giving and taking support:

- *Be aware of the specific challenges you face and the help that you likely need:*
  The early years are particularly important. The more self aware you are of the challenges you face, the easier it is to ask for the right support.

- *Learn from good and bad leaders:*
  Learn how they expand their spheres of influence and give and take support effectively.

- *Business is about relationships:*
  Make giving and taking support a habit. Practise it. Even if it means going out of your way to give of your time and energy.

- *Share your network and contacts:*
  As you do this consistently, new support and opportunities will come to you as other women act similarly and open their networks to you. Win-win.

- *Support other women:*
  As you move ahead in your career try and consistently support other women. This is the critical piece that will help truly balance out male-female leadership ratio over the long term.

In her spare time she studies mandarin, gemology and practices martial arts. Things that can be quite singular pursuits.

But her day job reveals a different persona. As the head of the Executive Education Department at the **Lee Kuan Yew School of Public Policy** at the **National University of Singapore, Louise Beehag** works and collaborates with leaders from all over the world to "Inspire these leaders to improve lives and transform Asia".

Positioned in Singapore, arguably one of the best public policy laboratories in the world, the School geographically has the perfect vantage point to witness - and contribute to - the rise of Asia. The School provides a platform for public policy practitioners, scholars and expert practitioners from around the world to come together and share ideas. It plays host to a steady stream of distinguished individuals including Tony Blair, Kofi Annan, Robert Zoellick, Aung San Suu Kyi, Paul Kagame, Amartya Sen and Elinor Ostrom, amongst others.

"My role is to custom design training programs for mid to senior level public officials. So far we have trained more than 10,000 people from around 80 countries, including prime ministers, vice ministers, mayors and CEOs of foundations and banks. We work closely with countries as diverse as India, China, Myanmar, Sri Lanka and the Gulf states, and have varied courses for them - urban planning, sustainability, dealing with ethnic conflict, leading organizational change, public financial management. I build relationships and work with people from very, very different backgrounds," shared Louise.

> *"Be inclusive. Do not disregard people because of their position, role, age, and level of education or background. Everyone's voice is valid, and often the best ideas come from the most unexpected places."*
>
> *Louise Beehag, Head of Executive Education, Lee Kuan Yew School of Public Policy.*

Louise grew up in an inner-city suburb in Sydney, Australia with two sisters and parents sharing a very tiny two-bedroom, 12-foot wide house. Her grandparents immigrated to Australia after WWII in search of a new start and better opportunities for their family.

"My grandparents and my mum, who was a child at the time, arrived by boat with very little and couldn't speak a word of English. My grandma worked tirelessly in a train station coffee shop, and my grandpa worked two jobs - a cobbler by day and a bus cleaner by night - to provide enough for their family. As a result my mum was able to go to university" shared Louise.

Through this, Louise learnt the value of hard work, tenacity and working together to improve lives.

"As a grand daughter, I felt both proud and sad that my grandparents went through so much so my sisters and I could have a better life," shared Louise.

It was at this point that she knew that she wanted to do something that had a positive impact on the lives of others.

"My parents were very supportive, and focused on our academic and life education. I do feel their approach was strongly shaped by the sacrifices their own parents made. My sisters and I were bright, and could have gone to selective schools, but my parents chose to send us at the local co-educational public school because they felt it better reflected the real world and would help us become more open minded, understanding and empathetic," shared Louise.

She continued; "This school was officially classified as "disadvantaged" by the education department as most of the kids came from very low socio-economic backgrounds. It was a very culturally diverse school, and as a consequence everyone was in a minority, myself included. Many of my friends' parents had not finished school themselves. Many of the students had difficulties with basic literacy and numeracy, and had quite a few struggles at home that made it difficult for them to focus in the classroom, including drug and alcohol abuse, or family members in jail".

"Our teachers were fantastic. Really amazing individuals. They cared about each student, and would go out of their way to create a supportive environment, one where kids could flourish. No matter how big or small their dream, the teachers would work together with students to help them achieve it," she added.

It was an environment that taught Louise the value of equality and collaboration. "I have always enjoyed talking to people, listening to their stories and perspectives. I grew up in an environment with a very flat social structure. It doesn't matter who you are, whether a cleaner or a CEO, it's how you relate to others and what your principles are that matter."

It also helped her understand the positive influence her parents were playing on her life.

"My mum is a psychologist and my Dad an electrical engineer by trade (but a unique combination of philosopher and dispenser of practical advice by disposition). They have always been great role models for me for collaboration and empathy. They are both nurturing and empowering and had an open door policy for our home. Over the years my friends would often pass by my parents' house to get advice on a range of personal and professional issues. Mum and dad would stay up all night talking to them, always with plenty of food on hand and a spare bedroom for anyone that needed it.

At school, Louise aced her examinations and got excellent grades.

"I was at a crossroads. I got almost 100 on my final school exams, was in the top 3% of the state which meant that I could choose to do law or medicine at good universities. The problem was that I really had no idea what I wanted to do with my life. I had a vague and lofty notion that I wanted to make the world a better place (as many idealistic university students do). I sat down and considered my personal values, and as a result I chose to undertake a broader, more general degree of Economics and Social Sciences, with a double major in Government and International Relations and Human Geography. In retrospect it was the best decision. Understanding the interplay between economics, government, social policy and so on gave me the grounding and perspective needed to work with diverse and often opposing viewpoints in my future career. I ended up enjoying it immensely and got distinction average, which gave me the opportunity to do an honors degree," she shared.

Her interest in collaborating with others to solve social and economic issues led to Louise doing a major year-long practical research project after graduating, with girls growing up in disadvantaged areas of the inner-city.

This focused on how more collaborative and inclusive government policy can help to build young peoples' resilience. She worked with local government, State government, schools and community groups and received First Class Honors for her work.

In 2006 Louise took up a role as the Local Action Plan Project Coordinator at the City of Sydney Council and the key objective was to improve Sydney for its residents. "It was my dream role at the time. I was excited and nervous and I really wanted to do a good job."

She commented, "I was in my early 20s and was put in a position where I was responsible for driving change management in an organization with hundreds of employees. I had to convince much older, more experienced people to do things they didn't necessarily want to do and felt had been imposed upon them."

"There were so many senior female role models to look up to – the Lord Mayor herself, quite a few Councilors, the CEO of the City, and numerous executive managers. It created an environment where gender was not an issue; it was all about performance and results. I also had a great mentor, an older colleague, who took me under his wing and provided me with invaluable professional guidance and encouragement. I have never had a mentor since, and I strongly encourage young women to try and find one. His advice and guidance gave me confidence which has lasted even till today," shared Louise.

"I worked with diverse units across the Council, from town planning to economic development, strategic planning to social policy. I worked with big businesses, residents, a multitude of community groups," continued Louise.

"I took the time to speak with each of the senior heads of departments, as well as the more junior staff (who would have to implement the changes). I listened to their concerns. I treated them with respect. I had a genuine interest in them as individuals, and the work they were doing. I showed them that we had common drivers and goals. Within a few short months I had gained their trust, demonstrated the benefits of the changes, and the positive effect started snowballing. Very soon I had people who were originally completely against the changes, coming to me proactively with positive suggestions about more things they could do personally in their units to contribute," she shared.

"In retrospect, I think my gender and my youth were probably an advantage, as I came across as non-threatening. I worked hard and earnestly because I felt that we were creating a more livable city for current and future generations, and establishing better, more inclusive processes within the organization. As a result, I was able to get people from vastly different disciplines and viewpoints to sit in the same room and collaborate. Together, we developed and implemented over 300 shared projects across the city, which was an incredible achievement," added Louise.

"These results proved the notion of equality and opportunity for all. And the power of collaboration - I began to value diversity of backgrounds even more. More perspectives mean better solutions," she added.

Louise believes that collaboration is hard work and it starts from being clear that you will persist despite the huge challenges that come your way. It takes guts and resilience to collaborate.

"While I learned empathy and how to look for the best in people from my parents, I think I got that resilience from my grandparents. Like I mentioned earlier, my grandfather survived WWII in Poland. He lost everything he had – his parents and seven brothers and sisters were killed, his wife and baby went missing, never to be found again and presumed dead. Eventually my grandfather met and married my grandmother (who, as a child, was orphaned and grew up in a strict orphanage run by nuns). They migrated to Australia, with my mother and uncle (11 and 9 years old at the time). None of them could speak any English, and turned up in this strange new land on the other side of the world to make a new beginning for themselves," shared Louise.

She added "My paternal grandmother grew up in rural Australia, one of five children, and was very poor. She didn't finish school, and moved to the city by herself at age 16. She became a nurse, met and married my grandfather, and made a life for herself. So I have had very good role models for being resilient."

Louise believes that sexism in the workplace is still a challenge for many women. "Of course I don't think it's anywhere as bad as it used to be, but it's still quite pervasive and can have huge impacts. Unfortunately most people are afraid to talk about it, often worrying that raising it as an issue might jeopardize their own career. In Australia we have a very unique and entertaining way of highlighting sexism displayed by public figures through the 'Ernie Awards for Sexist Behavior', which pokes fun at the ridiculous and offensive things that public figures have said in the preceding year. It began as a joke 21 years ago in response to the leader of the Australian Workers Union, a particularly sexist man called Ernie Ecob who famously claimed that women only wanted to become shearers 'for the sex'. A small group of women got together and threw a party to celebrate his resignation in 1993. Now, almost a quarter of a century later, the parties continue. These days they are held at Parliament House and attract 300 to 400 women annually. The 'winners' are selected through a 'boo-off'. It's a pity that misogyny is still alive and well, but it's great that women - and men - get together in solidarity to point out the ridiculousness of the sexist remarks, name and shame the offenders and make it clear it is unacceptable."

Louise has a few simple collaboration tips for our readers on giving and taking support and collaboration.

- *Use the first few weeks in a new job to introduce yourself to people, not only in your own department, but other departments:*
  When you're new, it's the best time to find out what other people do and how the whole organization works. This establishes relationships (and often friendships) and makes it much easier to collaborate in the future.

- *Be inclusive:*
  Do not disregard people because of their position, role, age, and level of education or background. Everyone's voice is valid, and often the best ideas come from the most unexpected places. Treat people with respect and take the time to listen and understand where they are coming from.

- *Do what you can to help others achieve their goals:*
  Everyone has potential. It is sometimes the littlest of things (some supportive words, or acknowledgment of strengths) that can help someone unlock their own potential and succeed. Equally, understand

your role in blocking people from achieving their goals; either intentionally, or through carelessness, you can have a big impact on another person's life.

- *Have the courage to stand up for your principles, but brave enough to let go of the roadmap for achieving these:*
  This is a hard one, especially if you have strong ideas at the beginning about what outcomes you want and how you plan to achieve this. Bringing in more voices can create unpredictability and uncertainty and reduces control. But I find that involving people in the discussion about how to achieve the vision ultimately results in stronger and more lasting outcomes.

- *Don't be afraid to ask others for help or guidance:*
  Often people are more than willing to give it.

At the Lee Kuan Yew School of Public Policy, Louise has been a great champion of collaborative success.

"A key part of how we work is bringing together the individuals who created change elsewhere in Asia and having them share - in person - their stories, their tenacity and their practical strategies for success with the class participants. This is very impactful.

I really enjoy working closely with our clients, understanding their histories, goals and how they want to develop. In order to design a program that is relevant and useful for them, we collaborate not only with our expert faculty, but also with a myriad of government agencies, multilateral organizations, corporations and civil society groups from across the region to expose participants to different ways of thinking and working that might be adaptable to their own contexts.

It's incredibly satisfying when I hear from past clients from Sri Lanka, India, Myanmar, the UAE and elsewhere and they tell me how they are adapting some of the things they learnt – be it in better water resource management, improved customer service, more inclusive social policy, new strategies to attract investment and raise the standards of living. The ultimate result is that we are achieving our mission – inspiring leaders, improving lives and transforming Asia.

Louise believes that women must come to grips with the challenges that face them today and take them head on. To this end, she insists that women as best possible must get educated."

Louise concluded; "My grandpa always said 'You can loose everything in life – your family, your possessions, your home, even your country. The one thing that can never be taken from you is what is in your head. Your education will stay with you forever and will lay the path on which to travel."

# Chapter 11

# BELIEVE
## IN YOURSELF

The University of Melbourne has done research on workplace success. Based on more than 100 interviews with professionals in large corporations in Melbourne, New York and Toronto, the pilot study found a strong correlation between confidence and occupational success. Belief in self determines the quality of your life. It determines the choices you make, the fears you harbour, and the success you eventually achieve. I spoke to three leaders who face unique challenges in their day to day jobs requiring them to have unshakeable belief in their abilities. Meet *Francoise Hostalier, former Deputy Education Minister, France*; *Yifei Li, Country Chair for Man Group in China*; and *Ninie Wang, CEO, Pinetree Senior Care services.*

"I knew it was dangerous. I knew my life was at risk. At worst, the road could be bombed or the Taliban could hijack my vehicle, but we were on a mission, and I had to do what I had to do," shared **Francoise Hostalier.**

Francoise was referring to one of the many trips she made to Afghanistan since 2002, where she was advocating for human rights and above all for women rights. Françoise has been many things – teacher, member of Parliament, Deputy Education Minister for France. She has been in and out of Government for the last 20 years. She is currently a **National Inspector for Education** in France. But above all Françoise has always been a woman who has deeply believed in herself and followed her own path.

"Women today face so many challenges. It is supremely important to believe in self, and abhor self doubt," she shared emphatically.

Born in Beauvais in 1953 Françoise journey towards self-belief was shaped as a child. Secure in a loving home created by her parents, she channeled her energy into an activity she loved most – swimming.

> *"Following your own light and belief in self will always attract the best possible outcomes for a woman in her career. You start playing to your strengths, and are firm and decisive in every course of action you may take."*
>
> *Francoise Hostalier, former Deputy Education Minister, France.*

"Swimming prepared me for success and helped me to believe that I could do anything I set my mind to. Swimming is tough, because you are alone in the water for two to three hours. It built not just my physical strength but also my mental strength," shared Francoise.

"More important, swimming taught me how to win and lose. It taught me how to celebrate my successes but also how to handle loss in a graceful manner," added Francoise.

Between the ages of 10 to 17, Françoise competed in and won many regional swimming contests. There were many losses too but she just kept going.

Francoise had many dreams, but adapted along the way to make the best use of the resources she had and the situation at any given point in time.

"I was not a good student. My teachers disliked me because I simply asked too many questions, and I was a bit undisciplined. But I persisted. I had many dreams. Of being an actor, a humanitarian, a journalist. But given my circumstances at the time I became a teacher," shared Francoise.

"I set my heart on becoming a mathematics teacher and passed an exam to be a teacher-student. My hard work paid off and I secured a scholarship for three years at Lille University, in the North of France but I was also required to stay in the National Education system failing which I would have to refund the scholarship amount," shared Francoise.

Early on, Francoise began to demonstrate great creativity in paving her path to success and never giving up.

At age 26 when she was teaching at a professional school with students mostly from the construction sector – male bricklayers, painters, etc. the students were unruly and difficult to manage. The male students had very little interest in the chemistry and scientific subjects that Francoise was attempting to teach them. But Francoise kept going. She invited her students to bring from home many of the household cleaning products they commonly used. She then helped the students test whether the products were acidic or basic. Suddenly chemistry and science seemed a whole lot more interesting to these youth from the construction business or background. 100% of her students passed their exams.

Then in 1982 Francoise was teaching a batch of female literature students mathematics, which they all hated. Instead of hammering away at teaching them mathematics in the traditional way, she instead connected the geometry and arithmetic to activities that the girls loved doing such as hand knitting, cooking and calligraphy. She helped the girls discover a whole different side of mathematics through this unique method of teaching.

Francoise taught for 18 years and over that time built a reputation as a creative, no-nonsense educator.

"Teaching is an amazing profession. It was what I really enjoyed doing. In retrospect, it allowed me to be all of the things I wanted to do earlier - actor, humanitarian, and journalist. A teachers job has a bit of all of this incorporated," she added with a smile.

In 1993, Francoise entered politics as a member of parliament. She became a member of the French Government in 1995 and was appointed Deputy Education Minister. Very quickly she started working on issues that really mattered.

"The first was in 1994 when as part of the liberal team we wanted to establish better measures to boost employment and the economy. I came up with the idea of a new concept of allowing people to work for a few hours- clean up the home, work in the garden or other odd jobs. At the time all jobs were through a contract or via the "black market" viz unregistered work. The resistance from many quarters was huge. Even my own party. But I believed it would make a valuable contribution to creating more jobs. So I persisted," shared Francoise.

Today, the law Francoise created has become the "le chèque emploi service".

"Today a lot of people use it in France," added a smiling Francoise.

Francoise shared that over the years she earned a reputation for being relentless in her follow up on issues that mattered.

One such issue was the war on drugs in schools.

"When I was Deputy Education Minister, I wanted to organize a program for the prevention of drugs and addiction in primary schools. A lot of people said to me it was impossible to speak on that subject with such young students. But I was convinced that it was at that young age that the best intervention and prevention was possible. Every Monday morning I met the Director of the primary level levels and tried to convince him to organize this program. Finally in January 1996, the Ministry finally issued a manual to all Primary schools in France," commented Francoise.

Francoise was delighted and amused when she received a letter from the Director of Primary schools who said simply, "I'm pleased to send you this manual. At last, you have won!"

"As a Member of Parliament too, I was renowned for my follow up or 'kind harassment'. When I wanted something for a dossier, I wrote or telephoned until I had a good answer. I built a reputation of believing in each of my cases and pursuing matters all the way up the hierarchy and in the Ministries when people saw a dossier was coming from me, they solved it quickly because they knew they would be harassed (kindly!!) until the end," said Francoise tongue-in-cheek.

Nothing however prepared Francoise for the challenges she would face as a woman leader in promoting human rights in troubled nations like Algeria, Bosnia and Afghanistan.

"For Algeria, 1995 to 1997 was truly a 'dark period' for this country. I was in contact with Algerian women and I supported them to organize conferences, meetings, manifestations in the streets, writing press articles or petitions to advance human rights and women's rights,' shared Francoise.

Francoise was also helping advocate human and women's rights in Bosnia, which since 1997 had been torn apart by the violence there. One specific project was helping the women who survived the "Massacre de Srebrenica" in which 8000 men lost their lives.

"I worked with an association called Mothers for Peace, France and we went to Bosnia every 11th of July since 1997 to support the survivors in their fight for justice and recognition of their human rights. We participate along with a group of other associations who were lobbying for this as well. We set up a memorial with all of the recognizable names of people killed during this conflict. We helped determine with the help of other specialists the identities of bodies discovered in mass graves. We stressed on the authorities that rape was a crime against humanity. And finally, through Mothers for Peace, France, we began to set up women's economic empowerment projects like the growing of strawberries," added Francoise.

In 2013 Francoise was appointed President of Mothers for Peace, France.

It was during her time in Algeria that Francoise also discovered Afghanistan.

"I was in Algeria when the "massacre de Bentalha" happened when le GIA's terrorism killed the people of the village of Bentalha. I was in Algeria to support the women who fought against terrorism. And my Algerian friends explained to me these terrorist actions were actually directed by the Taliban out of Afghanistan.

While it was impossible to visit Afghanistan in 1997, Françoise took part in actions helping afghan women to teach in clandestine classrooms. In 2002 she resolved to enter Afghanistan and first hand help that country and their people.

"People who knew Afghanistan well told me to be careful, and kept telling me not to go for fear of me losing my life," shared Françoise.

Not Francoise. Determined to follow through on her human rights agenda for Afghanistan, Françoise visited Afghanistan 23 times in under a decade, appearing at conferences, negotiating with the Government, helping human rights groups protest against terrorism and to support economic and development programs.

"Anything in life comes with risk. But as long as you anticipate the risk involved, understand them and plan to work around them, risk can be mitigated to a significant extent," shared Françoise.

"In life if you believe in something, you must understand the risk involved and your capacity to deal with it. And if you think its too dangerous and you cant make a difference, then don't do it. But if you do believe you can change something for the better you must," she added.

So in 2012, against the better advice of her friends, Françoise set out to meet the French military in Afghanistan in a very dangerous province, notorious for Taliban attacks.

"I was well prepared. In my case I knew that if my driver stuck with a group of cars and kept to the middle of the road I would be much safer, making a bomb attack a much lower possibility. I also had inside information that the safest time of day was between 7 am and 11 am, during which no Taliban were out on the road. I also enlisted the support of a driver I had known personally for six years. The car was stocked with supplies for any emergency," she added.

Francoise successfully made that visit. And as a result she was able to present her report to the President of the French Republic, Nicolas Sarkozy that served to prepare some directions for the Treaty between France and

Afghanistan signed the 27th of January 2012.

Francoise has similarly played a lead role in the peace process for Algeria and Bosnia. Her untiring human rights work has been lauded often.

"The biggest challenge I faced during these actions and even today is convince French decision-makers and media or the public that it is our responsibility to help this oppressed populations, to defend human rights, to support women and to educate children. Because the populations, in our comfortable countries, don't understand why we have interest for these people living so far from us," shared Francoise.

"Following your own light and belief in self will always attract the best possible outcomes for a woman in her career. You start playing to your strengths, and are firm and decisive in every course of action you may take," she added.

Francoise indeed has the next steps on her career path charted out already. At 60 with three children (a girl and two twins) and seven grandchildren Francoise is working on Francois Fillon's team to prepare for the presidential elections in 2017.

Francoise closed out our interview by sharing that she owes her self-belief to many things. Her parents first, and also the experiences they exposed her to.

"Every time I have self doubt, I look to the words of Rudyard Kipling's famous verse – You will be a Man, my son."

In a world where women are making their mark, Françoise is leading the curve.

Francoise had some very simple tips for young women professionals on how to build self-belief:

- *Learn to be self-aware:*
  Be aware of your capacity and strengths but also of your defects and try to correct them. Believe in your strengths and keep telling yourself 'I can do it.'
- *Be true to yourself and to your values:*

Don't cheat yourself; be always faithful to your values and to the line of conduct you have chosen.

- *Act with your heart:*
  Be always attentive to the needs and feelings of others. By listening to others and their opinions we can learn so much.

- *Never give up when you decide to do something:*
  At the same time, if you can see that your initial project has no reasonable chance of success don't hesitate to course correct and follow another path.

- *Make sure you maintain some balance between work and personal life:*
  So you can live happily and never regret the choices you make.

I was first introduced to **Yifei Li** in early 2014 and was immediately impressed with her diversity of professional experiences.

In 2013, Yifei Li joined the Rockefeller Foundation Board of trustees. It marked another milestone in an illustrious career. Yifei is currently **Country Chair for Man Group** in China, one of the world's largest hedge fund managers, which has assets under management of $55 billion.

> *"In life, you've got to take a no as a yes and keep marching ahead and keep believing in yourself."*
>
> **Yifei Li, Country Chair for Man Group in China.**

In welcoming her appointment Board Chair David Rockefeller, Jr. commented "Ms. Li joins us during a pivotal time in the history of the Foundation. The Board is committed to adding trustees who bring different skills and backgrounds, which will help develop the Foundation's next 100 years."

Before Man Group, Li was Managing Director of MTV Networks for Greater China and Executive Vice President of MTV Networks Asia.

Yifei is no stranger to success. In May 2001, she was selected as one of 25 Rising Stars-Global Leaders for the Next Generation by Fortune Magazine and was on the cover of Fortune. Between 2001 to 2005 she was selected as one of the 50 Most Powerful Women by Fortune magazine. She was also selected as one of Ten Women to Watch in Asia by Wall Street Journal in both 2005 and 2006.

Yifei has also been recognized as being responsible for leading the success of several MNCs in China through the 90s.

She attributes her success to the great opportunities China has provided with its high growth and market reforms in the past 30 years, and also because she holds a strong belief in herself.

"In life, you've got to take a 'no' as a 'yes' and keep focused and marching ahead. Belief in yourself is key to success is key to success," shared Yifei.

Yifei shared that her self-belief and confidence is grounded in deep curiosity and constantly learning and seeking new knowledge. That, on top of hard work is fundamental to any measure of success.

"In the early stages of career for a woman, it's all about learning and acquiring knowledge to do the job well. One must focus on getting to a point where you move from 'not knowing what you don't know' to 'knowing what you don't know'. Once you have the knowledge, people respect you for that, knowledge empowers us" she shared.

Yifei was born in Beijing in 1963. Her father is an astrophysicist, her Mom a teacher in Mathematics. As a child she was surrounded by books in every room in her house.

"I would read anything and everything to gain knowledge. I read all the classics – Tolstoy, Dickens, Hugo, and of course many classic Chinese poems, novels, etc. they were all fascinating to me, especially during and right after the Cultural Revolution when books were a rare commodity," commented Yifei.

At 10, Yifei also began to demonstrate a liking for marital arts. She started practicing. That taught her the value of self-belief through knowledge and hard work.

"I started to make real progress in learning good habits. The martial arts training helped me understand that one must go through hardship to achieve. At first I was a 'bench player' and looking back, I believe I was initially lazy. I was also not confident enough as I thought I was more of a book lover versus an athlete. But my coach pushed me hard and taught me that practice can create results.

When you train so hard you realize that life is full of such great opportunities. You realize success and failure are both part of the same picture. That has been so true in my career as well. Every time I have a set back, I tell myself I can come back from failure quickly," commented Yifei.

Yifei threw herself into the training. She trained for longer hours and far more intensely than she had ever done before. As the months passed the efforts began to pay off.

At 13, Yifei won a national championship in martial arts. Shortly after Yifei was selected to play a role in China's first martial arts movie after the ten-year Cultural Revolution.

Yifei went on to get a law degree from Beijing Foreign Affairs University and in 1985 went on to the USA for further studies, getting a master's degree in international relations from Baylor University in Texas.

Yifei returned to China in 1993 and was appointed general manager of MTV China and the country's chief representative for Viacom, MTV's parent company.

This was truly a uniquely challenging role. It was a time at which R&B and street dancing were becoming popular in China and Yifei, sensing the opportunity, managed to get programming to close to 300 cities in China reaching 400m households. She was even successful in persuading national network CCTV to co-produce China's version of the CCTC-MTV music awards.

"I knew this was a win win for CCTV and for MTV. CCTV got access to many upmarket hotels in the US, while MTV was able to expand the impact of its programming," she shared.

Expanding MTV in China was no easy task. Viewed within the context of an environment with many conservative Chinese officials wary of this new kind of music, Yifei had to dig deep into her understanding of Chinese culture, regulatory traditions and her negotiation skills to make progress.

"One of my key sources of inspiration has been the words of Confucius, who said that to succeed, one must walk the middle line and always strive for mutual benefits. I believed deeply in what I was doing, and I believed in my own ability. For some, walking the middle line is perceived as weakness, I perceive it as being strategic in building long term trust and respect and creating a win-win situation. I knew if I dealt with Chinese officials respectfully, and in a strategic, consistent manner, they would agree to many of our proposals," shared Yifei.

From 1999 onwards, Yifei created several firsts for MTV in China.

She brought in Britney Spears, Eminem and Jay Zhou to millions of young Chinese viewers, something that would have been considered almost impossible earlier.

There Yifei moved to Digital Advertising Company VivaKi. Then to hedge fund GLG Partners which was acquired by Man Group. In late 2011 she was appointed Country head for Man Group.

"My move to Man Group was such a big shift from MTV. But I believe in continuous learning and expanding my horizons," added Yifei.

Yifei is quick to add that the challenges she faces as a CEO are changing from those she faced as a younger professional.

"While in the early stages of career, it was more about acquiring knowledge and then demonstrating I was knowledgeable and earning respect, now it is about dealing with success with humility.

One interesting challenge as we move up the corporate ladder is not only winning respect of men but more importantly women.

How other women view your success is also a very interesting. You must also master the art of influencing and being truly collaborative with other women," commented Yifei.

"There are many challenges facing women around the world even today. Yet at the same time, women are incredibly influential as consumers and as influencers in society. Whether it is product purchase, TV viewership and consumption, social change, women are making incredible strides. There are so many inspirational women from which we can all learn.

One of the things I've enjoyed in my mid 20's to 30's was reading a lot of autobiographies of accomplished women. One of my all time favorites is the autobiography of Katherine Graham, former publisher of the Washington Post. She won the Pulitzer Prize in 1998 for her autobiography. She was a simple housewife who took over the newspaper after her husband committed suicide. She went on to become one of the most successful women in media in America.

I also have great respect for Hillary Clinton and enjoyed reading her autobiography: 'Living History', shared Yifei.

Over the years Yifei has leveraged her American education extensively. But she has always stayed true to her Chinese roots. Yifei has two children and insists on raising them the Chinese way. Her 19 year old daughter attended a local Chinese school instead of an International school in China before going to study at Yale University.

"I very much want my children to understand this great country. I derived a lot of professional skills from the US, but China is still my home." said Yifei.

Yifei's influence has gone beyond the corporate world and into the philanthropic community as well. Yifei is a global board member of GAVI (Global Alliance For Vaccines And Immunization), a global alliance established jointly by World Health Organization, World Bank, and the Bill and Melinda Gates Foundation. The mission of GAVI is to save children's lives and protect people's health by increasing access to immunization in poor countries.

Yifei shared with me a few tips on how a woman professional could nurture and leverage belief in self.

- *Aim high:*
  Do not say 'no' to yourself!
- *Keep learning:*
  I constantly upgrade my knowledge by reading.

- *Commit to whatever you are doing:*
  Do it well.
- *Demonstrate passion and energy for what you do:*
  That is infectious. Your self-belief has a greater effect on others than you could ever imagine.
- *Persevere:*
  Success is often just around the corner. Believe that how you respond to failure will define your next success.

Yifei believes that her belief in self has been key to her success. She repeated to me something I had seen in earlier media mentions.

"I stay focused on my goals. Many times I tell my daughter, if one phone call doesn't make it happen, 66 calls will make it happen."


**Ninie Wang** is 36. Possibly the youngest heroine in this book. She is also **CEO** of **Pinetree Senior Care Services.** Pinetree delivers in-home professional long-term care services as well as training support to the family caregivers of the customer. Doctors and nurses visit senior citizens at home, monitoring their health, providing chronic disease management, medication enforcement, restorative exercises and psychological support.

Based in Beijing and Shanghai, China, Ninie has a simple philosophy.

"Success for me starts with self-belief. I believe in myself and I believe in the goodness of people in general. This philosophy has sustained me over the years and is core to my success as a leader," she shared.

The path that Ninie has set herself on in China has indeed required belief in self and in the goodness of others.

"Care for the aged is everyone's business as ultimately all of us will be old," she added.

It is estimated that by 2020 the number of over-65 year olds in China could be 250 million. By 2050 China will become the most 'aged' among the emerging BRIC countries. In today's China, the one child policy has had an impact wherein the responsibility of caring for the elderly-the parents and two sets of grandparents-falls upon the single child who may not have the time or the resources to meet this challenge.

Alarmed by the lack of healthcare facilities for China's rapidly aging population, Ninie set up Pinetree in 2004 to provide affordable home healthcare to this rapidly increasing group.

She shared, "Pinetree symbolizes long life and good health in Chinese culture, and the pronunciation qing song is same as easy, worry-free. I have been passionate about creating a service for our elders to live a longer, better-quality life."

"Pinetree's mission is to build China's top trusted brand for senior healthy living. Whether it is sons and daughters seeking to provide their parents with quality home care solutions that allow their parents independent living, or senior citizens themselves seeking trusted products and services such as home care, wellness, and insurance, Pinetree aims to be their first destination," she added.

Ninie's road to success started in her birthplace – the city of Shashi (later renamed to Jingzhou after merging with neighboring cities and counties) in Central China in the province of Hubei.

"My Dad is from Xian and my Mum from Nanjing. I was always fascinated by the long histories of these beautiful cities. I have always been attracted to things with age," she shared.

> "Success for me starts with self-belief. I believe in myself and I believe in the goodness of people in general. This philosophy has sustained me over the years and is core to my success as a leader."
>
> Ninie Wang, CEO, Pinetree Senior Care services.

"As I grew up my parents always respected my point of view and let me participate in family discussions and major decision-making. At 11 I was very lucky to join the first experimental class at the best local high school, Shashi No.3 Middle School, together with 59 other students chosen from over 20,000 applicants. We were given the opportunity to study at our own pace and develop our interests other than just preparing for exams.

At one point the president of our school came along with our class master for a home visit. Before he left, he remarked that he had never seen such a "democratic" household, and that he thought it was perhaps why I could be so confident both in classes and other activities," shared Ninie.

Ninie is quick to acknowledge the role her teachers have played in her success.

"Throughout my education I benefited from having great teachers. The most important thing they taught me was not knowledge itself, but how to look for it. I read broadly thanks to their advice. It was the combined effect of my teachers and the books that made me believe that I could make a difference," she commented.

At 17 Ninie left her hometown and went to study a BA in International Finance from UIBE, China. It was only two years later that she realized she did not want to work in Finance but rather in Marketing.

In 1999 Ninie joined Motorola in Beijing.

"Away from home, I began to see what was happening to my older friends. I would go back and visit them and see their deterioration – both physical and mental. I began to recognize the pain they were facing and started thinking about how I could help them," she commented.

But the pain and challenge to the aged was not limited to Ninie's hometown. She slowly began to realize that the aged across china were facing the same issue.

"I saw the systems in China were simply not geared to give support or a better life to so many of these people. At the time I was working on pioneering mobile Internet via Motorola. Despite the huge opportunities in the Motorola role I began to feel that there was much more beyond that. I wanted to do something that would truly help me to change lives. I could not see myself making a life-changing difference in what I was doing nor could I feel long term passion for the telecom industry," she shared.

Easier said than done. Ninie found herself torn between the security of her job and what she really wanted to do.

Determined to do more with her life, Ninie continued to visit her aged friends, and continued to understand her problems and challenges.

In 2002, Ninie left her lucrative job in Motorola and decided to pursue her dream of caring for the aged.

"Financing the study was a small challenge. My savings were far from enough. I had to borrow from my family, my colleagues at Motorola, and got a scholarship from the school (Alumni Fund). The first book I read after joining INSEAD was The Alchemist. When I came to the part saying 'when a person really desires something, the whole universe conspires to help you achieve it', my determination became even stronger," shared Ninie.

"I thought of joining an NGO, or becoming a public servant or starting a business. Finally, I decided that I wanted to start a company working for the aged. I wanted it to become a big intervention and not a mom and pop store," she added.

Despite her long standing friendships with several people several decades older than herself, Ninie realized that she did not know enough about either the problem or the potential solutions.

"It was a turning point. If I truly believed that I wanted to make a big difference in this field of work, and believed in myself, I knew I had to invest in myself and professionalizing my skills before I started out setting up a business."

In 2002 Ninie invested her savings into studies at INSEAD, and started doing her MBA from INSEAD in France and Singapore. Her studies at INSEAD provided the catalyst to get more insight into the aged.

"I wanted to learn from the best. I took all the entrepreneurship courses I could find. And while at INSEAD worked on the plan of Pinetree," she shared.

At INSEAD every student on campus also learned of Ninie's passion to help the aged.

In 2003, Ninie was ready to start Pinetree with the help of a few friends who contributed 5000 USD each. At INSEAD, Ninie had also won 6000 Euros for winning the Roland Berger Business Plan Competition, which was also invested in Pinetree.

"I started working with about 20,000 USD, then in November 2004 raised 200,000 USD from two angel investors. I also got a lot of support from the NGO community. Soon after I started Pinetree, I got to know scholars from Gerontological Society of China and China Institute of Research on Aging. From them I learned so much about the subject and got connected to the international community of gerontologists and geriatricians," shared Ninie.

Ninie faced head on the challenges most entrepreneurs experience.

"Getting to understand and reach our target customers was the first one. Many people make assumptions about what the aged need, so did we. The only way to find out was to try things out and see what would actually work. Then we also had the challenge of finding the right people for the team. We encountered unethical 'alliances' between our administrator and external suppliers, self-acclaimed 'princelings' who wanted to charge for every piece of 'free help', people who were otherwise very capable but didn't share our philosophy at all and ended up diminishing the morale of everyone else, friends who offered to help but couldn't get used to the entrepreneurial life-style due to family commitments, etc. etc.

In hindsight, all these challenges were necessary for us to grow and mature. I fully understand why a serial entrepreneur is more appreciated, and am even more grateful for the trust and support from my initial investors, my friends and business angels.

I didn't encounter any particular difficulty being a woman but I did keep getting the comment of 'being a female entrepreneur' as if it was an achievement in itself," added Ninie.

"Initially we called our enterprise the Pinetree Life Institute. Our purpose was more focused on bringing seniors up to speed on information and skills that would better enable them to interact with their children and grandchildren. We did that for about a year and a half," shared Ninie.

But Ninie's initial offering had missed the target. Chinese elders saw the services as nice to have but not critical. They did not want to spend on something that they considered unnecessary.

"It was frustrating. We had to go back to the drawing board and listen to what these elders were telling us. We also had to revisit the initial research that we had done," shared Ninie.

Ninie went back to the INSEAD network and looked at research across over 30 developed countries to see what was the most sustainable business model for the care for the aged.

"Finally we realized that homecare was the answer. Providing the aged with healthcare services at their homes itself. Restorative long term care for seniors, especially after hospitalization so that their quality of life is such that they could still be active to the best extent possible at home with their families and in their communities." shared Ninie.

In 2005 Ninie relaunched the Company. Almost immediately the new concept took off! In the same year she became a member of the Gerontological Society of China GSC (with its parent organization being China National Committee on Ageing).

Commented Ninie, "One thing we learned at Pinetree was that we needed to keep our services affordable to the general population with an average package of about 150 dollars per month depending on the individual's particular care needs.

Ninie continued, "The Pinetree model is simple. We have service centers in high-density residential areas across a city, which enables fewer than 15 mins travel time for our nurses to a patient's home. Our nurses walk or use bicycles and public transport. The better the scheduling, the more patients a nurse can visit. That scheduling of time and travel is critical to our success," explains Wang.

As Pinetree took off, Ninie continued to network within the industry. She worked diligently to support the international programs of the Gerontological Society of China (GSC). In 2008 she was appointed as the International Director of the GSC.

In 2009, she became a China Social Welfare Service Standard Committee Member as well as a Member of Presidium for National Union of Long-term Care, and most recently, was elected as Standing Director of China Association for Life Care.

"The Chinese government has been very supportive. Being a pioneer in the field gave us the chance to give input to policy makers while they design the framework of aged care service industry development. In China, it is very common for Chinese businesses to be led by women, I believe it's quite a gender-equal environment here," she added.

Ninie estimates that most of today's nursing homes will eventually be replaced, by models that provide more senior-friendly, quality care, be it home-based, community-based, or integrated.

"For those who need intensive 24-hour-care-support, before a better way of delivering care is found, institutions will still be an option. As advancements are made in both medical science and technologies, innovations such as (and beyond) breakthrough treatment for chronic diseases, ubiquitous healthcare, smart home/city, etc. would make it unnecessary to take any elderly outside of their original living environment for receiving care," commented Ninie.

Nine's passion for Pinetree has had many implications on her personal life.

"I am fortunate that in China, being a woman is not as much of a disadvantage as compared to many other countries around the world. Yet the focus I was placing on pioneering Pinetree was clearly taking a toll on my personal life. In China, most women are under pressure to get married by age 30. My parents were afraid that I would be an entrepreneur who would stay single my whole life. I managed that pressure by reassuring my parents that I would indeed marry when the time was right and I found the right person," she added.

Ninie talked about the few attributes that have helped her believe in herself and what she is attempting to do in China.

- *Stay positive:*
  Make positivity a habit. Life is beautiful no matter what the challenge. In this line of work, we have to put in a lot of effort to change perception of people towards the aged. Some negative people want to hide their elders away without dignity. There is a lot of suffering. A lot of pain. But we continue our work with the belief that we are making a difference. And

for that, despite all of the negativity or suffering around us, we have to stay positive.

- *Surround yourself with good people:*
  Your success cannot be built just on your individual ability. It is dependent on the people you connect with; the people who you bring in to work with you, and the quality of the people you partner with to propel your ideas forward. When I get credit for setting up Pinetree I give it back to the hundreds of professionals who work for and with Pinetree. Recently a Television program asked me to accompany them to one of the Pinetree home visits and pose for the camera. I replied that that would not be credible. I would rather have the professional who is actually taking care of that senior at home on camera than me.

- *Keep learning:*
  Ironically, ageing is a very young science. Every day, new theories are being tested. To continue to believe I have the right to succeed over the long term in this business, I must be constantly learning.

- *Choose something you are most passionate about:*
  When you love doing something or working on something, you will reap the benefit of courage in your conviction. Your belief will be infectious and inspire other people.

- *Take a calculated risk:*
  At some point, all the research, background, etc. will have have to give way to the fact that you have to risk sometimes in life. Not foolish risks, but calculated risks.

Pinetree has grown explosively over the past few years and today serves 150,000 customers through 300 units in Beijing and Shanghai.

Success in Beijing is now enabling Ninie to spread the organization across China.

"We estimate that by 2020 we will have a client base of millions of patients through tens of thousand of nurses and over 1,000 local service units. This will be a critical help in a country where the demand and supply for care for the aged has a huge gap," concluded Ninie.

# Chapter 12

# LEARN TO NETWORK

Networking is critical to success. According to the US Bureau of Labor statistics, 70% of all jobs are found through networking. Three of the world's best networkers - **Kristin Engvig,** *Founder of Women's International Networking (WIN)*; **Su-Mei Thompson, CEO,** *The Women's Foundation, Hong Kong*; and **Christine Tan,** *Anchor, CNBC Asia Pacific* shared with me their formulas for effective networking.

**K**ristin Engvig is the founder of **Women's International Networking (WIN)** – an independent global leadership organization that inspires women worldwide. WIN is most known for its flagship event the Global WIN Conference and an increasing number of regional WIN Conferences.

WIN has become the reference for modern women working internationally, conscious men and those organizations active in the field of women's leadership, development, diversity & inclusion, and wholeness.

Kristin started her life in beautiful Kristiansund, Norway. She grew up on the wild, west coast of Norway, surrounded by mountains leading to the open sea. Whether it was living so close to nature with unpredictable weather (including some scary hurricanes), the rich community of Kristiansund itself (built on four islands and connected by bridges), the fact that the city had been bombed during World War II and rebuilt with beautiful colorful houses, or the dream of travel evoked when looking out at the ocean, Kristin understood at a young age how important it is for people to be connected, to respect nature, to help each other and to do something in life that will leave the world a better place.

> *"Networking and hard work has been key to my success. Network with purpose! Surround yourself with sustainers, believers and champions. Develop different relationships and sensibilities. And finally, build and nurture a network. You will never know when you will need it."*
>
> *Kristin Engvig, founder of Women's International Networking (WIN).*

She comes from a large extended family and one of the core principles she feels she learnt from her mother was to work hard, be honest, to care and to make sure everyone feels Included.

"My Mum was always ensuring that we went to a cousin, an uncles, an aunts or grandparents' birthday and our family gathering was important when growing up - a ritual of making sure everyone felt included," shared Kristin.

Kristin comes from a family of photographers that can be traced back to 1872 when her great, great, grandfather not only ran the local cinema, one of the first in Europe, but also took some of the most significant photos in Norway at the time. Although Kristin, the oldest and hence the natural inheritor of the family linage, could have chosen photography, her parents were keen to let their three children choose to do whatever they wanted to do.

They did. Kristin went on to study marketing, acting, business and to travel the world. However, just like any photographer, she brought with her a core essence and belief - that of ALWAYS making sure people are put in the right light.

"As a young person, I loved sitting at the table with the adults and listening and learning. I loved hearing my dad, my grandfather and my aunt discussing politics and I learnt so much. Likewise when family members came back from a trip, whether Africa, Germany or America, we gathered together to look at the photos and to listen and share. It was a kind of family networking, where the focus was on net - as in safety net. Where you were able to try, to fail, and to feel you really mattered. We all felt accepted and included. I learnt from how people were helping each other - whether it was building a cottage together or baking cakes. I learnt the essence of striving to be a noble person, working hard and building trust," shared Kristin.

But as Kristin sat and looked at the sea she started to dream about travelling. Her parents had already brought her and her siblings to most of the mountaintops, fjords and islands in the region; by boat, car, skiing, and on foot.

"I wanted to go abroad. I wondered what was out there, beyond the ocean, where I could not see so clearly. Then when I was a teenager, we finally travelled to Oslo, Sweden, Denmark and Spain. As soon as I turned 17, I applied to become an exchange student in order to travel on my own. I knew that with my parents it would be another ski trip to yet another Norwegian mountain - I wanted more," she shared.

Kristin travelled as far away as possible to Melbourne, Australia. There she met exchange students from around the world, learnt English and made friends. She understood more about other cultures and developed an even bigger appetite for travelling. Then she returned to Kristiansund and worked hard to finish her last year of high school, and to get good grades to get into the University in Oslo, where she attended the Oslo School of Business Administration.

"I loved being a student and was involved in many student and social activities. I was in AIESEC (international student association), took leadership roles, worked part time and made many friends in Norway and abroad. I began to understand that it is not only about what you know, but that who you know gives you energy and makes life fun. One of my student jobs was working for a well-known advertising agency conducting market research. We interviewed people, did product testing, and worked on the advertising campaigns pre and post launch. This involved a lot of listening to people, and collecting data both analytically and empathetically. These years of doing interviews provided good training for listening to what was about to come, and what was about to emerge. In Australia, I had met a group of Japanese students and I became interested in their ways. One day I received a message from a young Japanese woman from Osaka about coming to Norway with a group of Japanese students. I immediately became involved in the project and organized a group of students to host them in Norway, as well as opportunities for learning, company visits and cultural exchange. Whilst writing my final thesis, I found a job in Japan working for the Scandinavian Tourism Office and Norwegian Export Council (Innovation Norway), where I did PR and market research. I combined this with writing my thesis, and doing research on Japanese tourists coming to the Nordic countries," shared Kristin.

Connecting with people around the world seemed to come naturally to Kristin. She seized every opportunity to understand new cultures.

"After working in Japan, completing university, and working in market research work, I applied to do my MBA in International Management and Economics in Milan, Italy at the SDA Bocconi University. After Japan, Italy was my second dream country and I had a need to go there. What was going to be a year in Italy with my boyfriend, later husband, became 12 years. It was in Milan that networking became a way of life," added Kristin.

"After my Masters I started to work for a large American bank and operate in the city of Milan. Yet again the logic of what you know is important, but who you know and who knows you could be even more significant, resonated with me. Since I had not grown up in Milan, gone to school there, or have family that could offer direct support, I understood that something needed to be done to recreate a network. I also learned that people remembered how you made them feel.

Likewise, when working in big multinational organizations, I was confronted with corporate politics and activities that I considered a 'waste of time'. In addition, not everything was equally transparent, just, natural or efficient. If you didn't work late or engage in politics, I didn't think you had many career prospects. There was also another way; a co-worker's promotion seemed to be directly linked to the length of her skirt. I felt that although this had nothing to do with me, if I was a part of this office culture, it meant I was okaying it. I was not, so I resigned. I then worked as a consultant, predominantly in Eastern Europe and Russia. I realized, as I triple locked my door in Moscow, that as a travelling business woman, my life could be so much easier if I had a local contact," shared Kristin.

For Kristin those were life-changing experiences. She slowly started to feel that everyone was not as fortunate as she had been. Being born in a peaceful country, in a nice family, in an egalitarian society with a female prime minister, it became apparent that her situation was quite unique.

"I thought about what I could do to contribute to increasing the possibilities for all those women and men, those that I had met and who didn't see other possibilities? What can I (we) do to inspire those that are fortunate and resourceful, but who are wasting their time on politics, wondering whether they are smart or not, what to wear and how to look, when our world is falling to pieces, and awaken them to the fact that their resources are needed in the world, right now, to do something really useful? Let's network to wake people up, to open up possibilities, and to make sure more can become possible – together," shared Kristin.

Kristin became active in a local women's network in Milan, she coordinated a lot of their work and in 1994 she became their president.

She commented, "I loved being with the women, connecting and making connections. It was a mutually beneficial arrangement, I felt useful, and I was in my element. I was also involved in the alumni association of my business school. I started to know an incredible amount of people. I loved it. During this phase of my life, the 'market researcher' in me started to listen to the economic system - what was it? Why do we run our companies this way, with so little care - for young people, for women, and for the planet? Why can't we put some caring into the formula of success?"

I saw a lot of possibilities for how things could be done differently through effective networking. I had found my mission. I started to listen to the women, to the companies, to the way of doing things. I also started to listen to me, to what's inside and what's beyond. A new era began. From Yoga to Corporate Networking," she added.

Kristin came up with idea after idea. But the one that resonated most with her was the idea to host an annual leadership conference for women. A place to network, to prepare for the future and to learn new skills and behaviors. To heal and to grow, to find new ways of running businesses and to become protagonists in the lives of women who attended the conference and in the lives of others.

"I was passionate and enthusiastic, and even though many people thought I was crazy, too young, a foreigner, no money, nobody, and didn't believe in me, some did. Enough to make it happen.

Starting WIN was incredibly difficult in the early years (actually it is still kind of difficult). I have done it all through networking. We started with no budget and nothing other than supportive friends and contacts. It meant I had to learn how to do everything. But we had a team, and the first Women's International Networking (WIN) Conference happened in Milan in September 1998," shared Kristin.

Everyday challenges continued to come Kristin's way.

"One year an organization was going to give WIN a venue for free as, during the dates of the conference, it was empty. Then suddenly they needed it themselves. This was three weeks before the event and I found myself without a venue. I went to the Dean of the Bocconi School of Management where I had studied and where I had been actively involved as a volunteer in the alumni associations. The Dean, knowing me from my work in the association and believing in my idea, generously helped finance the rent of another venue," shared Kristin.

Then WIN took off and over the years Kristin has been relentless in networking her way into the corporate world and securing their ongoing support.

"I have relationships and these have been built over many years, where the rule of the game is to contribute and to generously receive. I support the idea with all of me, and others support with money, sponsors, speakers and so on. In the first year, I had 5-7 corporates supporting with things like coffee, paper, and lunch. From the second year, more came on board. It took 4 years before we could make it professional and move from a 100% volunteer run organization to a staff / volunteer run group," she shared.

Now, pioneering this work, companies such as IBM, Shell, Whirlpool, Unilever, HP, Yara, IKEA, and another 90 or so multinationals, have been strong allies and over the past years, numerous corporate programs have been set up to encourage authenticity in business, women leadership, creating inclusive cultures and allowing diversity to flourish.

"Much of this follows the inspiration received at the WIN conference and through networking with purpose with other companies. E.g. IBM sharing their long experience with mentoring programs with Du Pont, Medtronic and DSM etc. Du Pont sharing their processes with Shell. It is fun to have all been part of this journey. Exchanging, learning and sharing - that's networking with purpose. Doing it as whole people and growing vertically, that is the joy part - the networking with joy and passion," added Kristin.

"I have fought very hard to create and protect WIN. It is now easier to attract people to attend - we model, develop, empower and connect leaders with this more feminine, authentic and globally conscious way. A new way is emerging. The difference from so many other ways is the wholeness, the authenticity requested in the new way of building relationships, and in networking with purpose and joy. It has to be clean, clear and free of any manipulation. It becomes a subtle art and it is totally creative."

Kristin pursues her mission throughout the year, hosting 'Mobilizing Women Events' in different countries and holding quarterly 'Corporate Networking Group' meetings where professionals meet to discuss topical issues in the corporate world. She works together with a team of women from all continents. The organization is run on feminine principles, cultural differences and genuine relationships. If you manipulate, you are out. There are plenty of stories of participants and companies who have connected at WIN and who have come back with a new idea, a new way of doing things and the support to do it.

Kristin believes that women have a unique reason to win in the world of business as well.

"The world today is based too much on masculine values of competition, of over production. Women can bring in caring and sharing and looking after each other, listening to our emotions as well as the excel spread sheet," she shared.

"Today, women are leading. Men are with us. We can do many things together, both women amongst women and women and men. Young and old generations, its an exciting time if we work together," she added.

Kristin has created power-networking principles at WIN, which are as follows:

- *Be open:*
  Work on yourself, become conscious and aware of when you are judging others and yourself.

- *Be ready to connect:*
  Share what stimulates your intellect, excites your belly and makes your heart warm – connect at many levels, LISTEN, sense.

- *Be quick to contribute:*
  Be a solution to another's problem - whom else do you know, share what you have to contribute with. You matter!.

- *Be ready to take risks:*
  Step out of your comfort zone.

- *Commit (stand by what you say you will do, become a person dedicated to something. Your 'brand' is formed over time, who do you want to be?).*

- *Never accept the unacceptable:*
  Don't tolerate what is not good for you; if you accept what is not acceptable, it is reinforced. Be courageous. This is a very important point. Be a person with character. Be noble.

- *Be light and have fun:*
  Laugh, have a sense of humor, bring joy, do more of what you like, be generous to other people and listen to them when they talk about something they are enthusiastic about... it is the joy principle, and it is lovely).

- *Be prepared to experience magic:*
  Yes, expect magic to happen, it already does. This world is such a magic place and some magical solutions are certainly needed.

Kristin also has some personal tips for networking 'beginners' at an event:

- *Others may be uncomfortable about networking too:*
  Try to put them at ease. In so doing you'll make yourself feel more relaxed as well. Go up and introduce yourself to people standing by themselves.

- *Introduce yourself clearly:*
  Tell people who you are, what you do, where you live and something else about you that is positive, beautiful and that you feel passionate about. It only takes a minute.

- *Handing over a business card:*
  This can help if there are language difficulties and will ensure that you can be found again.

- *Give somebody the benefit of an introduction:*
  Being introduced is a wonderful experience, puts people at ease and makes networking much easier.

- *Thank people for the gift of being introduced:*
  Acknowledge an introduction and refer to the source. Be clear, be transparent, have fun, use all your senses, be in your body, stand on your feet, and ... breathe!

Kristin's WIN has spawned numerous regional conferences every year. 10700 women leaders have to date attended the LIVE WIN Conferences and hundreds of thousands are part of the network.

Kristin currently lives in Switzerland and stays attuned to emerging trends that shape our world, and continually encourages women and men to live creatively and authentically, so that together we can all create a sustainable future. She frequently speaks at conferences for companies and organizations all over the world and writes frequently on women's journeys. In Kristin's own research and "journey life" (as she calls it), and essential to her vision and being, is her passion for family, community, creativity, acting, yoga, Zen, and continuous learning.

"Networking and hard work has been key to my success. Network with purpose! Surround yourself with sustainers, believers and champions. Develop different relationships and sensibilities. And finally, build and nurture a network. You will never know when you will need it," concluded Kristin.

*"I do have a pretty big Rolodex but honestly it's not the size of it that matters. What counts is that I know most people will take my calls and return my emails. This has been an enormous advantage since the old adage still definitely applies that to get something done, it's not what you know, it's who you know."*

*Su-Mei Thompson, CEO, The Women's Foundation, Hong Kong.*

**P**erpetually busy, charmingly articulate and super-connected, these phrases all seem to be equally true of **Su-Mei Thompson,** Chief **Executive at The Women's Foundation, Hong Kong.**

Su-Mei lives life at a relentless pace. Besides running The Women's Foundation - one of Hong Kong's leading NGOs dedicated to the advancement of women, she was appointed to the Equal Opportunities Commission by the Chief Executive of Hong Kong in 2013, is an advisory board member of Intelligence Squared

Asia, a Board member of Opera HK, a council member of her own alma mater The Cheltenham Ladies College and also writes on women's issues for the South China Morning Post.

Su-Mei grew up in Malaysia before being sent to Cheltenham at the age of 12. She went on to study law at Cambridge and Oxford where she earned a first-class degree in the BCL, the Oxford equivalent of a LLM.

In 1989, she became a part time lecturer and tutor at Kings' College, London. The same year, she joined Linklaters in London.

"To be honest, I never set out with the conscious design of needing or wanting to build a network. Even as early as University, I've been the same way. I just like meeting new people, I like to help others and I like to connect people who I think will enjoy each other's company. So all along I've been doing what comes quite naturally to me," shared Su-Mei.

At Cambridge, Su-Mei organized a drinks party for 300 budding lawyers and persuaded Perrier Jouet to sponsor the event. As a young lawyer at Linklaters in London, she ran for and was elected to the Executive Committee of the National Trainee Solicitors Group comprising 17,000 trainee and newly qualified solicitors, while also serving as a member of Young Justice, a legal rights pressure group.

"I absolutely loved being part of the TSG which brought me into contact with young lawyers from all over the UK. As the Executive Committee member in charge of communications, I was responsible for the newsletter which went to all 17,000 members and this was an incredible way to hone my early interest in connecting people and persuading them to actively support a common agenda which in the case of the TSG in those days centered on improving the quality of training young lawyers in the UK were receiving," she shared.

After stints with Linklaters in Brussels and Paris, in 1993, Linklaters asked Su-Mei to go to Hong Kong where she has been based ever since. She worked for the firm for a further three years before joining Walt Disney Television as Regional Director for Legal and Business Affairs.

After four years at Disney, Su-Mei joined Asiacontent.com as General Counsel and SVP for Business & Corporate Development. After helping the company to list on NASDAQ, CEO Chris Justice tapped Su-Mei's organizational capabilities and astute inter-personal skills to head the business development and corporate development functions, which included managing Asiacontent's partnerships with dotcom pioneers CNET and DoubleClick, and liaising with investors who included Hambrecht & Quist and Viacom.

"Asiacontent was an amazing experience. I loved the entrepreneurial spirit and camaraderie of being in a start-up, and the feeling of endless possibilities to be explored. I think I met more people - from other entrepreneurs to venture capitalists, from techie-geeks to media moguls - in the 12 months I spent at Asiacontent than in the whole of my business career upto that point. It was an amazing moment in time – business deals were getting done in Starbucks, start-ups were getting bigger valuations than established behemoths, and the Internet was driving ever greater access to information and 24 hour connectivity."

When the bubble burst, the go-getter in Su-Mei decided to consolidate her business and management skills by pursuing an MBA at IMD in Lausanne, Switzerland. Here she became the first woman to graduate on the Dean's list and shortly afterwards, she secured a job with Pearson to run the Financial Times in Asia.

Despite the chaos that followed the outbreak of SARS in 2003, Su-Mei oversaw the successful launch of the new Asian edition of the newspaper with an eye-catching marketing campaign which saw Hong Kong's IFC2 tower (them the tallest building in Hong Kong) wrapped in a giant FT newspaper for three weeks.

"In a way our timing was serendipitous because we were able to position the launch of the FT as a sign that post-SARS, Hong Kong was back as an important financial and commercial centre. As a result, we got a lot of support from the Government and the business community."

Under her leadership, the brand established several important partnerships in the region and made significant inroads into India and China. In the year after its launch, the Financial Times was the fastest-growing international business publication in the region.

Su-Mei's own growing Rolodex, combined with the relationships enjoyed by the FT with government leaders, key regulators and business titans, also enabled the FT to mount several high-profile conferences in the region.

"I remember asking then Mayor Lee (later President Lee) of Seoul who would be on his dream list of speakers for the FT's inaugural Asian Financial Centres Summit in Seoul in 2006 and without missing a beat he said he wanted Alan Greenspan and Rudy Giuliani. Well, we managed to secure them both, which I think says a lot about the convening power of the FT."

Su-Mei got married in 1996 and had her first daughter in 2005. In 2006, while pregnant with her second daughter, she joined Christie's, the global auction house, where she helped to map the company's future growth across Asia and managed Christie's network of regional representative offices in 13 locations.

Of her time at Christie's, she says she is particularly proud of the new country heads - both women - who she hired in Indonesia and Singapore who are running these markets to this day. "Finding the right individual - with the right background, network and personal drive - who would excel in the role wasn't easy. I didn't use a search firm – I did it by tapping my existing contacts, Christie's connections, talking to our key clients and meeting candidate after candidate."

In 2007, Su-Mei had her second daughter and decided to take a year off to bring up her children.

She shared, "It was pretty terrifying stepping off the corporate ladder after being a corporate slave for over 20 years. My time off helped me understand why so many women who take a career break feel unnerved by the experience and how much confidence, courage and determination it takes to get back into the saddle. That was definitely part of what motivated me to accept the offer to run The Women's Foundation to ensure this and related issues which women face are being discussed and addressed."

Established in 2004, The Women's Foundation is a non-profit organization dedicated to improving the lives of women and girls in Hong Kong through groundbreaking research, innovative and impactful community programs, and education and advocacy. The Foundation's three key focus areas are challenging gender stereotypes, increasing the number of women in decision-making and leadership positions and empowering women in poverty to achieve a better quality of life for themselves and their families.

Under Su-Mei's leadership, in the last five years, the Foundation has embraced an ambitious agenda and launched a number of new programs and initiatives, spanning life skills and gender awareness training for at-risk and under-privileged teens, financial capability training for marginalized communities of women, a comprehensive strategy to stimulate demand for, and to promote the supply of, women on boards and in executive roles, initiatives to address the under-representation of women in technology, a campaign to highlight the role of media in creating and perpetuating gender stereotypes and research on women entrepreneurs in Hong Kong.

Commenting on the Foundation's flagship Mentoring Programme for Women Leaders, Su-Mei says "We launched The Women's Foundation's Mentoring Programme for Women Leaders in 2009 and over the past five years, the programme has gone from strength to strength. Every year, we match 50 seasoned female mentors who are leaders in their fields with 50 aspiring female leaders. Over the course of a 12-month programme cycle, mentors and protégés enjoy a one on one mentoring relationship, inspirational speaker events, skills workshops and networking gatherings. We have had so many touching stories of protégés who tell us how their mentor opened doors for them that led to opportunities they never imagined or how their mentor helped them get through a difficult personal or Proffessional period and emerge stronger on the other side.

"One such example was a couple of years ago when protégé Vicky Wu was in the process of leaving Goldman Sachs to set up zaozao.com, an online fashion site. We matched her up with Fiona Marin, founder and CEO of luxury accessories brand, KOTUR. Vicky credits Fiona as an incredibly important factor behind the successful launch of zaozao.com - a one of a kind crowd-funding shopping platform for jewelry, accessories, and handbags by emerging designers in Asia," shared Su-Mei.

Similarly, The Women's Foundation matched protégé Alice Yuen who was struggling to write a business plan to set up her own physiotherapy practice.

"She graduated as a Physiotherapist from Hong Kong Polytechnic University and had no business background. We matched her with Anne Farlow, a Cambridge and HBS graduate, who had had a successful career in private equity. Alice credits Anne with giving her the commercial advice and confidence she needed to launch the Alive Healthcare & Physiotherapy Center which is now a thriving enterprise," continued Su-Mei.

Su-Mei has also been instrumental in setting up the 30% Club Hong Kong, which is leading the charge for more women on corporate boards, by engaging male chairmen and CEOs and persuading them to sign on as advocates for change. Already some 60 chairmen of leading companies have signed up to champion bringing more women onto corporate boards.

Su-Mei continues to expand her already extensive network, particularly beyond Hong Kong's boundaries. She is increasingly in demand as a speaker at global and regional forums and conferences including, most recently, the Annual Meeting of the World Bank Group and IMF in Tokyo in 2012 and the Women's Forum in Myanmar in 2013.

I asked Su-Mei who her networking role-models are.

Her reply was quick.

"David Eldon, former Chairman of The Hong Kong and Shanghai Banking Corporation Limited, is someone I really respect and admire. He has so much integrity and warmth, and is unfailingly courteous and good-natured. It's no wonder that he's remained so active in, and is feted by, the business community even after retiring from HSBC in 2005," she shared.

"I am also a huge fan of Helena Morrissey - CEO of Newton Asset Management, and founder of the 30% Club. Besides her busy day job, Helena is actively involved in the arts and in education initiatives and recently chaired the independent inquiry into the Lib Deb party in the UK. She somehow manages to fit all this in while bringing up nine children. She exudes positive energy and is irresistibly charming, which is a very potent combination," she added.

Su-Mei shared with me her top few tips on effective networking:

- *Always take pains to make a good first impression:*
  First impressions are like ink stains; they persist and take a long time to fade.

- *Do your research beforehand and ask questions to show you care about the other person:*
  You need to be a good listener. It's not just about delivering your elevator speech - effective networking is about establishing a rapport with the other person and that only comes from a two-way dialogue.

- *Practice interrupting!*
  You need to find a way to make your voice heard and your presence felt particularly when everyone else is being very assertive around you.

- *Foster good relationships with a wide circle of people:*
  Not just with people from work or in a business context. They will help maintain perspective in good and difficult times, and will be an important source of encouragement and support if and when things go wrong at work. And beyond your friends and family, get involved in the community in some way whether through a charity, your church, a club or a political or other cause. Your life will be richer and more enjoyable as a result.

Su-Mei concluded our interview by sharing how much a part of her success her network has been.

"People have always been incredibly generous with their help, expertise and encouragement. Now almost 25 years after I first started working, I do have a pretty big Rolodex but honestly it's not the size of it that matters. What counts is that I know most people will take my calls and return my emails. This has been an enormous advantage since the old adage definitely still applies that to get something done, it's not what you know, it's who you know," she shared.

Su-Mei continues to enjoy Hong Kong with her husband Marcus, their daughters Tallulah and Allegra, and their four rescue dogs.

S he has been working in television for over 20 years. Since the start of her career she has built an incredible circle of connections with C suite executives such as Ratan Tata, Chairman Emeritus of Tata Sons; Cher Wang, co-founder and Chairperson of HTC Corporation; Jin Liqun, Chairman of Board of Supervisors of the sovereign wealth fund, China Investment Corporation; Kwek Leng Beng, Executive Chairman of Hong Leong Group; Richard Elman, founder of commodities giant Noble Group; Abdul Wahid Omar, former CEO of Maybank; Carlos Ghosn of Renault & Nissan and Sir Gordon Wu of Hopewell Holdings. She has filmed on the Great Wall of China, been in the thick of the action during the SARS crisis and has covered major events like the Asian Economic Crisis, the Dot Com Bubble Crash and the US financial meltdown.

Meet **Christine Tan** - the Singapore based anchor for **CNBC's award-winning** and **longest-running feature program 'Managing Asia'** where she interviews top executives and CEOs of companies operating in Asia.

In a business where getting to the top executives of the most powerful companies on the planet defines her day-to-day success, Christine is one of the best networkers in the world.

"Getting that elusive CEO to talk to me requires me to build up extensive contacts and networks. Building that circle of contacts and influence is linked to how credible I am as a journalist. Credibility has to be earned through sheer diligence ploughing through tons of research and working your contacts," shared Christine.

*"Networking is about putting in the hard work and proving to people you can go the distance. I believe that in success, 10% is based on luck. 90% is hard work. Every new contact is a challenge."*

**Christine Tan, Anchor, CNBC Asia Pacific.**

Christine grew up in Singapore, schooled at the Catholic Junior College and then went on to New Zealand for her studies. She holds a Bachelor of Arts degree in Sociology and English and a Master of Arts degree with Honors in Sociology from the University of Auckland, New Zealand.

"I realized early on that if you spoke well and engaged in conversations, it was always easy to connect with people. Having a sense of humor always helped. I was always the first to laugh at a good joke, even at myself if I did something silly. I also found I learnt a lot more by being a good listener. And I was very discreet with things that people told me in confidence. And that helped me strike up good and meaningful relationships," commented Christine.

Christine has more than 20 years of journalistic experience under her belt. She worked 7 years at Television Corporation of Singapore, now known as MediaCorp where she helmed the 7pm daily news and later on went on to host the company's flagship business programme Money Mind.

She left to join CNBC in 1999. "I had outgrown my previous job and when the opportunity came up to join a global network, I jumped". She has been working with CNBC for more than 15 years, hosting daily programmes like Squawk Box, Asia Market Wrap and Worldwide Exchange. But she found it was anchoring the network's flagship CEO show 'Managing Asia' that she had to work her networks the hardest.

"When you first start out, it's always difficult to make and strike meaningful contacts. The way you do it is by doing good interviews and making sure you are always on top of the game with breaking news and information. It's a slow process where you build up trust and credibility and that helps to opens doors in the end"

"My role as Anchor for Managing Asia required a whole new level of networking. It meant tireless research to get the right CEOs, and at the right time!

I love to "chase" the ever-elusive CEO to talk to me. I love breaking news with CEOs that other networks find hard to get. It's a thrill I thrive on and something my Senior Producer and I share passionately.

Public events where I play a part in moderating panel discussions are one of the best ways to strike up good contacts. CEOs attending these forums and conferences get to "know me" when I am up there on stage doing my job. Of course, having a good smile always helps," she shared.

"Asian CEOs are always more media shy than western CEOs. They tend to operate under the radar and shy away from publicity. Sometimes, it's about respecting their wishes not to appear on camera that gets you closer to them. And sometimes being patient pays off," added Christine.

That patience really paid off when Christine landed the most elusive interview with property magnate Kwek Leng Beng, who is listed by Forbes as No. 2 on Singapore's 50 Richest list with a net worth of US $ 7.1 Billion.

"It took me 10 years to get Kwek Leng Beng from Hong Leong Group to talk to me," shared Christine.

"There was also Eddie Teh, former Group Chief Executive of PSA. He was a very private man who didn't see the need for any personal publicity. I reached out to him several times and one day, he just said yes," she added.

"I did the only TV interview that Eddie Teh ever gave in his career. It was a real win over my rivals in the industry," shared Christine.

Christine is quick to recognize the team effort of her colleagues at CNBC and the support of the CNBC network.

"To be fair, it's not all me. Being part of such a great global credible business network like CNBC plays a big part in reaching out to CEOs. The constant daily coverage of high quality breaking news is something that CEOs and tycoons pay close attention to everyday when running their businesses and empires. No other network gives you that coverage. If you are a CEO, you want to go with a station that will make a big impact, if that's the only interview you'll ever do," added Christine.

"Part of building a network and influencing a CEO to come on camera is also about being a responsible journalist consistently and asking tough questions but in a fair manner on camera," she commented.

Christine offered some simple tips on how her networking success could be replicated:

- *Be deliberate and plan your networking:*
  It's about being at the right place at the right time. This takes a fair amount of planning and does not happen just by chance.

- *It's about focus but at the same time patience:*
  Be persistent but not pushy.

- *Never compromise on your integrity:*
  There is a lot of talking and convincing but never any compromise on integrity. I have rejected interviews where I've been told not to ask a certain question or touch a certain topic. At the end of the day, you want to do everything you can to keep and build your credibility. And whether CEOs say it or not, that 'rejection' helps to build respect for who you are as a person. As a journalist it is very important.

- *Don't be afraid of rejection:*
  I'm not afraid to fail. Like I said earlier, it took me ten years to get that one important interview. Often when you reach out, your target may not reciprocate that good will. Work through it and find another person who could help you meet your objective or influence the person you are not having very good luck connecting with. Through failure and rejection you get stronger. You learn what to do differently the next time!"

- *Finally, networking is about putting in the hard work and proving to people you can go the distance:*
  I believe that in success, 10% is based on luck. 90 % is hard work. Every new contact is a challenge. Every interview is a discovery. Every CEO is always interesting. I am constantly open to new things; exploring different ways to do things better.

Christine has made a huge impact on the business world and is widely recognized as one of the best in the business.

She was a finalist for Best News Anchor in 2001 and 2002 at the New York Festivals. She received the Best News Program award at the 2004 Asian Television Awards on behalf of The Asian Wall Street Journal. The same program also won a finalist award  at the 2004 New York Festivals for Coverage of a Breaking News Story. She also won for Best Current Affairs Presenter award at the 2008 Asian Television Awards.  Christine also received the Silver World Medal for Best Anchor at the 2009 New York Festivals Television Programming and Promotion Awards. Recently she was "highly commended" at the 2013 Asian Television Awards.

"Awards help build more contacts and networking gets easier. When you've made a name for yourself and people know you, it's always a little easier to get that elusive CEO. "In my profession, networking and building that so called circle of influence is about making that impression on CEOs that they will remember forever. It's about creating an experience where they enjoy talking to me on camera. At the end of the day, CEOs want to be engaged, they want to know I've done my research and that they're not wasting their time. And nothing makes me happier when they say to me at the end of the interview "Gosh, you've really done your homework!"

"That to me is success," concluded Christine.

# Chapter 13

# LEARN
## HOW TO
# INFLUENCE

Old command and control organizations are a thing of the past. The new buzzword is influence in a highly complex world of differing opinions and philosophies. For women in particular this is a much needed skill given the current lower percentages of women in leadership positions at the very highest levels of corporate power. I interviewed **Clarisse Reille,** *Chairperson of the Grandes Ecoles au Feminin;* **Micho F. Spring,** *Chair, Global Corporate Practice and President, New England, Weber Shandwick and* **Emily Sperling,** *President, ShelterBox USA.*

Clarisse Reille has switched between some of the most powerful roles in business and in Government. **Clarisse** is currently **General Manager for DEFI, the French Association for the Economic Development of the Apparel Industry.** She is also the **Chairperson** of the **GEF** (Grandes Écoles au Féminin). GEF includes the alumni associations of the top ten Universities in France - Centrale Paris, ENA, ESCP Europe, ESSEC, HEC, INSEAD, Mines Paris Tech, Polytechnique, Ponts Paris Tech, Sciences-Po Paris. In all, GEF currently has over 42000 members.

> *"The world of the future is dependent on influence and collaboration like never before. Today we live in a world, which truly has no boundaries and many stakeholders with very diverse points of view. Nobody can oversee or control everything. Consumers are all-powerful and have the means through social media to impose their power even on large corporations. So soft influence and collaboration is truly important."*
>
> **Clarisse Reille,**
> *Chairperson of the Grandes Ecoles au Feminin.*

Throughout her illustrious career there has been one leadership philosophy that has helped her most – the power of Influence.

Clarisse is the iron fist in a velvet glove.

"Life is long and therefore even though we cannot have everything at one moment in life, we can still have many good things at any point. Balance is very important. Respecting the stakeholders we deal with is even more important. And so is getting things done in a win - win way versus an adversarial way," shared Clarisse softly when we had our first discussion.

"I have found that I get the best results by working in a soft, non-threatening way to build consensus," she added.

Clarisse shared that she learned the art of influence as she grew in her career and learned a lot from mistakes she made in early years.

"At the beginning of my professional life, I thought it was sufficient to have a good analysis of a situation, think about the most rational solution and that this process would be sufficient. How naïve I was. The straight line is very seldom the most efficient. I learned the soft, collaborative way through experience and also because I respect other people and their points of view. Rather than focus immediately on the result, it is often much better to focus on the relationships and building trust with the person. The results will then come."

Clarisse grew up in Lyon to parents who were of Italian origin. Her grand parents on her father's side fled Italy to escape the Mussolini fascist regime.

"They crossed the Alps on foot. My mother was Italian when she married my father. I have no siblings, but my family was loving and caring, with strong values and a deep respect for people. I still call my parents almost every day!" shared Clarisse.

Growing up Clarisse's primary focus was to be a very good and serious student and she always had at the back of her mind that she would be able to "thank" France for welcoming her family. She remembers a quiet life with wonderful supporting teachers. But she also learned the negative impact of carelessly spoken words. A schoolgirl once told her she was 'eating the bread from the French' because of her Italian origins. That made Clarisse resolve that she would never use negative language in her communication.

After secondary school, she studied mathematics and physics, then she graduated from Ecole Centrale de Paris, which is one of the top ten universities in France focused on a multidisciplinary and scientific approach towards the industry. Because Clarisse felt the need to have a broader view on the world she studied international economic policy, public administration, and sociology.

In 1984, at the age of 26, she started her professional life at the Ministry of Finance and she quickly became a key member of the Foreign Trade Ministry.

"It was a hectic but fascinating period but within just three years I felt the need to get more Corporate exposure and so in 1987, I joined BioMerieux - one of the leading companies in medical diagnosis. I started in Florence, Italy where I managed a company just acquired by the group. I faced some key challenges. First, I was the youngest member on the team and I was

French (though of Italian origin). Also, I was one of the very few women on the team," shared Clarisse.

As part of this assignment, Clarisse had to manage various teams - research, development and production and she quickly turned around the company.

"This was a very rewarding time in my career. I had to discuss issues and find solutions to many problems in a very emotional Italian environment. I learned that to influence, I had to first listen to all kinds of people in the Company in the environments they were comfortable in. Even the junior most employee taught me something," shared Clarisse.

In addition, she felt as a French woman, it was absolutely necessary to be fully aware of the results of the Fiorentina Squadra of football to be fully recognized by her Italian team!

Within three years, Clarisse's achievements were recognized and she was moved to the Headquarters of BioMérieux near Lyon in France. She assumed several roles of increasing importance. First she was made responsible for an expansion plan of one of the major product lines and she had to manage all aspects - research, production, logistics and commercial. Subsequently, she was appointed Vice President of the group for Business and Scientific Development. During this period, she travelled extensively. But she also faced a unique challenge. Clarisse had to work with the researchers and help them foster creativity. She did this by using multiple brainstorming sessions where the researchers could build on each other's scientific ideas. In short she brought out the most creative ideas from a highly talented but technically oriented team.

"I learned the power of being not just a devil's advocate but also the importance of what I call being an angel's advocate – using gentle persuasion and brainstorming to influence discussions, and bring out the best in my people," commented Clarisse.

In 1993, Clarisse joined the Cabinet of the Industry Minister. She had to overlook many sectors such as consumer goods and healthcare. In those positions, it is highly necessary to be able to reach consensus with almost opposite parties. One of the most difficult subjects: to reinforce intellectual property rights for the companies. She had to spend weeks and weeks to listen, to convince the parties opposed to this project. In any case, she was certainly right to make this move because she met her husband at the Cabinet: love at first sight! In one year her life changed radically. She got married and soon expected her first child.

Clarisse began to then give more attention to creating a strong balance between family life and work. Her family became the top priority.

"Soon after the birth of my first daughter in 1995, I received an offer to lead as Managing Director for a major company, based in Milano. My husband was very supportive, but if I had taken the position, it would have meant we would have had to split our family. We talked and both felt that the family was most meaningful to us and the cement of all the many meaningful things we wanted to achieve. I turned down the position," shared Clarisse.

But that did not stop Clarisse's upward journey. In 1996 she became a Member of the Board of Management of the CDR, the Credit Lyonnais defeasance structure, and was put in charge of a 10-company portfolio worth 1 Billion Pounds in sales. In 1999 she joined Marsh, Paris – a world leader in insurance brokerage as a member of the Executive Committee and Managing Director.

Today as Chairperson of GEF Clarisse continues to practice the art of influence in many ways and use her senior executive experience to coach and teach young women professionals.

"One of the great challenges that women face in our part of the world is the poor representation of women at very senior levels of large Companies. To demand for interventions is a waste of time. But to bring men onboard to this agenda slowly and convincingly with the right data that makes business sense, in a collaborative way is far more powerful," shared Clarisse.

One of Clarisse's key programs to do exactly that is a Breakfast with CEOs program that has invited the CEOs of some of the largest companies in France to have breakfast with a group of 200 members of GEF at a time.

"This one program has had a tremendous impact on the CEOs of these large Companies and on the young women professionals we bring them in contact with. It is an amazing win-win situation. The women who attend, tremendously benefit from the CEOs' knowledge. For the CEOS themselves, they leave convinced that they need to do more to empower and develop the talented women professionals they have just met. In all, we have already had 30 of France's most powerful CEOs to these breakfasts. This includes Jean-Paul Agon, CEO of L'OREAL; Christophe de Margerie, CEO of Total; Henri de Castries, CEO of AXA; Baudouin Prot, CEO, BNP PARIBAS; Louis Gallois, EADS; Henri Giscard d'Estaing, CEO, CLUB MED and many others.

"Many of the CEOs have gone back to their Companies highly impressed by our young women professionals and almost immediately start diversity circles etc. Some of the best examples include Alstom, Saint Gobain, BNP Paribas, Renault, Societé Générale and Orange.

A few months back we invited Patrick Kron, the Alstom CEO to come and speak. That very afternoon after his visit, he called for a diversity study within the company and in just a few weeks he implemented a new diversity strategy.

"The young women professionals also benefit so much. Because they get a chance to network amongst themselves. They realize that wherever they are, they face the same difficulties. They begin to support each other so much more," added Clarisse.

"Yet only two of those CEOs who came and spoke to our members were women. It is a humbling reminder of how far we yet have to go," she said. "But we are grateful for every step forward," she added.

Clarisse has also leveraged GEF to influence important laws and legislation in France.

"A law in France now imposes quotas in big companies with a target of 40% of women in a few years. The members of Parliament decided to vote for this law after discussing with GEF. They realize how important such a rule is. Because if not imposed the stereotypes are so strong that nothing moves," shared Clarisse.

She added, "We are also influencing via the several studies that GEF carries out in partnership with some of the leading Companies in France."

For its fifth survey, conducted with the support of ten leading companies in 2012 the "Grandes Écoles au Féminin" network asked graduates, men and women, of its ten member schools about the major challenges that companies and organizations will have to meet - the way business leaders get to the top today - the qualities that will be essential for future leaders - the actions needed to make things change positively.

One of the key conclusions of the survey was that 84% of the graduates believe that the appointment of more women to top management positions would change, in a positive way, the qualities and profiles of the leaders of businesses and organizations.

"We use this hard data in soft ways," smiled Clarisse.

I asked Clarisse why she took up this role as Chairperson of GEF and what drives her to the great passion she has for the job.

She responded, "The alumni association of my school actually asked me to take up this role. What influenced me was a study they were doing at the time. One of the questions was "As a woman do you feel strange or alienated in the role you are in". I was shocked that over 65% of respondents said YES. All of these women felt alienated in their roles but faced many similar challenges as women professionals."

"The world of the future is dependent on influence and collaboration like never before. Today we live in a world which truly has no boundaries and many stakeholders with very diverse points of view. Nobody can oversee or control everything. Consumers are all-powerful and have the means through social media to impose their power even on large corporations. So soft influence and collaboration is truly important," she added.

Currently Clarisse s role at DEFI is focused on helping young French designers to go abroad.

"In this role I deal with a lot of people that are truly passionate about the work that they do. For me it is very important to be in touch with beauty. I believe that the art of Influence is just that – a thing of beauty," she concludes tongue-in-cheek.

Clarisse had five power tips for influencing.

- *Respect the stakeholders you deal with:*
  If you demonstrate this respect at every step, work will get done in a win win versus an adversarial way.

- *Focus on building trust:*
  Rather than being single-mindedly focused on the result, focus first on building trust with the stakeholder. As that trust develops, the results will come.

- *Listen to all kinds of people in the environments they are comfortable in:*
  Listen across levels and you will be surprised just how much you can learn from people even at the most junior level. Once you have these insights, it will be far easier to influence.

- *Collaborate, collaborate, collaborate:*
  No one can control everything.

- *Be truly passionate about what you do:*
  The people you are trying to influence will see it, and they will begin to buy into your narrative too.


**M**icho F. Spring is **Chair, Global Corporate Practice** and **President, New England** for one of the world's most powerful Public Relations consultancies – **Weber Shandwick.**

CEO. Deputy Mayor. Chief of Staff. Awarded the Order of Isabel La Catolica Award presented by King Juan Carlos of Spain. One of the "20 Most Powerful Women in Boston" by Boston Magazine. These are all titles that this powerful woman of influence has held during her illustrious career.

But Micho's story of influence and success began during the Castro revolution in Cuba when she had to flee to the US along with her family.

"It was 1960. I was 10 years old. And we had to leave everything we owned behind as well as family, status and influence to escape Castro's threat to send all children, including me, to the countryside for 're-education' -- to Pioneer School. Until that point I had enjoyed a very sheltered environment. Overnight, all of that changed," shared Micho. "I learned how fluid and elusive status and influence can be."

> *"To influence you need a very specific objective or goal. You must want to get something important done. Then you must find the path of least resistance – you need to know which hands to hold and which arms to twist to get there."*
>
> **Micho F. Spring, Chair, Global Corporate Practice and President, New England, Weber Shandwick.**

Micho's earliest impressions about influence came from her mother, who in pre-Castro Havana, when women were expected to stay home, was on the Board of Directors of Cuba's most influential newspaper and was a consultant to McCann Erickson, a leading global advertising firm.

"I often marvelled at the work my mother did even though I was very young at the time," Micho said. She helped McCann's global clients, such as Esso and Coca-Cola make their advertisements culturally relevant to Cuban audiences. She even got me to model for an Esso ad when I was 8! My mother was always positive, courageous and tenacious -- she had a beautiful smile, behind which was a steely determination. It takes courage to break down barriers and reset things in a positive way, especially given the challenges she faced leaving Cuba."

Micho was also heavily influenced by her father, who was a doctor in Cuba, at a time when being a doctor was more akin to public service. Micho remembers many nights during her childhood when her father was awakened in the middle of the night by the phone at his bedside calling him in to provide medical help to someone who needed it. Micho cannot remember a single time he did not respond to the call.

The move to the USA was challenging and Micho remembers her mother's admonition to blend in, become an integral part of their new country, and focus on looking forward. "If you look back, you will turn into a statue of salt," she often said, in reference to the story of Sarah in the bible.

"She reminded me not to speak Spanish on the bus so that I did not seem different in New Orleans, where we first lived, so I would blend in. When we left Cuba, we went from being part of an elite to being a minority overnight. I learned the difference between status and influence, between assertion and persuasion. I saw my mother, for example, persuade a dentist in New Orleans to take care of my braces for free because we had no money to pay, as I sat in the dentist chair, horrified to hear her ask. 'In my country', she explained to this surprised dentist, 'doctors don't charge each other out of professional courtesy'. My father was indeed a doctor, but he was still in Cuba and I am not sure the courtesy applied across national borders!" added Micho.

Micho continued to be amazed by her mother's ability to influence.

"At the Convent of the Sacred Heart, an exclusive girls' school in Manhattan's Upper East Side, my mother persuaded the Reverend Mother, as again I watched in horror, not only to grant me admission two weeks before school started, but to give me a full scholarship because we had no money. My great Aunt, she explained, had left all her money and her silver to the Convent of the Sacred Heart a few generations before. My teeth were straightened and I got a first rate education at Sacred Heart 91st Street, for which I am forever grateful, but more than that, I learned all about the power of persuasion and the importance of communications to influence and get things done and achieve your objectives. Through all this, my mother never once lost her dignity or her humor. I learned that everything communicates, and that having a goal, understanding the environment and then having a clear picture of whom you need to influence and how in order to get the right result is crucial. And of course, I learned that it often takes courage, which was the most important  lesson from my mother, particularly when the answer at first is no," shared Micho.

So when Micho was told by her college counselor that it was impossible to get into Georgetown University, where she very much wanted to go to college, she researched what the least popular major was -- it was Portuguese -- and she applied for it, persuading the Dean of Admissions that she firmly believed Brazil was the country of the future.

And Micho was right!

Micho attended Georgetown and Columbia Universities, served for four years in New York City government, and then received an MPA from Harvard's Kennedy School of Government.

"In fact when I decided to pursue a Master in Public Administration at Harvard even though I had not finished my undergraduate degree, I persuaded the Admissions Dean that my four years in between working for the Mayor of New York were the equivalent of the credits I was missing.

I think my ear is trained never to hear NO. NO just challenges me to find a way to get to YES -- it energizes me, particularly when it is the established power networks that are in my way. It has served me well as a woman often challenging the status quo and hopefully has served my family and my clients," shared Micho.

Her most valuable lesson on learning how to use influence to get things done, however, came on day one after joining the staff of Boston Mayor Kevin H White in 1976.

"To me, that was one of the toughest environments as a woman. Boston City Hall was an Irish white male bastion. They did not know what to think of a young Hispanic woman with a name that sounded Japanese -- I was foreign in so many ways. The biggest challenge I faced as a woman was breaking down barriers and breaking into networks that historically excluded women," shared Micho.

Micho found support however, in a man who believed in women in leadership -- Mayor White.

"Mayor White called me into his office on the first day of my new job as a junior staffer and asked me to look out of the window at Quincy Market below, the crown jewel of his administration, which had just opened -- his proudest achievement. He pointed to a huge, unattractive billboard the market's developer had put up that said, For Rent, call this number".

"You see that sign on top of that building," the Mayor said, barely looking up from his paperwork. "It does not belong there and MUST come down. I want you to get that done." The meeting was clearly over.

"I had absolutely no idea how to get this huge sign taken down," shared Micho. "I was terrified."

In the next few weeks Micho had to do research and ask for meetings with the head of Development, the Buildings Commisisoner, the Public Works Department, other staff members and permitting authorities, none of whom she had met and none of whom had to respond to her, and figure out who had the power to make the developer take the sign down and how to persuade them to do so.

Three months later, after many negotiations with multiple stakeholders, Micho got the sign taken down.

She realized that Mayor White had given her an important test of how to exert influence without having control -- key to being an effective staffer and getting things done against the gravity and the power of the bureaucracy.

"It confirmed my belief that to influence you need a very specific objective or goal. One must want to get something important done. And then finding the path of least resistance to your goal is key. This is a very important skill to have, especially for women in the workplace," she shared.

That single challenge changed Micho's whole mindset.

"To this day I believe that was a very  important lesson I learned among so many from the Mayor. I learned that influence is figuring out a way around traditonal patterns, finding the leverage points in an organization, reading the signals, and understanding this can be a major weapon in getting things done. And the importance of never taking no for an answer."

Micho went on to serve on the staff of the Mayor for eight years, the last four as Deputy Mayor for Policy Management as well as Chief of Staff. During her time there, she witnessed first hand how conservative men's attitudes were to women in the workplace.

"When I was Chief of Staff to Mayor White, I had to conduct the performance reviews of all 42 city commisioners against very specific policy goals we were trying to accomplish.  One of our goals at the time was to increase the representation of women in the Fire Department. The

Fire Commisioner at the time did not take the goal seriously and I was determined to hold him accountable for the goals we had set a year back, which the City was under court order to attain. During his performance review I shared that he had failed to meet this goal and he would not have a salary increase. He was furious, since this would affect his retirement. He looked at me and said 'I can't promote women because they keep going out on maternity leave.' I was visibly pregnant with my daughter at the time."

But neither that commisioners' attitude nor that of Micho's other male colleagues could stop Micho from making a difference in her work. During her role at the Mayors' office she helped steer the city through its worse fiscal crisis, successfully ran the cable franchising process and was part of the team that helped transform Boston into the world class city it is today.

In 1984, Micho was pregnant with her son when the Mayor retired and she left City Hall after running the transition to a new Administration. As she looked for new career opportunities, she was shocked to hear criticism about her plans to continue working even though she was pregnant.

"Come back to us when you are serious," some of the interviewers told her, not even bothering to hide their bemusement that she would seek employment when she was six months pregnant.

Micho persisted and finally was recruited as CEO for a start up Company -- Boston Telecommunications Company.

"At that time, the telecommunications industry was mostly male and I was often the only woman in the room. Attitudes toward women in the corporate sector were far behind attitudes in government, so I found much more resistance to being taken seiously as a CEO. Delivering business results was key -- there was less margin for error because I was a woman, and I had to work twice as hard to establish my authority at meetings. But I felt I had earned an organizational behavior degree at City Hall that served me well, and knowing when to assert and when to beg was extremely useful. The fact I know how to close the deal and bring in business was very helpful.

In 1992 Micho joined a strategic communications firm called SawyerMiller Group, which would finally become part of Weber Shandwick.

At Weber Shandwick Micho began to unleash the full power of her ability to use communications as a key vehicle to influence outcomes on behalf of clients.

Her practice focuses on enabling corporate clients to use communications to support their business strategies, enhance and protect their reputation, and respond to public policy challenges. During her tenure at Weber Shandwick, Micho has counseled clients across industries on a wide range of reputational issues, including CEO succession, mergers and acquisitions, litigation and regulatory matters, and corporate responsibility. Her current clients include Liberty Mutual, McCormick, Houghton Mifflin Harcourt, Brigham and Women's Hospital and Massachusetts Institute of Technology (MIT).

"Influencing attitudes, habits and policies on behalf of our clients has become my full time profession. I came to understand that communications is key to influence and it is the currency of change," shared Micho.

Micho shared with me several examples of her influencing skills in action.

The first example was when P&G acquired Gillette in 2005.

Micho commented, "P&G bought Gillette, an iconic Boston based company, at a time of great anxiety among Boston's business, political and civic communities. Several key Boston based institutions had recently been sold to outsiders, notably Bank Boston, the city's most prominent bank, and the Boston Globe, our major newspaper. When Gillette announced it was selling the company to Cincinnatti based P&G, it felt like a deathblow to the city's pride. Matters were made considerably worse by the outgoing CEO of Gillette's remarks in a speech to the Boston Chamber of Commerce, where he was critical of the city and the way he had been treated and acknowledged he had never moved to Boston while running the company."

Micho received a call from P&G's Charlotte Otto, then P&G's Chief External Relations Officer asking if Micho could help P&G generate a more positive environment, as they entered the Boston market as a key player.

"Charlotte and I met and reviewed options. We determined the damage was such that we needed to go beyond extending Gillette commitments and defining the obvious economic benefits having a company like P&G

could bring to the region. Since P&G markets to women (as opposed to Gillette, which markets predominantly to men), we decided we would launch a campaign to get women leaders in this region excited about the prospects of P&G having a significant presence in Boston. We developed a list of women influencers and went to work, and organized a way to reach every one of them through small breakfast meetings and open forums, and we defined the benefits of having such an iconic company as a new player in Boston. Within 60 days the fever had broken. We also engaged the economic development community, the universities where P&G conducts research, and announced a series of CSR initiatives, but the backbone of the campaign was our women influencer strategy and it turned the tide. P&G's acquisition of Gillette is considered one of the most successful in the history of the Company," shared Micho.

Another great example came in a highly controversial area of tissue sample collection and genome mapping.

"Ardais was a new start up focused on building a high tech tissue bank, where hospitals could store tissue samples and researchers could retrieve them as genome mapping opened up the possibilities of much more targeted cures and personalized medicine. Ardais raised the capital and attracted the talent to establish the gold standard in the field, but no major hospital wanted to be first for fear of being perceived as trading on their patients' tissue samples.

So what could we do to reassure a major hospital to take the first step? I recommended a risky strategy -- that we go after an editorial from our region's newspaper of record, the Boston Globe. If we could persuade the Globe to do an editorial endorsing the concept and naming Ardais as the ethical gold standard in this new category, we could get a major hospital to sign and the business could proceed.

We put together a team to explain the concept and the safeguards to patients that included medical ethicists and even a Rabbi. We marched into the Globe, and while we were all waiting in the hallway, the Editorial Director saw me, and said for every one to hear – 'Micho, you are not with the tissue snatchers, are you??' This was not an auspicious way to start the meeting. We spent the next hour answering every possible question. We persuaded the Globe. They published a glowing editorial and the next week one of Harvard's leading teaching hospitals signed the agreement to move forward, breaking the ice and paving the way for other hospitals across the country," shared Micho.

Micho is today one of the most celebrated women professionals in Boston.

Over the last four decades as a government, civic, and business leader, Micho has helped shape public debate on numerous issues in Boston and beyond. She has managed many political and advocacy campaigns and is a frequent independent media commentator. On multiple occasions she has been named one of the "20 Most Powerful Women in Boston" by Boston Magazine.

Micho currently sits on the Executive Committee of the Greater Boston Chamber of Commerce, is a founding member of the WBUR Group Executive Council, and is a Founder and Chair of Friends of Caritas Cubana. She holds numerous board memberships, including NBH Holdings Corp, the John F. Kennedy Library Foundation, The Boston Foundation, and the Massachusetts Women's Forum, of which she is a past President.

Micho was inducted as a Legend into the Ad Club's Hall of Fame and recognized as a Distinguished Bostonian by the Boston Chamber of Commerce. In addition, she received a Lifetime Achievement Award from the Greater Boston Chamber of Commerce's Women's Network, the Women Who Give award by the Women's Lunch Place, the Give Liberty a Hand honor by the Massachusetts Immigration & Refugee Advocacy Coalition (MIRA), the Jorge Hernandez Corporate Leadership Award, and the Order of Isabel La Catolica Award presented by King Juan Carlos of Spain.

Micho shared with me the five simple  steps she uses in her "Influence Process."

- *Have a clear purpose:*
  Before you attempt to influence, you must be clear about your objectives what it is you want to influence.

- *Listen carefully and make sure to understand the environment:*
  Figure out who your allies and your opponents are as well as the pressure points you need to target. Train yourself to read the room.

- *Connect the dots among peoples' agendas:*
  Know where they are coming from. See what could be a win-win versus a win-lose.

- *Prepare, prepare, prepare:*
  Throughout my career I have been better able to influence when I had all of the facts and was better prepared than my opponents.

- *Believe in the power of sisterhood. Ask other women for support and support other women:*
  Secretary of State Madeline Albright once said that there is a special place in hell for women who do not support other women -- and I strongly believe that. Join women's networks or start them!

- *Remember that everything communicates:*
  Be conscious of what messages you are sending both formally and informally by what you say and do. Symbols are powerful.

"Influence is after all knowing which hands to hold and which arms to twist!" added Micho.

Alongside her illustrious career Micho has faced another challenge that many women across the world face. Breast cancer. She has reapplied her influencing ability to meet this challenge with similar courage.

"I was diagnosed 10 years ago, and it stopped me in my tracks. I am lucky that we caught it in time so that it is very much in my rear view mirror. But what I think was transferable was my ability to look for things I could influence in order to have some sense of control -- for me, after I finished radiation, it was to focus on diet and exercise. I became very disciplined about eating healthy and exercising regularly, which studies show is very helpful in avoiding recurrence. And I try to help other women going through it, because having that network was crucial in getting me through that initial shock," she shared.

Today Micho enjoys the simple pleasures of life.

"I love running, swimming, yoga, and am an avid reader of history, particularly biographies. I have been married to my husband Bill, whom I met at Harvard, for 38 years and he is my soulmate -- the nicest guy I ever met. We are blessed with a growing family, and I spend most of my spare time trying to influence my grandson Julian (5), granddaughter Vera (1) and newborn grandson Mason," concluded a beaming Micho.

A s the **President** of **ShelterBox USA**, managing millions of dollars worth of relief funds, **Emily Sperling** describes herself as a **social entrepreneur**. When we first spoke, she was in the midst of organizing relief for the Philippines in the immediate aftermath of typhoon Haiyan.

"If I am to be effective in the rapidly changing, crisis linked environment that Shelter Box operates in every day, I have to be agile in terms of influencing people to support our basic mission – of instantly responding to disasters and humanitarian crises by delivering equipment and materials that provide shelter, warmth and dignity to vulnerable families around the globe," shared Emily.

ShelterBox helps thousands of families who lose everything in a disaster every year. Each ShelterBox supplies an extended family with a tent and essential equipment to use while they are displaced or homeless. The Company charity has now worked in more than 90 countries, responding to earthquakes, tsunamis, floods, typhoons, hurricanes, volcanoes and conflict.

> *"I learned about the basic motivations of each of the members of the team. I understood what made each of them do what they did with such passion, and then I worked to foster their unique talents and create growth opportunities for them within our small organization."*
>
> *Emily Sperling, President, ShelterBox USA.*

Emily grew up in Florida to a talented Mum who was an artist – a goldsmith who worked tirelessly to look after Emily and her elder sister as well as care for Emily's ailing father.

"While my parents divorced when I was six years old, they remained very close until my father's death six years later. My Mum is a true warrior. She worked multiple jobs to support us, including teaching jewelry making. My mother's passion and compassion toward my father provided my motivation – to be able to help people leverage their talent and look after their families," shared Emily.

Emily also claims that her role model for influencing people was her grandfather.

"My grandfather was city commissioner for the town of Sarasota, Florida. And was incredibly adept at the art of influencing people. By the age of 9, I was already spending a lot of time with him, understanding what he did and seeing him in action. I learned from him the importance of integrity and building trust with someone as a solid foundation for influence. The biggest gift I received from my grandfather was the special skill of making people never want to disappoint you," shared Emily.

Then when her father passed away when she was 12, Emily threw herself into her studies and equestrian sport. She was also surrounded by a large extended family that had very high expectations but at the same time was very supportive.

"My refuge was equestrian sport. It is an expensive sport so all of my Mum's disposable income went into this pursuit. Mum recognized it as a passion of mine (just like creating jewelry was for her) and in the early days time at the barn gave us something we could enjoy together, particularly while healing from the loss of my dad. And I was very, very lucky to have the support of a riding instructor with whom I became very close. She recognized that for me and other kids the sport could be extremely expensive – she gave me the opportunity to work off some of the costs. With her encouragement in my early teens I began managing her barn, teaching lessons to other students and training other people's horses to pay for my involvement in the sport," added Emily.

In 1993 a chance meeting with a schoolmate's dad influenced Emily to study agricultural economics. In March 1998, Emily took her first permanent role as Manager for Communications and member services at the Cape Cod Cranberry Growers Association. This was quite a complex task. As part of her role there, Emily provided communications, fundraising and membership services for the association and its mission to support the cranberry growers of Massachusetts.

"Among the most challenging tasks requiring tactful influence was working out disputes between cranberry growers and their neighbors who were unfamiliar with the farming practices employed adjacent to their properties. The situation was unique. An expanding commuter train line from Boston down into southeastern Massachusetts created tremendous housing growth. The majority of the open space available in that area was located near active cranberry farms. At the same time, the cranberry market crashed and the price growers were paid for their fruit dropped immensely. Many Cranberry growers were dramatically impacted by the market and were faced with the potential of losing farms – many of which 100+ years old. People wanting to move to the area, coupled with the fact cranberry growers owned a lot of the open space and were facing financial crisis due to the cranberry market drop, led many growers to sell some of their land to home builders. Suddenly bogs that had been previously buffered by acres of land now had houses abutting their properties. In many cases, the residents didn't seem to understand what it meant to live next to an active farm and this led to complaints about noise, pest management tools and growing techniques. Emotions often ran high," shared Emily.

Emily began to quickly understand the importance of getting to the root cause of a problem, quickly and definitively addressing misinformation during the influencing process and also the importance of slowly getting closer to people you have conflict with versus stepping back away from them.

"My colleagues and I spent a good deal of time bringing residents and growers together. In most cases, they were very willing to speak to the residents about their complaints and fears. We would approach the neighbor; offer information about normal growing practices and a chance to visit with the growers, face-to-face.

The importance of addressing the root cause of issues before they become a crisis also became clear at this time. The root cause of the cranberry grower/neighbor conflict was unmet expectations and misinformation. When the real-estate agents sold the homes they themselves didn't fully understand what activities would be taking place on the adjacent property during the other seasons of the year. So we held 'cranberry 101' workshops for real-estate agents to educate them on what homeowners could expect and encourage them to connect the prospective homeowners with the growers before the purchase was made. Doing so would set expectations and establish a relationship between property owners before issues arose.

The strategy worked. Slowly the two groups became increasingly tolerant and collaborative," said Emily.

"To this day, I believe cranberry growers are among the most community-friendly farmers in the USA," shared Emily.

In 2000 Emily moved to another assignment that would stretch her – as Director of student recruitment and alumni affairs and executive director for the University of Florida – College of Agricultural and Life sciences. Here she faced the tough task of recruiting and retaining students for the University's fourth largest college comprised of 20 academic departments and two schools. She also had to engage a rapidly expanding alumni base of more than 25,000 graduates.

"The biggest challenge I faced in this job as a young woman was distinguishing myself from the students who were not much younger than me while trying to influence faculty and alumni leaders much older than me to embrace change to ensure a successful future for alumni programs. This became acute between 2004 and 2006 when I decided to tackle the misalignment between alumni trends and the infrastructure our college had to support programs. The majority of our alumni programs were geared toward those who graduated in traditional agriculture majors, while overtime, college enrollment particularly in non-traditional majors related to pre-med, business and social sciences grew exponentially. The college that once housed mainly students from rural areas studying agronomy and animal sciences now had more students from larger metropolitan areas studying microbiology, nutrition and family sciences. With the growth of student enrollment in these new majors, one could see that within just a few years the number of alumni from non-agriculture majors would surpass those from farming-related majors. In addition, the rapid growth of enrollment meant the alumni base was also becoming younger. Therefore, our alumni engagement programs needed to change to reflect a much more diverse alumni base and it was my job to inspire our college's alumni board to lead that change," shared Emily.

While the board, comprised of all men from traditional agriculture programs who graduated from college decades before, was fairly amenable to change, Emily had to use all of her influencing skills and efforts to accelerate change at a rate that would outpace the impending influx of 'new' alumni.

"I was 29 years old and just seven years removed from being a student myself when I tackled the change. I realized during this period that it was unlikely a relatively inexperienced leader in her 20s would be seen as having the expertise needed to convince the alumni board members, many of which were 40 years my senior and from an era when young women wouldn't have been serving in the position I was, that a paradigm shift in alumni programs was needed. But that didn't mean I couldn't create change and influence a positive outcome for all involved.

I learned through this experience something I find valuable in influencing decisions today: the influencer doesn't necessarily need to be the messenger," shared Emily.

Emily realized that her best chance at creating change for the alumni program came in the form of playing facilitator to the change process and not trying to be the authority on collegiate alumni trends. She gained the trust and confidence of the alumni board by organizing a facilitated retreat where board, faculty and staff members worked together to create a vision for the alumni organization.

"We agreed we wanted an organization that would not only promote fraternity among alumni but also create a network to enhance the college's academic programs. To do that, the process required looking at the undeniable change that had occurred in the composition of the student body and how that would impact the alumni group. Exposing the board to external sources and best practices at other colleges of agriculture facing similar changes in alumni demographics also added third-party credibility to the argument for change. So too did having authority figures, like the dean of the college who the board admired deeply, echo the need for change," added Emily.

In the end not only did the board agree to develop programs that would better address the needs of a more diversified alumni body, but it also became clear that the composition of the alumni board did not reflect the rapidly diversifying alumni group. As a result additional board members representing wider geographic areas, majors and ages were added within six months of the facilitated meeting.

"Accepting that in this situation my greatest chances of influencing change would be to serve as the person organizing the change process versus being the vocal visionary ultimately led to the outcome I had hoped to achieve for the college. And in the process, my credibility with the board increased to a point that allowed me to be a more visionary leader for the time I remained with them," commented Emily.

Between 2006 and early 2010 Emily worked with the Economic Development Corporation of Sarasota County as its Community Relations Director.

Then on January 12, 2010 the Haiti earthquake happened and Emily received her calling.

"At the time, I knew the person who was running ShelterBox USA. The organization was doing great work in the field during the time of the Haiti earthquake distributing relief supplies to the victims. Yet ShelterBox did not have the infrastructure it required to grow. They had gone from an organization handling just two Million USD of relief funds to over nine million USD of relief," shared Emily.

Emily was asked to come onboard and joined ShelterBox on April 1, 2010 as Director of Operations.

Right away she realized that her influencing skills would need even greater practice at ShelterBox.

She set about getting to understand ShelterBox intimately.

"In my new role I was very energized by the importance of our mission and the seemingly limitless growth our organization could experience. While most organizations plan strategically for steady growth, sometimes rare opportunities force a rapid growth spurt as was the case following the Haiti earthquake. Things were changing rapidly in our organization and the support infrastructure, including our administrative operations and governance structure needed to advance quickly.

I was aware it could be challenging to influence change as quickly as needed. Not only was I new to the organization, but the position I filled was new. Two of our five-member team joined within two months of my arrival so most of the staff was new. While the organization still maintains a small staff in the USA today, prior to 2010 the organization remained largely volunteer run. The board of directors was now governing an organization with a growing budget, opportunities and now a capable staff which meant a transition of some of the day-to-day organizational duties held by volunteers to staff could be undertaken, "shared Emily.

Yet Emily knew that the conditions were right to rapidly transform the organization. A board comprised of volunteers that truly held a passion for the mission, an executive director that was progressive and thrived in what can sometimes be the chaos of rapid change, and a capable and motivated staff.

"But that didn't mean it would be without its challenges, especially as the small staff and board would be not only tasked with improving the organization for the future, but asked to do so while already stretched by handling extremely high levels of activity in the wake of the Haiti earthquake," she added.

As the director of operations, Emily was tasked with overseeing and engaging others in the evolution and further strategic development of the organization. Along with key staff members, she was able to quickly gain the trust of the board and volunteers needed to advance change by relying on experience and staying true to ShelterBox's values.

"We shared best practices and scenarios from other organizations we previously served and experiences we lived. As staff, we lived the organization's values. The same organizational values that drove our relief operations in the field would be the same that would drive improvements in our administrative operations-among them: speed, innovation, collaboration and accountability.

In the first few months, we took the time to review and improve processes. We rethought how things were done. Doing so would not only help us improve the organization longer-term, but also help us get through the high volume work that came with increased donations, opportunities and response activities of the Haiti earthquake. Within a year, the administrative operations of our organization were running smoothly and more efficiently than ever. We were chasing new opportunities, gaining a higher profile among the NGO community and ultimately increasing our ability to help more families left vulnerable from disasters and humanitarian crises," she added.

In March 2011 Emily was appointed President of ShelterBox.

"My team is comprised of professionals all under 40. They operate in a very dynamic environment. Where the rules of the game are always changing – dictated by where and when the next big disaster occurs. They do not take kindly to a directive style of management as each of them are unique individuals working with the kind of zest that you would rarely find in the corporate world," shared Emily.

But true to form, Emily set herself to the task.

"I learned about the basic motivations of each of the members of the team. I understood what made each of them do what they did with such passion, and then I worked to foster their unique talents and create growth opportunities for them within our small organization."

Emily continued, "I also understood how they interacted with the steady pool of over 400 volunteers who are our primary executors of the work we do. And most important of all, we discussed together the aspirations and goals of ShelterBox USA. We reconfirmed our commitment to the organization's values and we agreed the problem solving process always begins with the question "what is the right thing to do?"

ShelterBox USA operations continued to grow under Emily's nurturing.

But growth in a fairly young disaster relief organization can be challenging, explained Emily.

While large-scale disasters often catch the world's attention and the funding required for response, ShelterBox is responding to 25-30 disasters each year that don't make the news or public agenda. Under Emily's leadership, the team is very focused on raising the support needed to respond to those disasters as the families impacted in them are just as deserving of assistance.

The organization has made significant progress in building an engaged supporter base by explaining the impact their support can have through sharing individual survivor stories.

"An individual donor can make a significant impact on a family affected by disaster. Not just by providing them with the supplies they need in the immediate aftermath of disaster, but also in the longer-term as their intervention can ensure the family more quickly recovers in all aspects – health, livelihood and community engagement. The simple fact that a donor, a stranger from afar, cared enough to provide support to a family they have never met, can provide those survivors with the hope they need to go on. In working with many of our donors, I've also learned that they are equally inspired by the resilience of the disaster survivors they are helping," shared Emily.

That resilience is something Emily has witnessed first-hand. She explains a disaster response she participated in during severe flooding on the Amazon River in Peru 2012.

"Three ShelterBox response team volunteers and I were deployed to work with villages in Peru to distribute emergency shelter and other supplies to families whose homes were washed away in floods. These families had been living in makeshift shelters or overcrowded schoolrooms for weeks and needed the safety and security of temporary shelter for the following months while more permanent housing was built farther back off the river to protect them in future floods. While those impacted lost their homes and possessions, they were determined to rebuild their communities and return to a sense of normalcy.

Like most of our deployments, we faced complex logistical challenges working in remote areas. The villages were only accessible by water and therefore our supplies had to first travel by riverboat from a larger town upstream, then by small boats from adjacent ports to the villages and ultimately be carried by hand through shin-deep mud once on land. But even more challenging, was establishing an approved plan across the municipal and regional governments involved and the villages we aimed to help.

As in many initiatives requiring partnership, conflicting priorities, egos and timelines can put project success in peril. In this case, not every entity involved was working with the same sense of urgency we felt, as they were busy addressing other priorities or facets of the response. That meant precious days were spent chasing approvals and tackling one roadblock after another -- all while vulnerable families remained unsheltered.

With no authority over those we needed help from, we assembled a group of allies to solve this problem. The team of influencers included a local translator who knew how the municipal system worked, a sympathetic local government worker eager to ensure his region was helped and a citizen leader from one of the villages we were trying to assist.

Each member of the team was assigned tasks associated with their circles of influence. The local government worker helped us pinpoint exactly which municipal and regional leaders held the authority to sign-off on the plan and ensured we were given time with each; the translator used his knowledge of the local area and municipal system to deliver our team to the offices of each coordinating body for meetings to understand their needs and priorities and the citizen leader worked within the village to come to agreement about the distribution plan and families who would be receiving priority assistance," added Emily.

Emily continued, "Successful leaders understand their ability to influence has limitations and know the importance of engaging others in influencing change or completing initiatives.

The exercise of assembling a team of local influencers in Peru was successful. Immediately we were able to begin distributions across four villages along the Amazon River and ultimately hundreds of disaster survivors were provided with the shelter and supplies they needed to begin rebuilding their lives."

In 2012 Emily received an important industry recognition that underlined her ability to influence people towards a common goal – the Biz 941 Best Boss 2012 award.

I challenged Emily on the role that gender played in success at an organization like ShelterBox.

She responded:

"To me one of the challenges that women face today is that sometimes recognition and success becomes more dependent on gender than merit. I am gender blind. I'm quite put off when women are selected for something just because they are women versus because they are more qualified or a match for a particular job, award or opportunity. Anything short of evaluating women equally and on their merit is an injustice to all involved, in my opinion."

She continued, "In the previous generations I think the gender pressures were more external. In my generation (Emily is 39), the pressures seem to have shifted to the inside. The biggest challenge women face today is the conflict they feel every time they have to make a choice between their family and their job."

Emily and her staff and volunteer team continue to inspire others to help families impacted by tragedies around the world. In the last two years, with the help of generous donors and volunteers, the ShelterBox network has responded to nearly 60 disasters and humanitarian crises, including Typhoon Haiyan/Yolanda, the largest to ever make landfall, impacting the Philippines and conflict in Syria displacing more than two-million people into neighboring countries like Iraqi-Kurdistan and Lebanon and earthquakes, flooding and storms in Africa, South America and the United States.

Emily's role is constantly evolving. And the pressures on her time are significant.

"We never know when the next disaster will strike," she added so we must be continuously prepared.

Emily offered up her top five tips for using influence to enhance your success:

- *Be clear about your objective:*
  You have to know where you are trying to get people to go before you start out the journey.

- *Put yourself in the shoes of the person or organization you are trying to influence:*
  Try and find the common ground between your objective and theirs.

- *Learn from everyone:*

  Learn from the people who are great at influencing but also learn about what not to do from people you do not want to emulate.

- *Be value based:*

  Values are central to efficiency. When in doubt as to what decision to make, values serve as a good cornerstone.

- *Keep your word:*

  Trust is the basis of influence. Once trust is established between you and the opposite party it will be easier to find a win win solution vs. constantly opposed views.

Emily shared with me that the art of influence also extends to the home. Her husband and she have aligned on a life mission statement. And that is serving to balance out priorities at work and at home.

Emily Sperling is a continuous student and practitioner of influence!

Chapter 14

# TAKE A RISK.
# FOLLOW YOUR DREAM

The bigger the risk, The bigger the reward. But is that is really true?. To find out I spoke to **Laura Desmond,** *Global CEO, Starcom MediaVest Group;* **Marina Maher,** *CEO, Marina Maher Communications; and* **Hiroko Wada,** *Consultant, author, coach.*

Risk and reward have always gone hand in hand for **Laura Desmond.**

That's how she got to where she is today—**Global CEO of Starcom MediaVest Group** and the only female global CEO inside the Publicis Groupe (parent of SMG and one of the world's largest advertising and public relations conglomerates).

And that's why she sees such opportunity for female leaders in today's media world.

"Women do really well in communications," she said. "We represent the consumer, we empathize with the voice of the consumer—and our clients are looking for that. Women need to embrace this fact and, in some form or another, be risk takers. Take what's old and known to you and see how you can create something that's new and needed."

> "Women do really well in communications. We represent the consumer; we empathize with the voice of the consumer. Women need to embrace this fact and, in some form or another, be risk takers. Take what's old and known to you and see how you can create something that's new and needed."
>
> **Laura Desmond,**
> Global CEO, Starcom MediaVest Group.

Laura comes from a long line of risk takers. And it's the risks taken by the grandmother she was named after that most inspired Laura as she's made a name and a career for herself.

"My grandmother was a true trailblazer," Laura said. "When she was just 14, she left her family's farm in rural Indiana and moved in with another family in Chestertown, Ind., so she could attend high school. When she wasn't in class, she cared for the family's children in exchange for her lodging. And then, after graduation, she moved to Chicago, where she earned a degree in surgical nursing. She was a nurse for over 35 years at Little Company & Mary Hospital in Chicago, Illinois."

Laura was also heavily influenced by her parents. Her father taught Laura about dreaming big, taking risks and that she could be anything she wanted. Her mother, meanwhile, supported Laura's success by following and measuring every step of her daughter's journey.

"My mom, in her own way, is a risk taker too. She worked as a nurse for 10 years before having children. Then she raised me, from the start, to pursue my own goals and to be comfortable competing in all arenas—sports, in the classroom, after school activities."

At 16, Laura learned that her father had cancer. Alongside her studies, she dedicated all of her spare time to helping her family to take care of her father.

In 1987, at the age of 22, Laura began her communications career with Leo Burnett. By 1993 she was the European Media Director on the McDonald's account working for Leo Burnett, overseeing the account and gaining valued experience with European markets. By 1996 she was overseeing global accounts such as Coca-Cola and Kellogg.

She credits her early success with one of those clients, Coca-Cola, to one factor: having the guts to tell the client when and where they were doing something wrong.

She shared, "One of the biggest things I learned at Coke was the things I said 'no' to were more important than what I said 'yes' to," she said. "At the same time, it was critical that I showed my clients what the agency and its people could do. At the time, we were unseating an incumbent agency that had worked for Coca-Cola for 50 years. We won the business because we took deep and calculated risks on talent, resources and capability. We were laser-focused on where we were world class and didn't waste a minute trying to be something we were not with Coca-Cola."

"I started with three markets with Coca-Cola. and by the time that assignment had ended a few years later, we had expanded the business to 17 markets. Today, we work for Coca-Cola in more than 30 markets globally, including their largest – U.S., China, and Mexico," added Laura

In 2000, Laura moved to SMG as part of a global team that started this new media specialist business unit.

Her first role there was CEO for SMG Latin America, with the primary responsibility of setting up a business from scratch in eight Latin American markets. That's when she said she faced one of the toughest business challenges in her career: building a business when many established sister companies saw no value in the new media business unit.

"The biggest risk I took in this role was to stand up to these established sister companies who were not supportive of our start-up venture in media. Their focus was to block progress not support or enable it. But we just would not let the opposition stop us. We knew we could be a real growth engine for our parent company, and we went after that growth. It was daunting to insist on independence in a region that valued legacy and tradition," said Laura.

"Many a time my counterparts and peers went above my head, around me and to my clients to get their way. But we stuck to our guns and we were fortunate that our clients gave us their backing. We were also quite determined to ignore the risks of failure," she added.

When she left this assignment in 2002, Laura had doubled the size of the business, tripled profits and won a record nine pitches in a row.

In 2002 Laura was appointed as CEO of MediaVest USA, a top 5 media agency in that was, nevertheless, faltering.

"We faced considerable challenges at the time. Clients were unhappy, employees were unhappy. We had to move quickly. We listened and appealed to our dissatisfied clients. I was straight with them. I asked for time and told them exactly what they could expect from me and the agency if they gave us time."

She made the most of that time, creating a clear vision of what MediaVest's purpose would be– 'Innovation that works' (based on the heritage of MediaVest)—and created a leadership team that was flat-structured and broad-based across the agency. She also demanded that everyone at the agency focus on personal responsibility, accountability for their part of the turn around, and differentiated products and services that no one else could match in the industry.

"We did not lose a single client in my first year," she said. "In fact, we won three of the biggest business pitches in the first 18 months – Coke, P&G and Mars. These were unprecedented results."

Adweek named MediaVest agency 'Network of the year' in 2003, 2004 and

2005. And by 2005, MediaVest was the biggest business unit inside SMG and a top U.S. agency in billings.

In 2006 Laura was appointed CEO of SMG Americas and in July 2008 she took the top job as Global CEO of SMG, which now works with some of the most innovative and iconic brands in the industry, including P&G, Coca-Cola, Microsoft, Wal-Mart, Spotify, Comcast and Samsung.

Laura is quite simply one of the most powerful women in the world of business today. She reflected on the ongoing challenges women still face today.

"Women are 50% of the population but still fewer than 5% of FORTUNE 500 CEOs," she said. "I joined the board of Adobe in May 2012 and realized that the lack of women leaders in the technology industry has reached near crisis stage. If you look at Google, Facebook, Amazon and other leading companies, their managements are now waking up to the reality that there are so few women at the top, and these companies are all doing something about it. "I'm also encouraged to see women breaking through in sectors like technology, biotech, and data/analytics. Yet there are still so few women at the top. So it makes even more sense for women to step out of their comfort zones and take a risk.," shared Laura.

Sometimes, she added, risk presents itself in different ways.

"When I was promoted to my role as Global CEO, I was significantly impacted by my predecessor's leaving, because she was an important mentor to me. She had, in fact, done a great job in promoting my career. Now it was time to do it on my own, balancing brave leadership, risk taking and a mature approach."

Once she accepted the position, Laura set about setting the business on a brand-new path, expanding it beyond its traditional-business boundaries.

"I was taking big risks, but in my mind I had a clear vision of where I wanted the company to go and that we could achieve our goals," she said. "Once I was clear about this vision I made several changes to my team, moving from a completely decentralized structure to a more centralized but flatter global structure."

"I wanted to ensure my senior leaders oversaw large parts of the company but were interconnected by functional and business areas," she added. "This meant a highly matrixed structure with twice the communication expected than previously. It also meant to deliver a far more rapid, global speed wherein leadership is expected to not only know their area very well but also be clear about how that area connected to other people on the management team."

She also changed the whole way SMG understood and presented itself. "We decided to stop calling ourselves solely "a media company", and redefined our business as a business of ideas, data and experiences," she said. And, at the same time, she took a big gamble on digital. She and her team started to create a future ready communications company that was future-ready that would integrate traditional communications with the new digital one.

"We believe experiences matter, that they enhance lives and build brands," she said. "So we embarked on the challenge to transform the company from nearly a 100% traditional, analogue media company to a company with a 50% digital and 50% traditional media. In just four years we have achieved our goal of being a balanced, future ready company. To do this we focused on reskilling and retraining our traditional talent base, and also bringing in new talent in radically different areas of data, analytics, cultural anthropologists, specialists in social and mobile, and software engineers. The combination of reframing and remaking the company from within has worked, but there's still so much more to do."

This single strategy put the company on an accelerated growth path as compared to the industry. Over the last five years, SMG has averaged + 9% growth. The group is No. 1 in China, the U.S. and in emerging markets. In the U.S. alone SMG has a six-point market share lead, at 17% of the market. Its closest competitor is at 11%. This share point advantage has doubled during this time. Globally, SMG is also #1 with $40bn + global billings.

"We have the largest partnerships with Twitter, Google, Facebook and are considered one of their strongest innovation partners on behalf of our clients," Laura said. Balancing and combining innovation and operational excellence is our number #1 job.

So taking risks is clearly paying off for Laura. But is this a skill someone is born with? Or can it be taught?

"Both," Laura said. "Risk takers are born and made. There are only two things: ability and desire. What made Michael Jordan a great basketball player? Not just unbelievable ability but also an amazing desire to work hard, reshape his skills as he got older and learn new ways to adapt as competition changed as well."

Laura acknowledged that there were times in her career when she faced almost absolute failure and that it was her ability to take risks—to keep pushing—that most helped her deal with disappointments.

One such time was when SMG lost the General Motors account in 2012.

"We lost for the wrong reasons," she said. "Those reasons were, a chief marketing officer who wanted to create change, being caught in the middle of turmoil as GM was coming out of bankruptcy and playing it too safe as opposed to leading GM through the transformation."

"Once I realized we would lose, I made a deal with myself: We would lose, but we would lose the right way—with our head held high. We would take care of our people to the greatest degree possible and only make cuts that we had to given we were losing our second-largest business. I was determined to learn from the experience and to do what was needed so we would not repeat that kind of loss. To lead change with clients, to anticipate better, to become a stronger global network with unified operations," she added.

"What happened? We're a stronger company today— almost two years later. Still number one, closer with our clients and in a better position to lead. Why? Because we focused on losing as best we could and rebounded as quickly as we could. We didn't ask what happened - we said, it happened, learn from it and move on," shared Laura.

These lessons underscored the importance of being honest and transparent within the company especially in 2008-'09, when she and her team faced the global financial crisis.

"When we saw we were going to lose revenue and our clients were cutting back, I knew we had to be honest about that inside our company, no matter how tough a message it was," she said. "It also showed me that forces could overtake you. Rather than fight something that big, we tried to make ourselves more nimble and knowledgeable during the recession so we could help clients through the impact to their business and so that they could rely on us for key data, information and truth."

There is a direct correlation between risk and reward, Laura explained. "We live in a world where our clients or companies in general want us to do more with less. But many companies are also willing to reward risk even if it fails. That certainly is the culture we have built at SMG."

And it's by sticking her neck out that she's been able to forge her way in what is still largely a man's world. "The challenges of being a woman professional are many. For me, early on, it was simply overcoming being the only woman in the room—and the youngest person in the role As I got to mid-to senior-level ranks, the challenge became one of balancing a strong leadership style with the silent perception of 'being overbearing.'"

Today, Laura encourages young women to focus on breaking through in the big sectors of tomorrow.

"Success, power and prestige follow big money. Women must learn to play in the big leagues. And for that you must take some risk. And, learn from everything you do – the success, the joy, the loss and the failure.

Her top picks on how to take prudent risks are as follows:

- *Learn from  failures yours and others:*
  Learning from failures quickly and watching other people overcome challenges has helped me save time and make the fewest possible mistakes myself.

- *Don't let your frustration or negative emotions cloud your reasoning:*
  I've sometimes seen people over react to things like being passed over for a promotion. Anger makes them lose self-awareness. They start thinking they can do things they cannot and take foolish risks instead of reflecting on why they were passed over in the first place. This is the time they should face their fears, not get frustrated or run away or self-destruct.

- *Make decisions:*
  I've seen bosses be the nicest people, but in the end, they are unwilling to make the tough calls because they don't want to risk being disliked. As a

result, people in the organization stop taking risks and stop being brave. Your team will only take risks when they see that their leaders can make tough calls and can be decisive.

- *Never bottleneck. Instead delegate:*
  I've worked for bosses who would never make a decision, which was fine. But they prevented decisions being made too. And this is a recipe for disaster. I once had a boss who would profess to be available – but would often not be available. What I learned—delegate, delegate. Don't bottleneck. If you can't be available to make a decision, then trust others to do the right thing and make the right call. You can't hold up the company just for your own need for control.

- *Collaborate:*
  I've also learned that collaboration can be another great way to minimize risk. I picked this up from one of the greatest basketball players of all time: Michael Jordan. There was a time when he was not winning because he refused to pass the ball. Amazingly, he learned how to pass more. The more he passed the ball, the more his team won! From that I realized that collaboration could be a very powerful tool to insulate against risk and to generate greater results.

Today Laura is pushing relentlessly toward ever-challenging boundaries for SMG and Publicis Groupe.

Her focus for the company for the next three years is to pivot SMG to the future growth areas of the industry.

"We are making big bets on mobility, on content and on ventures. In the same way we were successful in turning SMG from an analogue company to a digital company, we believe that the next wave of change is evolving from a mass at scale to a 'one to one' scale.

"Risk has paid off for me," said Laura, who now lives in Chicago with her partner. "We are passionate about our Michiana home on the duneland shore of Lake Michigan, and find time to enjoy our hobbies of sailing, gardening, golf and cooking. I'm fortunate to have a wonderful circle of lifelong friends who have been wonderful supporters and keep me grounded."

No book on inspirational women would be complete without the charismatic **Marina Maher;** CEO of the New York headquartered **Marina Maher Communications, (MMC)** a division of the Omnicom Group.

With the personal motto of Avanti, Avanti! Marina is one of the most powerful women in the International beauty business who has built one of the world's leading agencies for developing relationships between women and brands.

Marina has worked every aspect of the public relations business: as a copywriter, media director and account manager; on the corporate side and in agencies; and in U.S. practices and abroad.

I left writing about Marina to the very last chapter of my book on the world's most inspirational women. The simple reason – we share a unique friendship. She has been my PR counsel, critic, mentor and friend. Seeing her live her motto of Avanti, Avanti over the years that I have known her, personally inspires me.

Marina's secret for success is simple. She is willing to take a risk and go after her dreams.

Growing up in Chicago, Marina was influenced by her Father, who was both an entrepreneur and an artist. "My father ran a very successful business," shared Marina, "but also found time to paint and sculpture, showing his work at galleries in Chicago. It never occurred to me that I couldn't do the same."

> *"Having your finger in pop culture is what enables you to keep conversations consistently interesting and fresh. And helps you to make the right judgments in business and take the right risks."*
>
> *Marina Maher,*
> *CEO, Marina Maher*
> *Communications.*

"I started my first business when I was 12, providing entertainment for children's birthday parties. It was a real business and I made my business cards out of construction paper. The typeface was whatever the Smith Corona typewriter produced. I would hand out my cards to the doormen of all the high-rise buildings near where we lived in Chicago. That was my first experience with PR and word-of-mouth. I loved it—I was booking clown acts and magicians, making little kids happy and Mothers proud. By age 14 the business was thriving. But my parents made me shut it down as it started to interfere with my schoolwork.

I vowed I would start another business, some day," she added.

After completing college, Marina had her first encounter of the challenges facing women in the work place when she started her first job at a magazine and scheduled a meeting with her boss.

"There was an editorial spot open that I was hoping to be promoted to—I knew I had all the skills for a job. But when I asked about it, he responded, 'You are terrific. You are the person best qualified for this job. But why should I promote you and then watch you go off and have children in a few years, never to return to the workforce?"

That was a harsh reminder to Marina that the world indeed looked at men and women differently.

Marina continued her role in editorial at the magazine but left after 18 months because she could see she wasn't going to advance there.

"And the environment didn't suit me: it was slow moving and not fast-paced. However I was a good writer, so I got a job in Public Relations—and loved it from the very first day. It was fast-paced and I got to work with the media and figure out angles for stories. I was hooked!

As she progressed to mid-management level in her career, Marina noticed that other women started helping her to succeed.

"I didn't expect to be involved to the golf outings (and by the way I still don't play golf!) but I did start noticing in the office that I was not invited to every meeting. That meant I was out of the loop and could easily have made a mistake. But the secretaries of the male executives helped me. The secretaries attended the meetings to take notes (think Joan in Mad Men), and they kindly gave me the notes so I could follow the corporate agenda and also see where my opportunities might lie.

It wasn't until years later that Madeleine Albright said: 'there is a special place in hell for women who don't help other women.' But in the early days of my career, no one thought that way," continued Marina.

Marina claims that risk taking comes easy to her because she understands where the world is going.

"To succeed in the communications field, that thrives by sparking consumer conversations, you have to know what's new and what's next. I have an innate intellectual curiosity about people, their jobs, how they started in their careers and how they met their spouses. You'll often find me talking to our staff, clients, the person next to me on an airplane as well as women in a supermarket or behind a cosmetic counter. I have a genuine curiosity about people and what makes them tick, why they buy something—or don't. I read constantly – about the social and digital worlds, consumer trends and pop culture and probably watch over 100 movies a year. Having your finger in pop culture is what enables you to keep conversations consistently interesting and fresh. And helps you to make the right judgments in business and take the right risks," shared Marina.

In 1983, Marina took the next calculated risk that would change her life. She founded Marina Maher communications. Since then she has built MMC into the preeminent marketing-to-women public relations agency. The Company counts blockbuster clients such as Procter & Gamble, Kimberly-Clark, Merck, NovoNordisk and Pfizer on its enviable roster.

Marina's leadership and dedication to agency staff has resulted in the agency consistently being cited as a "best agency to work for." Her top team is almost 100% female, an indication of the commitment that Marina demonstrates to women overall.

Marina is widely recognized as one of the nation's leading authorities on marketing to women, with particular expertise in beauty, consumer products and consumer health brand building. She has played a key strategic role helping such brands as COVERGIRL, Clairol, U by Kotex* and WonderBra achieve iconic status.

Marina's secret has always been that she is able to take risks that others consider 'too risky'. They could not have been more wrong. Marina's incredibly sharp understanding of how pop culture trends will impact consumer behavior ensures that her 'risky' campaigns are in fact highly calculated risks.

My friendship with Marina started in 2003 when I transferred from Singapore to the United States on assignment with P&G to lead the Hair Care External Relations team. We had the unique opportunity to work on what was then one of the largest portfolio of hair brands in the world, with MMC being the lead for iconic brand Head & Shoulders. Iconic yes, but challenged by a host of wannabe hair care products envious of H&S' success.

The brand marketing team wanted to attract more users and Marina and her team made a case for expanding Head & Shoulders' equity to beauty, creating a campaign entitled "Head Turning Hair." This was a risky strategy, as at its core, H&S was an anti-dandruff shampoo, yet Marina and her team, headed by lieutenant Nancy Lowman Labadie, believed the brand could be so much more.

Inspired by Marina's vision of broadening the appeal of H&S to a much larger audience, the team signed on an unlikely endorser for the brand - The first ever celebrity hair stylist on Broadway, Jason Hayes.

To underline H&S' beauty credentials Jason did hair makeovers for several of his star clients with a "mystery shampoo and conditioner". When his clients were amazed with the results that the new product was delivering on their hair, Jason then revealed that the product was in fact H&S, subsequently securing the strongest of recommendations of several of this star community for the brand!

The leverage of a Broadway hair stylist was risky but effective. On an annual basis, over 35% of the brand's overall positive mentions in news media were traced back to Jason Hayes. Not bad for an 'anti-dandruff' brand which now seemed to literally cover such a wider stage. By 2006, H&S was already in the most mentioned brands in the Hair category.

Marina's ability to take risks was also fully evident in the mid 90's when Marina and her team launched Wonderbra in the USA without any advertising support. The challenges facing her and the team included the parent company's key concern about a potential female backlash against objectifying women.

Undeterred, Marina along with Nancy Lowman Labadie created a 'product as hero' strategy, putting Wonderbra (and not scantily clad models) at the center of the launch, creating the image of the brand as a "must have" fashion accessory.

Marina created unique angles such as the 'Cleavage caravan' and 'Bra wars are coming' to capture the imagination of the news media and fire up interest in Wonderbra. Amazingly, they never showed the product but used fully clothed models to demonstrate the dramatic difference the Wonderbra created in a fashion silhouette.

With PR as the primary marketing tool, Wonderbra raced to record share of 36.5%. In New York, one Wonderbra was sold every 15 seconds. Wonderbra went on to become a cultural phenomenon.

Then on Kotex MMC again created a pioneering, new and potentially risk strategy that that paid off in strong results for the brand.

"A few years ago, MMC had the good fortune to change the way menstrual products were marketed to women when the agency launched a bold and breakthrough product called U by Kotex for client Kimberly-Clark. To capture the attention of young women, we took on the category by being culturally disruptive and consistently innovative. We ditched the euphemisms about menstruation that competitors were still using (remember girls dancing in white skirts and Mother Nature giving you a 'gift'?) for 'real talk' conversations and gave women a voice to drive social change," shared Marina.

Led by MMC's Diana Littman Paige, MMC secured major segments on network television – which had banned Kotex advertising that used the word 'vagina' – and other millennial friendly outlets like TMZ. We sparked conversations in social media, and gave women an opportunity to create a new vocabulary to discuss menstruation and vaginal health, facilitated by U by Kotex.

"In doing so we changed a category and a generation's view of periods and catapulted U by Kotex to an 8% share, ultimately driving the total Kotex brand share to 20% for the first time in more than a decade," shared Marina.

Marina today enjoys a reputation second to none for building brands that speak directly to women. She mentors some of the top executives in public relations and marketing and frequently provides senior level marketing counsel to global CEOs, presidents, CMOs and communications leaders. Fluent in French and Italian and with business experience in markets around the world, Marina shapes many of her client's global marketing campaigns.

She is a member and former Board Director of the Council of PR Firms, an industry organization that promotes the profession and sets quality and ethical standards. She also serves on the Board of Governors of Cosmetic Executive Women and the Beauty Industry Advisory Board for the Fashion Institute of Technology Masters Program.

In her offices in New York, Marina continues to groom an almost all-women team of communicators that are shaping the destinies of the most powerful brands in the world.

Marina is proud of the unique culture that she has developed at MMC.

"MMC's agency culture is extremely important to me. We ask our people to work hard and adhere to high standards of client service. At the same time, women today place a high priority on workplace culture and want an environment that emphasizes teamwork and community. They crave opportunity and want their contributions to be meaningful and recognized. They flourish in a flexible and supportive environment where they are valued enough to work autonomously.

So we have created the kind of culture at MMC that allows the best talent to flourish in this environment. We encourage them to pursue their passions and hold them accountable for their results. We encourage them to offer opinions and measure our leaders on their ability to listen. Everyone in the agency belongs to a management group of their peers where they are empowered to tackle agency strategy and issues," she shared.

"Today's young women belong to history's first 'always connected' generation, where they are 'always on,' whether at work or not. At the same time, having a personal life, being with their friends and family and having a multitude of life experiences are just as important as their careers. We have created a flexible work culture, which includes a liberal time-off policy to pursue their interests out of work, including summer and 'personal' days throughout the year. We also have options to work from home or to work reduced hours. In return, our staff approaches everything with a "can do" spirit," shared Marina.

"The Millenials on our staff are very focused on helping others in need; in fact research shows it is their third highest priority. So last year to commemorate our 30th anniversary, MMC undertook a staff-recommended cause initiative to fund the education of 30 girls through an organization called 'She's the first'. She's the First educates girls in the developing world, helping them be the first in their families to graduate from secondary school. The program was completely aligned with the agency's DNA of empowering women. And to up the ante, we offered a trip to visit the school in Uganda that our She's the First sponsored girls were attending for the staffer who raised the most money for scholarships.

Seven MMCers took up the challenge, but everyone at MMC contributed in some way, whether it was attending a fundraising event, mentoring the participants, bidding on swag at an auction or just handing over $50. The cause united MMC-ers into a community, which began to view each fundraising event in the context of how many girls' educations were funded vs. how much money was raised. An MMC-wide bake sale funded three educations. A 'Date Auction' raised enough for 11 educations, and so on.

From March, when the competition kicked off until August, MMC raised $25,000! Instead of funding 30 educations for our 30th Anniversary, the agency raised enough for 43 educations. Sending those girls to school was life changing for them. But it changed the women (and men) at MMC, too. Human Resources noted that no other cause project had mobilized and excited the entire agency the way this one did," added Marina.

She added, "And the impact went well beyond the immediate benefit of funding girls' educations. Internally it gave real-life examples of agency culture to our 50 new hires in 2013 and is also being used in recruiting. The contestants realized the value to their career of participating in the challenge because it helped them develop important on-the-job skills. Learning how to ask people to contribute to their cause will serve them well when they have to negotiate a raise and promotion or ask for business from a prospect."

Marina has a few tips for young women professionals on how to create a habit of taking calculated risks in business.

- *Do your homework:*

  Every meeting is an opportunity. So whether you are interviewing for a job, pitching a company for its business or networking at an event, always take the time to research the people you'll be meeting. Having knowledge about them reduces the risk of awkward conversation or asking an inappropriate question. So dig beyond page one of a Google search. Look up what they've posted recently on their blog and social channels. Your interest in them will naturally increase their interest in you. You may even find out you have a common connection that could open doors for you.

- *Negotiate your way to success:*

  Many women are better at compromise than conflict. They are averse to starting discussions that shake the "status quo." A lot of business is about negotiation—whether it's about salary and title, or ensuring that your idea for a campaign prevails. Yet it is one of women's greatest weaknesses in business. I could scream at all the times I was told, growing up, to "be a nice girl." In business, you have to take emotion out of the equation and negotiate with a lot of coolness. Really skilled negotiators work out compromises that are a win for everyone. I highly recommend taking a course in negotiation or, at very least, read a few good books on the topic. You can practice by role playing with a friend and by incorporating negotiating into your life by cutting a better deal with your cable company or bargaining at flea markets on weekends. For most women, negotiating doesn't come naturally, so start doing it—every day.

- *Networking = oxygen:*

  Networking is essential to the growth of my business – not just for meeting potential clients, but also for attracting top-level staff, gathering competitive intelligence and learning how your clients' products are perceived. Find ways to stay in touch with people you meet in your business life. That assistant product manager you meet in your 20s could be running the company in your forties. Sometimes women shy away from this because we feel phony — or that we are using someone. It will feel more natural if you network around your common interests, like volunteer work or serving on a committee for a trade organization. Don't be afraid to ask one of your influencers for a favor. Or ask for their advice, such as how you can connect with someone they know. More times than not they will make the introduction for you.

- *Figure it out:*
  Sometimes we're concerned that asking too many questions will make us look uniformed, or just plain dumb. Usually that's not the case. Be curious about your profession. Ask questions. Dig deeper. Pick out the people you admire in your company and watch everything they do. Consume books, media and trade publications. Curiosity keeps your mind active and inspires creativity. And it pays off in spades when your colleagues perceive you as the smartest person in the room – just because you ask questions.

- *Pay it forward:*
  As much as women have advanced in business in recent decades, there is still a massive gender gap at the top. Women make up only 15 percent of Fortune 500 executive officers and 15 percent of law firm equity partners. Only 21 Fortune 500 CEOs are women. It's not a risk to your career to help others—where would I be today if those secretaries hadn't helped me, long ago? We need more role models to encourage young women looking to enter the business world. So commit to helping other women on the way up. To paraphrase Hillary Clinton, let's put some more cracks in that glass ceiling!

**H**iroko Wada has been a pioneer her entire life. She has been listed by Fortune Magazine as one of the most powerful women outside the US in 2004 and by Mainichi newspaper in Japan as one of the most outstanding women of the year in 2007.

But the journey to the pinnacle of the business community in Japan started in 1977 when she took a chance and applied for a secretarial role at the worlds largest consumer goods company – P&G.

"I had a hard time finding a job or career that met my expectations. Back in 1977, women were hired to handle clerical work and serve tea to men. They were expected to quit jobs when they got married or pregnant. I was unable to find any company wanting to hire me.

One day I saw a newspaper advertisement by P&G wanting to hire an experienced bilingual secretary. I had no eligibility except that I was bilingual. I decided to take a risk and apply. As expected, I was turned down for the secretary's role. But P&G asked me if I was interested in applying for a marketing job. So I went in for the interview," shared Hiroko.

At the interview, an American marketing manager explained what marketing was and what they did. Even though she did not completely understand what it meant, Hiroko decided that it sounded interesting.

Hiroko shared; "I told the hiring Manager candidly that I am smart enough to understand marketing as long as you teach and train me to help me become what you expect me to become."

The manager liked Hiroko's transparent, positive attitude and she got the job, becoming the first woman to be hired in Marketing at P&G Japan.

"Since I was the first woman in Marketing, it was challenging as people did not completely get what I was doing. One day one of the secretaries asked me to take turns to serve tea to the other marketing staff. I considered reporting this to my Manager, but decided that if I accepted this additional task and later yet prove my ability to succeed in Marketing, it would help convince more women in the organization that any other woman could also work in Marketing!"

> *"The survivors in the business world are often not the biggest players, just the ones that most speedily learn and adapt to threats and risk."*
>
> **Hiroko Wada,**
> Consultant, author, coach.

A few months later, when she was promoted to Brand Manager, Hiroko influenced her bosses to stop wasting peoples time serving tea, and paper cups were introduced. This eliminated dishwashing. Later, thanks to Hiroko's intervention vending machines were installed. Staff time was no longer used to serve people tea.

"I think that Japan is very different from

other countries when it comes to women in the workplace. Things have gotten better but there is still a lot more to be done," shared Hiroko.

"The cultures in most of the working environments continue to expect men to be the leaders and managers. Women are expected to prove themselves to be truly exceptional while men are not necessarily tested so harshly. There is a lack of social systems that encourage working mothers to continue their careers after they have children. This is getting better but still not enough," she added.

Hiroko added that in Japan the culture still seems to expect women to stay at home to handle household chores and raise the children.

"Increasingly, men are sharing household chores but this is still the exception. Since a few years ago, men are also entitled to take childcare leave. But in reality very few take it as most of them are concerned that they may be made losers in the career race within their companies if they take child care leave," she added.

"Finally, there is still a lack of systems in Japanese companies to hire, train and promote women professionals just like men. Women professionals going up the corporate ladder need self-teaching to some extent. Men become very nervous when they discover their bosses are women. They also become nervous when they discover their direct report managers are women. Men prefer working with men up and down," she added.

"In such an environment very few women are willing to meet these challenges head on. The majority of women don't want to take a risk," she added.

But taking a risk is something that Hiroko has always been comfortable doing. And that has clearly helped her stand out in the industry.

When she was assigned to develop a sanitary napkin brand for market entry in Japan in late 1984, P&G was a late entrant into the category where three Japanese competitors were entrenched and dominating about 75% of the market.

"Even if P&G had already been successful with the sanitary napkin brand Always in the US, we had to re-formulate the product to meet Japanese needs, change the brand name, package design and its configuration and marketing plans. Also P&G had never seen success with any American product in Japan at the time. In the first two years of its development, I lead consumer understanding to come up with winning strategies and plans for market entry. It took us two and a half years to get approval to test market. Even with formal approval from top management to go to market in mid 1986 there was a lot of skepticism within the organization on whether Whisper's (the brand name finally chosen for the sanitary napkin in Japan) marketing strategies and plans were strong enough to succeed," shared Hiroko.

Hiroko diligently explained to her key managers that the Whisper launch plans were a calculated risk and were based on solid consumer understanding.

"Three months into the test market, we began to see early signs of success. By late 1986 we went national. Whisper became the top brand in two years of launch and stayed in the leadership spot for many years. Additionally, for the first time in its history, P&G Japan started making profits," commented Hiroko.

Whisper was so successful that Whisper products and its marketing strategy were reapplied across Asia. Hiroko even taught a 'Whisper college' to key managers from new launch countries. Her team inducted brand assistants from India, Pakistan and China as interns. As the years passed these very interns became the leaders of the Whisper rollout in their countries.

"The Whisper advertising called Ms. Whisper campaign became a global model as it built and sustained its business. This campaign received World Class copy awards and was selected for the Advertising Hall of Fame," shared Hiroko.

Hiroko's ability to take planned risks soon attracted even more challenging assignments.

In 1989, Hiroko was assigned to the Hair care category. At the time P&G's first hair care brand Rejoy two-in-one (shampoo plus conditioner in one product) shampoo launch was unsuccessful. Hiroko joined the team as marketing manager. The team was having a tough time facing the reality of an unsuccessful launch of despite all the hard work they had put in.

"I realized that we needed to work better as a team so went off site for two days and revisited the hair care vision, strategies and plans and what we could have done differently. I reiterated the need for better consumer understanding," commented Hiroko.

After doing in-depth consumer understanding, Hiroko and the team concluded that the existing global positioning for Rejoy (Rejoice) in Japan was in fact inappropriate for Japanese consumers. The global model positioned Rejoy as a two in one whereas Hiroko's positioning was based on superior conditioning versus other two in ones.

Hiroko pushed hard with her management to get permission to take a risk and test the alternative positioning in a local market to prove her theory. Reluctantly, she was given approval.

"The local market kept building business rapidly versus the national control. Finally, top management recognized the potential and gave us permission to expand the new positioning nationally. It helped turn Rejoy around, supported by ongoing product upgrades," added Hiroko.

Hiroko took the very same principles to design Pantene and Vidal Sassoon for the Japanese market.

"We needed multi brands to make the hair care category profitable. For Pantene, Ed Artz (then Chairman of P&G) assigned Japan and Taiwan to propose a new positioning. I lead the Japan team and we proposed and got approval for the "healthy hair so it shines" positioning. Again, we were asked to introduce it as another two-in-one shampoo. But we proposed to make it a system of shampoo and conditioner," she added.

"We were convinced the system approach would deliver higher business based on very high usage of conditioning in Japan (every shampooing comes with conditioning. 2x versus US market). Based on volume forecast studies we finally did take Pantene national with this positioning and it was a huge success," commented Hiroko.

Hiroko grew rapidly within the P&G system. As the first female Brand Manager, Marketing Manager and Marketing Director in Japan. In 1995 she became the first female Japanese General Manager in P&G in very challenging circumstances – the Kobe earthquake.

"P&G has a major facility in Kobe. When the earthquake struck I was in an apartment, which was brand new and just overlooking the P&G offices. The apartment did have some damage but I quickly established that I was overall okay. I saw other apartments that had been totally demolished. I looked out and saw the P&G building was still standing. So I walked down 10 floors from my apartment and rushed across to the P&G building. I could see through the glass doors of the lobby that there was heavy damage inside. The sprinkler system had turned on. At the time I was married so we packed a few things and drove to my parents place. The trip took us 11 hours instead of the normal 60 minutes," shared Hiroko.

Hiroko showed initiative and moved along with the leadership team to Osaka to take charge of the situation.

"The Company was amazing and made arrangements for many of us to stay at the Hilton hotel for almost a month. Our entire management team moved to Osaka to take charge of the situation. Amazingly, across all levels our people were still working, demonstrating their own initiatives. We managed to get our order system up and running and were able to keep all of our orders. We also made sure we paid all our people as normal. We set up a provisional office with 200 desks coming in everyday for four consecutive days (at the time we had about 800 people)," she added.

P&G also managed to get dozens of volunteers on motorcycles to deliver detergents, sanitary napkins etc. and many of their products to the affected communities.

On the 10th day after the earthquake Hiroko was appointed as General Manager of the Paper Division in Japan – the most important and profitable division of P&G Japan.

"A G Lafley (current Chairman and CEO of P&G) was then head of the business in Asia, and called me to give me tips on how to manage the situation. He also insisted on coming to Japan despite the obvious dangers and leading himself," shared Hiroko.

Personally, it was a challenging time for all of us. I recall fondly my beautiful cat called Maruko who I adopted after the earthquake. Sadly Maruko died suddenly in 2011 and I adopted yet another cat called Marumo," shared Hiroko.

Hiroko continued, "I was fortunate to have the support of P&G in every single role. I was exceedingly fortunate to be mentored by A.G. Lafley. He guided me into my role as general manager. I was the only Japanese GM, overtaking senior Japanese men. AG advised me to personally visit all function heads that were senior Japanese men to introduce myself and consult with them what to continue, stop and start doing to help me help them do better. All except one agreed to meet up with me and we had productive meetings."

"AG met me from time to time giving me feedback to help improve my leadership. I was one of the few Asian GMs. So this level of close attention demonstrated P&G's serious commitment to grow talent globally. I was very grateful for it," she added.

In 1998 Hiroko became the first ever Japanese Vice President in P&G. After an illustrious career of 23 years at P&G, Hiroko retired from P&G in March 2000 and joined P&G's Global Leadership Council as a retired officer. But a life of retirement was not for Hiroko.

In March 2001 she rejoined the workforce as President of Dyson Japan. At Dyson she quickly revamped its business strategy for Japan, developing a new Dyson model for the Japanese market. She also increased brand awareness to a significant level and drove sales to record highs in less than two years. Under her guidance the Dyson business made profits for the first time in Japan.

Then in 2004, Hiroko moved on as President and COO of Toys 'R' us. There she quickly developed strategies to re-energize the business. She re defined the Marketing function to start much stronger branding and consolidated four advertising agencies into one newly assigned agency for consistent marketing.

Here too Hiroko demonstrated her appetite for taking risks when she went against the standard US model of separating Toys 'R' us and Baby's 'R' us to create the first combo store to open in 2009.

"In 2009, I read in the newspaper a proud announcement of this new store. My understanding is that the combo store model has been a big success," shared Hiroko.

By then though Hiroko was already four years into being her own boss. In January 2005, Hiroko took the ultimate step of starting her own business as a management and business consultant.

She is today one of Asia's leading marketing and business consultants with clients like Toshiba, Panasonic, Asahi Beer, Otsuka Pharmaceuticals, Gunze (apparel company) and Yushin Shuzo skin care on her client list.

Hiroko believes that her ability to take risks and deliver results was based on some very simple principles.

- *Focus on the end point:*
  Be clear about what it is you truly want to achieve and specific outcomes

- *Try to make a career out of what you like to do:*
  Even better if you can turn that 'like' into love.

- *Cultivate a true passion for winning:*
  Irrespective of the difficulties that stand in the way, one must be relentlessly focused on winning.

- *Learn how to lead:*
  Leadership is not about title or position but a collection of critical behaviors – of being able to envision, energize both self and your people and then execute.

- *Keep learning from others and your own experiences:*
  The survivors in the business world are often not the biggest players, just the ones that most speedily learn and adapt to threats and risk.

Hiriko today enjoys her life as a consultant, teacher, author and mentor to men and women. She continues to be based in Kobe, Japan.